W9-AVG-887

Democracy at Risk

CHATHAM HOUSE SERIES ON CHANGE IN AMERICAN POLITICS

edited by Aaron Wildavsky
University of California, Berkeley

Democracy at Risk

The Politics of Economic Renewal

KENNETH M. DOLBEARE
The Evergreen State College

CHATHAM HOUSE PUBLISHERS, INC.
Chatham, New Jersey

DEMOCRACY AT RISK
The Politics of Economic Renewal

CHATHAM HOUSE PUBLISHERS, INC.
Box One, Chatham, New Jersey 07928

PUBLISHER: Edward Artinian
JACKET AND COVER DESIGN: Lawrence Ratzkin
COMPOSITION: Chatham Composer
PRINTING AND BINDING: Hamilton Printing Company

LIBRARY OF CONGRESS CATALOGING IN PUBLICATION DATA

Dolbeare, Kenneth M.
Democracy at risk

(Chatham House series on change in American politics)
Bibliography: p.
Includes index.
1. United States—Economic policy—1981-
2. United States—Social policy—1980- . 3. United States—Politics and government—1981- . I. Title
HC106.8D65 1984 338.973 84-19928
ISBN 0-934540-27-6
ISBN 0-934540-26-8 (pbk.)

Manufactured in the United States of America
10 9 8 7 6 5 4 3 2 1

For LINDA—*and* JAKE *and* MATT

Contents

Tables

Figures

Preface

I began this project as an effort to understand the sharply contrasting public policy prescriptions urged in the 1980s for curing the deepening malaise of the American economy. In particular, I wanted to identify the value premises that lay behind them and trace their probable economic *and* social consequences, all in the context of comparing our present situation with the only similar period in our history, the "Great Transformation" of 1877-1920. My thought was to see more clearly what may be at stake in our pending policy choices by looking at them against the backdrop of the momentous conflicts and changes of that period that so decisively shaped our contemporary social order.

The historical parallels are truly striking, as I shall show in the chapters that follow. Essentially, our society is being reconstructed by two distinct but sometimes linked sets of very powerful forces—apparently economic in character, but also social, political, and cultural. (Though only one of several fully integrated dimensions of social change, economic conditions are usually the most visible ones, and therefore often seem to be the principal driving force as well as the best means of measurement.)

The dominant set of forces is a long-term transformation, in which the kinds of work we do, where and how (and how well) we live, and how we think about ourselves and our future are all being fundamentally altered. We have been in a period of economic *decline* since the late 1960s; we can see the *transformation* in the contrast between the kinds of jobs that are lost and those that are gained each year; and we hope for some kind of economic *renewal* that will restore long-term viability to our economy.

The other set of economic and social forces that has us in its grip is a much more short-term one, but nevertheless powerful in its effects and sometimes difficult to distinguish from the deeper and more fundamental process of decline, transformation, and renewal. This is the all-too-familiar business cycle of inflation, recession, and recovery. In a period of transformation, the cycle swings wildly and rapidly from one stage to another, and I refer to it subsequently as a roller coaster. For example, with massive deficits fueling its rise, in two years the U.S. economy shot from the worst recession in 50 years to a recovery that set statistical records (but left millions in poverty and unemployment.) However, until the still-uncharted stage of basic economic renewal is reached, we shall probably continue to swing wildly from one extreme in the short-term cycle to another.

We are thus in the midst of a rare but crucial period of economic and social *choices*—choices the more compelling because they are forced upon us by necessity. We cannot preserve the present. Holding on to the status quo is not one of our options, because the forces of change are implacably destroying it every day. The question can only be, What form of change will result? As a stubbornly optimistic democrat, I have framed that question as, What form of change do we prefer?

In trying to spell out the nature and implications of these choices, I have reached what amounts to the major thesis of this book. Economic renewal is the equivalent of *political* renewal; there can be no effective economic renewal program, no policy redirection capable of coping with the transformation that is underway, without fundamental reconstruction in our political system. This reconstruction must occur in the form of (1) institutional changes, in which new governmental structures, mechanisms, and practices are created and old ones altered; and (2) electoral realignment, in which new coalitions come together in support of the basic changes of structure *and* policy that are made. Our present institutions, our decision-making processes, and our national political practices are simply not capable of producing the policies and the political support that are necessary to long-term economic renewal under today's conditions.

But these essential political changes can come about in very different ways. They can be instituted from above, perhaps out of concern for preserving the American economic system in the context of a national emergency—or simply because an opportunity presents itself. In either case, popular support might be secured for some reason unrelated to a specific economic renewal program, and institutional change justified after the fact as a necessary accompaniment. Or the essential changes can be brought about from below, in a democratic process in which a conscious popular movement plays a major role. Such a process may seem unlikely to modern Americans, but it would not have been so foreign to our predecessors in the American political tradition. Again, the importance of a historical perspective.

Our current political stalemate—paralysis of institutions amid a plethora of moneyed special interests, withdrawal by voters amid programless media manipulation—must and will be broken somehow enroute to economic renewal. It can be broken from above, by decisive action and manipulated acquiescence. Or economic renewal can be a democratic product, in which politics and economics both respond to popular preference.

This is why democracy is "at risk" in the coming period: our choice is not only about *which* economic renewal program to institute, but about *how* it shall be done. Stated bluntly, our choice is whether to *contract* or to *expand* democracy in the United States. Just as today's economic conditions will not permit retention of the economic and social status quo, neither can our political system remain as it is today. As in the latter half of the transformation period of 1877-1920, the scope and character of what we understand as "democracy" will be substantially altered. Translated, this point amounts to a refinement of my major thesis, which now becomes: the choice of an economic renewal program is simultaneously a choice about whether to expand or contract political democracy in the United States.

Now, no stubbornly optimistic democrat can pose such a thesis as an abstract academic matter and then walk away from it. I have felt it obligatory to try to show also what is necessary for a democratic rather than an authoritarian solution to the economic renewal problem, and that such a democratic solution is in fact possible. The key to a democratic solution, I argue, is found at the conceptual-cultural level of thinking about "politics" and "democracy." This is where history, politics, and economics—power and interest, if one prefers—merge together to produce definitions that shape public understanding for generations.

I have invested some early chapters in showing that Americans once understood "democracy" to include both political rights *and* economic realities—in effect, that people could not be politically equal if they were living under conditions of drastic economic and social inequality. A democratic society was (is?) one in which economic opportunities—real ones, not merely rhetorical ones—are genuinely available to all. Mutual dependence and collective effort were taken for granted; popular participation in various forms was widespread, and voting turnout in presidential elections regularly averaged over 75 percent of the eligible electorate. I argue that the beginnings of the modern equivalent to those ways of thinking and acting are visible in the United States today and that the continued existence of democracy (properly understood) depends on their expansion and realization in political institutions and public policy in the future. My goal is to show not only how and why democracy is "at risk" today, but that we simultaneously have a rare opportunity to preserve and enhance the democratic essence of our society. No risk, no opportunity: the two are inseparable.

The argument of this book is thus linked temporally to the entire era of transformation in which we find ourselves. Neither the short-term swings of the business cycle nor the vicissitudes of particular electoral results can change the basic long-term agenda that this book addresses. Until an economic renewal program and the attendant political revitalization have been implemented through one or another route, we shall continue to face the issues set forth here. I have used data from the 1970s and early 1980s, because they show clearly the decline and transformation that is underway. They may also indicate, as I argue in the last chapter, that we are in the early stages of political realignment in the mid-1980s. Such data change from year to year, but basic transformations take decades, even in our fast-changing times. The framework that I offer here, I believe, will serve to organize and give meaning to economic and political data and events for a considerable period of time.

For all these reasons, therefore, this is at once a book about vital macroeconomic policies and their consequences, government and business (present and future), American political ideas, the changing character of American political institutions and processes, and the future of American democracy. It is intended both for college students in these fields and for all the other places and people that are concerned about the future directions of the American political-economic system.

To be sure, there are some important matters that time and space considerations have forced me to reluctantly sacrifice. I would like to have dealt more comprehensively with the notion of economic growth, seeking to reconstruct that concept toward less dangerous and more humane terms. I wish I had more time to explore all the dimensions of the internationalization, economic and political, that is reshaping our world. And I have only touched upon the implications of the current technological revolution, which may make possible for the first time the diffusion of knowledge necessary to a genuine federal balance between the center and the peripheries of our political-economic system.

The old "isms" and labels, happily, are dead. Conditions have changed so much that those who are burdened by intellectual baggage of World War II vintage, and in some respects even as recent as the 1960s, will have difficulty understanding today's problems and prescriptions. But as yet we have only the dim outline of new concepts and frameworks to take their place. As we start to build a way of understanding the present and possible futures, it will help to give priority to questions about the evolving character and prospects of "democracy." By its nature, democracy involves the work of many people. I have sought only to show that a meaningful American version is already inherent in the thoughts and actions of many Americans. The eventual outcome depends, as it should, on the choices that people actually make in the next decade or so.

Many people have contributed to this volume. Steve Hodes and Orin Kirshner stand out for their invaluable research assistance and perceptive reading of early drafts. Two colleagues, Jeanne Hahn of The Evergreen State College and Dan Clawson of the University of Massachusetts, took time from their own work to provide me with the most demanding and constructive criticism that it has ever been my good fortune to receive. So much is owed to Linda Medcalf that this is truly her book, and it is almost redundant to dedicate it to her.

1. The Politics of Economic Renewal

The 1980s have produced economic anxiety and experiment unequaled in half a century. A small army of economic doctors has generated a wide variety of often contradictory remedies designed to permanently restore the once robust American economy to the vigor and capabilities formerly taken for granted. And we have learned to live amid hourly bulletins about the health and prospects of the patient.

By now it is conventional wisdom that our problems are not merely the result of a runaway inflation-recession-recovery roller coaster. They stem also from the emergence of a newly integrated world economy, a growing lack of competitiveness on the part of the United States in several vital categories, and a transformation from heavy industry to high-technology and service occupations. Several countries surpass us in key measures of economic performance. At times, we seem headed for a world economic role as manufacturer of exotic weapons and exporter of raw agricultural products.

The current American dialogue accepts the idea of economic decline and transformation, and puts forward alternative economic renewal programs. Prominent among these are cowboy capitalism, the Reagan administration's "free market" package of business-promoting policies, and Yankee capitalism, the trendy "industrial policy" bandwagon. Less visible, but perhaps equally important in the current political setting, are programs for full employment and economic democracy.

Almost unacknowledged in this compelling focus on economic problems and remedies is the fact that far-reaching political changes are inherent in any process of "economic" transformation. Economic analysts, and their economic renewal programs, tend to see the economy as an isolated mechanism—a clock or a car—whose workings can be understood and repaired without upsetting its social and political context. However innocent this may be, it is dangerously misleading. No analysis, program, policy, or transformation can be merely economic. Economic transformation and renewal are also, and equally, political transformation and renewal.

No early step is more vital than grasping the indivisible unity of economics and politics; the failure to do so results in seeing only half of what is at stake in the choices that have to be made. Nor are these political dimensions derivative in the sense of being mere products of economic forces and actions. Not only the advocates of economic renewal but also their critics have fundamentally misconceived the nature of the problem.

Thus, even the humane and liberal criticism of industrial policy by Charles Schultze, President Carter's chief economic adviser, almost completely misses the point. In a widely noted essay examined in detail later, Schultze denies the need for an industrial policy—primarily on the grounds that our political institutions and customary politics could not accommodate such a government role in economic and social life.[1] The economic problems that he sees are separate and distinct from the political institutions and practice that he takes as given, fixed, and permanent. To be sure, we are locked in a political stalemate, just as we are searching desperately for an economic remedy. But the two are inextricably linked. The remedy requires a break in the stalemate, and the stalemate must be broken to implement any real remedy. This inseparability of economic and political forces and consequences must be firmly established before we can proceed.

The scope of economic change alone has vast political implications. It is causing a massive shift of population within the country, altering the distribution of real income in basic ways and creating a new mix of jobs that demands different kinds of education and threatens to disemploy whole sectors of the middle-aged and blue-collar workforce. These changes and needs are finding expression in our politics in the form of new power balances, protest movements, policy pressures, and similar demands. In turn, responses to them in the form of new policies and programs will have economic outcomes.

But even greater political consequences are embedded in the unacknowledged fact that each economic renewal program carries with it *both* major institutional changes in the structure and practices of our political system *and* basic redistributions of wealth and power in the society. New institutions must be created and others modified in fundamental ways in order to implement any of these programs. More such changes are likely once the process starts. When institutional structures are changed, profound economic results will follow.

The patterns of redistribution that will be generated depend on the economic renewal program chosen. Cowboy and Yankee capitalism will result in American workers and consumers paying enormous financial and political costs for an experiment in rebuilding investment and profitability in the American economy. Full employment and economic democracy would reconstruct the economy in equally untested ways, but ones that would shift wealth and power toward the middle and lower levels of the social pyramid.

To understand our context adequately, or to evaluate the alternatives offered, we must see social life as a whole—economics and politics, society and culture. The "separateness" or compartmentalization of these concepts is a historical product, given us by the outcome of past struggles. Nor are the meanings of the central concepts of political-economic thinking the only burdens of history that we carry. The present is part history, part future—and understanding where we are and how we think requires a short detour into the past.

The Necessity of History

The 1960s and 1970s gave us social and cultural changes and generated political impacts that have not run their course. In many ways, Americans are still promoting, defending, or reacting against those changes. The current economic transformation, however, is cumulating powerfully with this first wave of change. As part of a pattern that is both worldwide in scope and comprehensive in character—at once social, cultural, economic, *and* political—it has far greater potential for fundamental social and political change.

For a precedent in American history, we must look past the Great Depression of the 1930s, back to the period from 1877 to 1920. In that relatively brief span a century ago, the United States changed from a rural, agricultural, insular country to an urban, industrial, world power. Prolonged and bitter conflicts of various kinds, a political realignment that lasted 40 years, a fundamental reconstruction of national government institutions, and a redirection of public policy were all part of this process.

The era of transformation on which we have embarked is thus another in a series that occurs at 50-year intervals, in which a new accommodation between capitalism and democracy is essentially at stake. Capitalism rests on the accumulation of private property and the freedom to employ it as the owner desires. As we know, it can be immensely productive under favorable conditions. But it results in a highly unequal distribution of wealth, as well as of power over people and things.

Democracy involves participation in public decisions for the dual purpose of having some degree of control over one's life and experiencing growth in personal qualities. It assumes political equality, which in turn depends upon rough equality of political resources—including wealth, social status, and power. Without such preconditions, participation is meaningless, and effective control and personal development are impossible.

There is therefore a continuing tension between capitalism and democracy in our history. Accommodations, in which democracy normally yields (whether this is widely recognized or not), historically have been achieved by one of two means. One is economic growth, permitting the distribution of a larger amount of economic rewards to the "have nots" while not threatening the possessions or political power of the "haves." The other is through the cloak of ideology, in which partial definitions of "democracy" have been developed and applied to a separate and distinct sphere of life called "politics" as a way of obscuring the basic tension.

Profound political implications flow from the social acceptance of particular definitions. There is no one true or correct definition of "politics" or "democracy." These concepts are not tangible, objective facts with an independent existence as things. They are not even neutral, mechanical ways of identifying the particular collection of relationships that we are willing to accept as making up "politics" or "democracy." Every definition of politics or democracy is in part an expression of what we think *ought to be* open to public debate and choice, plus an assertion of our own perspective or world view—our judgment about what the world *is* and *should be* like.

The definition of as vital a concept as politics or democracy is like the rules in a children's game. Every child learns early on that if he or she can only make the rules, chances of winning will increase enormously. Adults who join such games must resign themselves to losing graciously or face a frustrating period of trying to reassert the "real" rules for the game. So it is for "politics" and "democracy," the rules of the game of social life in the United States. A deep cultural struggle goes on all the time over how the society will understand what is included within the scope of these concepts. It is only rarely a conscious struggle, and those advantaged by the currently dominant version of either concept have an interest in avoiding or preventing explicit consideration of the issue. They simply teach it, insist upon it, as one of the "givens" of life.

The meaning of key concepts is intimately involved in the conflict and accommodation that regularly occur between capitalism and democracy. Indeed, to shape the general understanding of such concepts as "equality" or "freedom," or "capitalism" or "democracy," is to hold the future in one's hands. This point cannot be overemphasized and deserves full statement as a basic theme of this chapter.

The American political tradition contains competing definitions of democracy, and the perhaps temporary dominance of one version lies at the heart of the question of political change today. When democracy and capitalism began to take shape as descriptive labels for sets of human relationships in the early United States, people were not in the habit of making sharp distinctions between politics and economics. Instead, they thought of politics and economics as an integrated set of activities; "political economy" was a term that expressed their unity. Nobody doubted that the institutions and practices of the economy and the government each had powerful effects on the other. To think about democracy in those days, one had to think simultaneously about political rights and powers *and* about the roughly equal social and economic conditions that actually obtained *and were essential to the reality of the political rights and powers.*

As industrialization advanced and capitalism took shape, that rough social and economic equality began to give way to an increasing inequality of wealth—and with wealth, power. The growth of those inequalities, and with them the need and capacity of some to employ or direct many others, raised a serious threat to the principle of equality on which democracy rested. It was a threat to the political essence of democracy that could have resulted in open conflict between capitalism and democracy. The conflict was avoided in a social process that amounted to a major cultural victory for one definition over another. The social and economic dimensions of the concept of democracy were simply excised, and the notion of democracy came to apply only to strictly political and legal matters. The political world was split off from the economic world and treated as a separate compartment of life. What had been a *full* definition became a *partial* definition.

Thus a capitalist social and economic system could be compatible with a democratic political system, and many celebrated the combination as "capitalist democracy" or "liberal democracy." The game had been given capitalist rules (and conditions of sharp inequality), but it was *called* democracy. Some people did not accept this, of course, and kept asking for the *old* version of democracy. This older version is what I call the "full" version of democracy, in which economics and politics are seen as a single unit. The *partial* version, in which economics and politics are seen as separate compartments and democracy is applied only to one or the other at any given time, actually dates only from the middle of the nineteenth century.

Efforts have been made, semiconsciously and unconsciously, to build a substantial wall of separation between the spheres. But they have never been completely successful. In this book I argue that what is at issue today in the conflict between the various economic renewal programs is, first, the question whether those walls will be raised or breached. The choice of an economic renewal program, in other words, is related to the ongoing cultural struggle over the way in which democracy is understood in the United States. This is part of the nature of a time of transformation.

In each period of working out a new accommodation, there is both great risk of losing some of the democratic qualities of our social order and great opportunity for expanding those features. Change of *some* kind is inevitable.

The problem for citizens who would play some part in helping to make a better rather than a worse future is to recognize their choices before it is too late. For example, passive or even active defense of the rights and opportunities of our present form of political democracy may be ineffective amid the powerful pressures of this transformation. A new accommodation favorable to the democracy side of the enduring conflict may require instead aggressive efforts to expand current versions of political democracy.

In any event, my premise is that our times are distinguished by this once-in-a-half-century combination of risk and opportunity. This is why the question of choosing an economic renewal program is a decision about the future of American democracy.

Economic Renewal Programs and Their Implications

I have adopted the phrase "economic renewal program" to maintain contact with the economic focus of economists, journalists, and other social commentators. But I want to emphasize the scope of what is involved in the four major alternatives that now compete for acceptance in the United States. Economic renewal programs, as the term is used here, are combinations of macroeconomic policies, new or reconstructed institutions, changed political practices, and their associated new electoral coalitions.

The term "industrial policy" is both too narrow and too closely associated with one version of economic renewal for our purposes. It really means whatever a government does to manage its fiscal, monetary, trade, investment, tax, and regulatory policies to promote economic growth. In this sense, every country has *some* kind of industrial policy, even if the net effect of various statutes and programs is neither coherent nor purposeful. The term's usage in the United States arose from the advocacy of a particular combination of government policies and goals, and is therefore too limited for our purposes of comparison and evaluation.

Many different proposals for economic renewal have been put forward since the mid-1970s, when the need for some redirection of government policy and practice became apparent. I have arranged these in four broad categories that emphasize their commonalities and their essential contrasts with other groups of proposals. My characterization here is little more than a definition with examples of sources of political support, because each program is the subject of a full chapter in part 2.

COWBOY CAPITALISM: A "FREE MARKET" SOLUTION?

Cowboy capitalist proposals call for restoring investment, productivity, and growth through freeing those with capital to follow the incentives of the economic marketplace. They also intend to free business from regulation and taxation as another means of promoting productivity and growth. I use the characterization "cowboy" to suggest a widely shared nostalgic attachment to the idea of individual responsibility in a private enterprise system as well as the geographic, nationalist, and militaristic orientation of many supporters for these proposals.

Cowboy capitalism has ideological roots in the long history of our attachment to the notion of a free market with little or no government intervention, or "laissez faire." This principle has been strongly held by most Americans, particularly those who rise to prominence in the business world. The term is followed by a question mark in my caption because, as we see later, there are substantial deviations from free market theory in the programs and practices of cowboy capitalism.

In practical political terms today, once the ideological appeal has been put aside, cowboy capitalism has its base among sunbelt oil, construction, and high-technology corporations and military-industrial suppliers. Much political support also comes from small businesspersons and believers in the need for military strength to restore American primacy in the world. Widely visible advocates besides the leaders of the Reagan adminstration include such popular writers as George Gilder (*Wealth and Poverty*[2]) and Irving Kristol (*Two Cheers for Capitalism*[3]); supply-side leaders such as Congressman Jack Kemp and author Bruce Bartlett (*Reaganomics: Supply-Side Economics in Action*[4]); and the voice of monetarism, Milton Friedman (*Capitalism and Freedom.*[5]).

YANKEE CAPITALISM: BUSINESS-GOVERNMENT PARTNERSHIP

Yankee capitalist proposals call for an active government role in helping the nation's leading industries to greater profitability and growth, based on a new system of cooperation in which business dominates the other major "partners," government and labor. Not only is the "free market" deemed inadequate to the changed economic conditions of the day, but the idea of unlimited competition is seen as potentially destructive. The cooperation sought would require new consultative mechanisms and implementing means that have historically been termed "corporatist." The term is intended to indicate the extent to which one unified system has been created out of formerly distinct and competing interests, and that it is now subject to central control.

The "Yankee" label represents the primacy of eastern financial interests and a generally internationalist orientation among major supporters. The leading voices of this "industrial policy" version of economic renewal programs, however, have been prominent academics, such as Lester Thurow of MIT (*The*

Zero-Sum Society[6]) and Robert Reich of Harvard (*The Next American Frontier*[7]), and the investment banker Felix Rohatyn of New York. Their work has been closely followed by several Democratic congressional leaders and presidential candidates, and both legislative proposals and party platforms have been constructed along these lines. Business leaders also have shown interest. Several prestigious groups of executives have called for one or more components of such a program—but less often for the comprehensive policy package or a legitimate general role for government in the economy.

These two sets of economic renewal programs—cowboy capitalism and Yankee capitalism—are more visible than the others because they enjoy the support of leading members of the business community, prominent politicians and writers, and the media. They are grounded in the perspective that economic renewal depends, first, on improvement in opportunities for investment and profit. Supporters of each agree on the need for a rollback of the welfare state with its limits on business freedoms, expensive social programs, and resulting need for tax revenues. They also agree on the need to reduce the power of trade unions, redirect capital from consumption to investment, and expand American military capabilities. But they have different underlying interests, which cause them to take different directions when it comes to more specific efforts toward economic renewal.

The other two sets of programs, in contrast, have only thin support at the elite level. They would defend or expand the welfare state, defend the rights of middle- and lower-income people to at least their present share of the nation's income, and rank social needs above new weapons. Most important, they are concerned, first, with democratic participation and control and much less with the needs of business for new investment and greater profitability. In short, they proceed from the bottom up instead of the top down, and with democratic rather than capitalist priorities.

FULL EMPLOYMENT: JOBS BEFORE PROFITS

Full-employment proposals accept the capitalist system of property ownership and the basic idea of the economic market as the allocator of goods and services in the society. But they insist that the market can no longer provide either the proper allocation of resources to serve social needs or an appropriate distribution of income to serve individual needs. Full employment should be the dominant social goal and individual rights to a job at decent wages the means to assuring adequate income. Through an elaborate system of decentralized and participatory planning, advocates propose to use government to direct the economic engine toward achieving these ends.

Supporters of these proposals are found in the left wings of the Democratic party and the trade union movement. Some more liberal members of Congress associated with the Congressional Black Caucus have drafted implementing legislation. Many church and civil rights groups, led by former Secretary of Labor Ray Marshall and Coretta Scott King, have formed an umbrella organization known as the Full Employment Action Council to press for a broad commitment to full employment. Political thinkers such as Michael Harrington have joined in trying to make full employment a major goal of the Democratic party.

ECONOMIC DEMOCRACY: THE TRANSITION TO FULL DEMOCRACY?

Economic democracy proposals accept the private corporate system less willingly than the others, preferring to view it as a temporary reality or perhaps a transitional necessity. The market is rejected entirely as either an efficient allocator or an equitable means to achieve income distribution. Economic democrats see the economy as a set of social relationships among people rather than an aggregate of mechanical forces working on each other; they condemn the present character of the economy as wasteful, alienating, and destructive. Instead, they would set the entitlements of people at the center and try to run the economy—and the society—in a completely democratic manner.

This movement is a recent arrival and has a more limited political base than the others. But the vigor and scope of its critique has drawn much attention since the early 1970s, generating powerful impact on the substance of the public policy dialogue. Prominent advocates include academic economists Martin Carnoy and Derek Shearer (*Economic Democracy: The Challenge of the 1980s*[8]) and Samuel Bowles, David Gordon, and Thomas Weisskopf (*Beyond the Waste Land: A Democratic Alternative to Economic Decline*[9]). Support is found among some components of the Democratic party, local electoral coalitions like the California Campaign for Economic Democracy, and a few progressive union leaders.

INSTITUTIONAL CHANGES AND DEMOCRATIC IMPLICATIONS

Even more than sweeping policy changes and the resulting redistribution of wealth and income is involved in the question of which of the four alternatives is able to find the sustained electoral support necessary to carry out its intentions. Each of these economic renewal programs would create new or substantially modified national government institutions as an immediate part of the design for renewal. If the program were successful in doing so, it seems likely that further changes would be needed to adjust the rest of the system to the new realities or to more effectively implement their commitments.

I take up these institutional changes in some depth in chapters 9 and 10, and only indicate their scope and variety here. Cowboy capitalism, whose free market rhetoric might suggest little need for change in government institutions, has not only eliminated some but created others, and will probably end up adding or expanding more. A number of existing government agencies have been terminated or are scheduled to be, and the result will amount to major institutional change. It is easy to believe reports that the urgency of the dismantling task leads White House operatives to exhort each other, "Don't just stand there! Undo something."

On the constructing side, the Reagan administration has certainly not been idle. It has already substantially expanded the use of presidential commissions. Major issues such as the MX missile controversy, revamping social security, and the question of Central American policy have been depoliticized and negotiated in this private manner. Reagan's "New Federalism" or its successor and the call for a balanced-budget constitutional amendment convention indicate motion already under way toward other changes. There may be further needs for new institutions, however ad hoc they may at first appear, in order to carry out administration priorities. It may be considered necessary to find ways to gain legitimacy for circumventions of congressional limits on the power to wage war, or to develop new law enforcement capabilities in the event that domestic social control once again demands high priority.

Yankee capitalists are more ambitious institution builders. They need to develop a high-level consulting mechanism so that business, government, and labor can arrive at and perhaps implement agreements about national policy. Various advisory councils and planning agencies have already been proposed. New "development banks" have also been proposed, as have several ways of reconstructing the Federal Reserve Board. New institutions for managing import and export policy are also likely to be needed. All of these institutional changes have in common a detachment from direct contact with people, and in some cases from their elected representatives as well. There is a clear sense among Yankees that not only delay but danger is inherent in too much popular participation in economic decision making.

Yankees have also raised the possibility of changing the political representation process so as to enable government to act more quickly and decisively. Longer terms for elected officials, a stronger role for political parties, and greater integration of Congress and the Presidency have all been put forward as possible means of increasing the capabilities of the national government. While these may be proposals whose time is past, as I argue later, they at least show the directions of Yankee ingenuity. In some respects, full employment and economic democracy advocates concentrate on democratizing existing institutions instead of building new ones. The Federal Reserve Board is a leading candidate for democratization, which would in this case mean breaking the bankers' monopoly and installing a more representative Board of Governors. Other financial and business-promoting agencies and activities of the national government would also come under closer popular control.

But there is also a need for new mechanisms to implement some of the key changes that these programs seek. New legislation to prevent companies from closing their plants and disemploying large numbers of workers without notice has a high priority for both sets of proposals. This would require an enforcement apparatus with wide powers and many local offices. And a major effort at institutional development would occur in the creation of a vast local-state-national participatory planning system.

The risks to democracy that arise out of the proposed policy and institutional changes flow primarily from some themes shared by cowboy and Yankee capitalism. Both are concerned with the need for government to be able to act decisively and quickly, and when government deems it necessary, to be able to impose sacrifices on people. Both stress the goal of rising above "partisanship" on major policies or in emergencies, and the need to insulate officeholders from the pressures of special interests or people generally when important decisions are involved. And both must be prepared to maintain social control when people are suffering from hardships and austerity decided upon as a matter of national policy.

There are ways in which each of these shared themes or needs on the part of governing elites sound plausible and reasonable. We can all probably imagine circumstances where we would feel such capabilities would be at least temporarily necessary. But this is just the point. Cowboy and Yankee capitalism intend policy and institutional changes that serve the needs of business first and democracy second, if at all. In that context, such themes amount to a new claim that capitalism should take precedence over democracy whenever probusiness elites in government decide the two are at odds. The continuing capitalism-democracy tension would be resolved once and for all in favor of capitalism because in any serious collision between them there would always be the new rationale and legitimacy for cowboy or Yankee action in accordance with business needs. This is why democracy is "at risk" in the choice of economic renewal programs.

The Political Setting

The necessity of choice among economic renewal programs is clear. It is the decision of our decade, and one that voters will make explicitly and knowingly or by default in one of several ways. For example, voters might support President Reagan because they approved of military adventures like the Grenadan invasion and then find that they had endorsed a major redirection of economic policies. The choice comes at a time of unprecedented political volatility and growing polarization, when many different outcomes seem genuinely possible. Every major feature of our politics today testifies to the powerful impact of the cumulating social, cultural, and economic transformation. A brief review of some of these conditions shows the extent of the current volatility, hints at the new range of possibility, and sets the stage for a look at one of today's major sources of polarization.

Perhaps the most salient initial fact about American politics today is that of low and declining participation rates. Barely half of the eligible electorate is now voting in presidential elections, and less than that in congressional elections. The decline in turnout for elections has been continuous since 1960, and the proportion of voters who took part in the 1980 election was the lowest since 1948. Had it not been for substantial increases in the voting rates of blacks in the South in recent years, the drop in turnout would have been even more dramatic. Nonvoting is greatest among the less advantaged socioeconomic groups, who normally vote Democratic by about a 3 to 1 ratio, but there is significant nonparticipation at all levels of the social order.

Experts see different reasons for this massive abstention. For some time, it was taken as a sign that people were so well satisfied that they did not think it important to vote, and then that nonvoting by alienated and uninformed people was actually preferable. More recently, some have ascribed nonvoting to the lack of distinct programs or a real intention to carry them out on the part of political parties and their candidates.[10] Whatever their analysis, experts are agreed that if even a substantial share of this large body of potential voters were suddenly motivated to go to the polling booth on election day, they could change the direction of American politics. In the words of Arthur Hadley, an experienced observer of American voting habits: "These growing numbers [of nonvoters] hang over the democratic process like a bomb, ready to explode and change the course of our history as they have twice in our past."[11]

He is right. Major changes in American public policy are historically associated with dramatic increases in the turnout of previous nonvoters, as in the Jacksonian period and the New Deal, the two instances to which Hadley refers.

A second and equally unprecedented phenomenon is the dramatic drop in confidence in American institutions and their leaders. National surveys by several polling organizations have measured levels of confidence in the leadership of the basic institutions since the mid-1960s. Results are usually reported in terms of the percentages of respondents who say they have a "great deal of confidence" in the leaders of particular institutions. These proportions were apparently at their highest point when this sort of polling began, and have declined steadily ever since.

Medicine, education, and the military draw the highest levels of confidence, but less than 30 percent of all Americans said they had a great deal of confidence in such leaders in the early 1980s.[12] For the Supreme Court, the President, and the Congress, the percentages were 23, 12, and 12 percent respectively. These percentages were from one-half to one-third what they had been in the mid-1960s, and the decline was continuing. In late 1982, the average level of confidence in all American institutions was the lowest it had been in the history of these polls. The authors of the leading collection of these surveys, appropriately titled *The Confidence Gap,* concluded their book by characterizing our prospects as follows:

> The United States enters the 1980s . . . with a lower reserve of confidence in the ability of its institutional leaders to deal with the problems of the polity, the society, and the economy than at any time in this century. . . . Serious setbacks in the economy or in foreign policy, accompanied by a failure of leadership, would raise greater risks of a loss of legitimacy now than at any time in this century.[13]

Perhaps equally significant are the basic changes occurring in the population base of the American social order. Some of these changes are familiar, but their combination generates massive political impact. Relatively affluent, educated whites are moving to the sunbelt in a continuing stream, and jobs are shifting in the same direction at an even faster rate. By the year 2000, one out of every five jobs in the country will be in California, Texas, and Florida. Left behind in the Northeast and Midwest will be the older, declining industries, reduced numbers of jobs, and increasing proportions of minorities.

The ratio of elderly to younger adults is increasing sharply, and so is the proportion of minorities in the total population. This partly reflects rising immigration, legal and illegal, which now stands at higher totals per year than at any time since the early years of this century. In 1982, about a million people entered the United States legally, of whom 42 percent were from Latin America and 40 percent from Asia. Hispanics will become the largest U.S. minority in the 1990s, and California will have a majority of Third World people soon after. The black population is highly concentrated in the cities of the North and the Southwest, and Hispanics only slightly less so.

The consequences of all this movement will surely include basic shifts in the national political balance. The sunbelt picked up 17 seats in the House of Representatives after the 1980 census and is estimated to gain as many as another 19 after the 1990 census. California, Texas, and Florida together are expected to gain 11 seats. These gains also show up, of course, as added strength in the electoral college at presidential elections. By the election of 1992, the sunbelt (broadly defined) will hold a clear majority of Electoral College ballots.

Less clear are the public policy implications of these changes. What will it mean, for example, to have predominantly black and Hispanic populations in almost all the major cities, with nearly all-white surrounding suburbs? Hispanics include different groups with different economic and political interests, and they are highly concentrated in a few states. Is it reasonable to expect working coalitions between Hispanics and blacks? We know that there is a high potential for new minority political power, but not much about its prospects for realization.

Part of the reason that the consequences of all these changes are so difficult to foresee is that American political parties are weaker and less capable than at any time in this century.[14] We seem to be in the midst of a "dealignment" that has not yet come to the point of a new coalescence or "realignment." Both major parties have steadily lost their capacity to motivate voters or serve as the vehicle for organizing electoral majorities in the last decades. The mass media may have focused attention on candidates, or candidates may have gained independence by personally raising their campaign funds and taking advantage of other rule changes within the parties. In any event, people identify themselves much less strongly with political parties than they used to, and many more people call themselves "independents."

Most observers regret this decline because it implies a less organized, more chaotic electorate in which support for new policy directions is more difficult to achieve. Voters are better able to vote *against* something—for any number of distinctive personal reasons—than participate in working out a consensus in support of a specific alternative. In this context, highly organized groups of voters with intense attachment to a few specific goals can become particularly significant. The New Right's achievements of 1980 are a good example. Made up of voters who were reacting against the changes of the 1960s and 1970s, the New Right used its organized communication networks and numbers effectively to defeat several senators and help elect Ronald Reagan.

The election of 1980 illustrates some other points just made.[15] Reagan's victory by a 10 percent margin of the popular vote and a lopsided Electoral College majority was viewed by Republicans at first as a realigning "landslide," and by the administration later as a "mandate." But as the evidence began to be assembled, it looked less like a dramatic threshold and more like another expression of atomistic voter dissatisfaction with the incumbent and the times. For one thing, turnout continued to slide; most realigning periods are distinguished by sharply increasing turnout. Reagan's winning total was actually smaller than the number of votes cast for some *losing* Republican candidates in the past.

Next, several polls showed that more Reagan voters were voting *against* Carter than *for* Reagan. The nation's rejection of Carter was vehement, and was based on the combination of economic difficulties (high inflation, persistent moderate unemployment) and frustration over the continuing Iranian hostage situation. The leading source of pro-Reagan strength probably was the New Right voting bloc, particularly in the South and Southwest. But what all this added up to was that Reagan actually had been chosen for affirmative reasons by a minority of a bare majority (somewhere between 14 and 16 percent) of the eligible electorate.

Notions of a mandate were vast exaggerations but nevertheless useful to the administration as it sought to implement its program. Certainly Reagan succeeded in implementing the program he had promised to a degree that none but his most devoted supporters had imagined possible. Perhaps ironically, these very successes turned into a major source of polarization in the electorate as the impacts of policy changes began to become clear.

Two important components of the President's program were tax cuts and reductions in social programs. Tax cuts were enacted in 1981 to take effect over three years. Reductions in social programs were also enacted to take effect at various future times. These took two forms. One was a reduction in cash transfers, such as unemployment compensation, disability insurance, and welfare. The other was a reduction or elimination of some in-kind benefits, which are services or commodities provided by the government such as Medicaid, food stamps, or housing assistance.

Studies conducted by the Congressional Budget Office and various congressional committees in 1982 compared the impact of these cuts in taxes and social programs on American families at different income levels.[16] They found that reductions in cash transfers affected the poor more than the rich, but not by very wide margins. Reductions in in-kind transfers, however, hit the poor much harder than the rich. These findings were particularly important in view of the further finding that people in the lowest 20 percent of income levels received 56 percent of their cash income from the federal government before any of these cuts were made.

Not surprisingly, tax cuts helped the rich far more than the poor, who normally pay very little in taxes. But the net change in income distribution accomplished was a staggering redistribution of national income from the poor to the rich. The shares of national income received by the upper-income levels rose significantly, while those of lower-income groups dropped.[17] Reactions to this finding vary, of course, according to ideology, income, and other factors. As we see later, Reagan administration supporters view this as necessary to encourage new investment and ultimately more jobs; others see it as an example of Reagan's bias toward the rich. Reaction among the poor, minorities, and women against Reagan administration policies seems sharp and growing.[18]

Polarization and Prospects

It is tempting, but it would be an exaggeration at this point, to say that Reagan administration policies are accomplishing what the American left has been unable to do since the 1930s: create a political movement around the issue of economic justice in the United States. There is a substantial reaction among the poor, the elderly, and women against the unfairness of the redistribution that is under way. For those who are surviving on marginal resources, it seems simply outrageous to take from the poor and give to the rich. Economic theory, however optimistic, cannot persuade those who live the reality of life at the bottom of the American social pyramid. These feelings of unfairness about the Reagan program show up in several different opinion studies. In one series, for example, national samples steadily shifted from a two-thirds ratio expecting Reagan to serve all people equally (early 1981) to recognizing by wide margins (mid-1983) that he favored upper-income people.[19]

Many other indicia of a growing sense of Reagan administration unfairness on economic issues appear in later chapters. But the best characterization of reactions to Reagan policies remains that of polarization. Ironically, some of the greatest dissatisfaction with Reagan's performance comes from the leadership of the New Right and perhaps some significant share of their supporters. They consider the President to have been too modest in his efforts to reduce the growth of the federal government, too weak in his support for efforts to prohibit abortion and permit prayer in schools, and too soft in relations with the Soviet Union. In short, they view him as too much the captive of their nemesis, the eastern establishment.

This polarization to both left and right raises intriguing questions about the American political prospect. At the least, the spectrum of ideas and possibilities is widening substantially. One wonders what if anything remains of the center! The electorate is not only deeply polarized but also highly volatile, with almost half of all eligible voters standing outside the electoral system and threatening to turn it upside down. Business elites seem to have broad areas of agreement on what should be done, although with some differences on the specifics. Their economic renewal programs are ready. Most politicians follow what such "better people" want, but those programs seem likely to incur the opposition of large numbers of voters—and perhaps even more opposition from current nonvoters. Yet the choice of an economic renewal program cannot wait much longer. Economic decline, transformation, and all the accompanying loss of markets, unemployment, and other dislocations will not permit much more delay.

What will the outcome be? What factors will shape those results? No answer to the first question can even be attempted at this point, although it should be stressed that much depends on the action—or inaction—of millions of ordinary citizens. I think it is possible to begin an answer to the second question, and that conviction underlies this book. One vital factor is the way that we Americans understand the key concepts of our political life—the definitions and understanding about such notions as equality, freedom, capitalism, and democracy that our culture has given us and that our circumstances are steadily reconstructing. Problems, issues, needs, and events work on us in often unrecognized ways to shift our understanding of what is and what ought to be. I later suggest ways that such changes have occurred in our past and explore the possibilities that they may be occurring again in this new time of transformation.

Another factor of perhaps equal importance is the extent to which Americans come to see the social world as a whole, rather than as separate compartments. The notion of economics (capitalism) as a set of activities that is and should be separate from politics (democracy) is neither inevitable nor natural. It is a social and human creation with the most profound consequences. How this came to be and whether circumstances and experience can reverse it again are vital issues that will shape our future.

These assertions suggest continuing attention to conceptual developments, concern for historical background, and an integrated analysis of the current American social-cultural-political-economic system. Not surprisingly, those are the defining characteristics of this book. In the three chapters of part 1, I look first at the evolution of the key concepts and then in brief but comprehensive terms at our present political-economic context. In part 2, I try to give a responsible if not totally objective chapter-length presentation of the beliefs and proposals of each of the four major economic renewal programs. The several chapters of part 3 explore the political implications, feasibility, and prospects of the economic renewal programs with a special concern for what happens to democracy in the midst of this once-in-a-half-century period of political-economic transformation. I assume that a new accommodation between capitalism and democracy is inevitably in the works, and I critically explore every possibility that democracy has to emerge intact.

PART ONE

The Political-Economic Context

2. Democracy and Capitalism in American History

A tale is told in the folklore of many cultures, varying in setting but never in moral, about sibling rivalry between two children close in age. From earliest childhood, they absorb shared but different versions of the values of the family, and they compete for approval. The younger child is quick and confident and full of achievements, although ultimately flawed by excessive need for self-gratification generated by those same achievements. The older child is genuinely virtuous but lacks confidence, and is deeply drawn, as are people generally, by admiration for the other's accomplishments. Soon the older child leaves home—on a lengthy journey, perhaps—and suddenly the younger asserts full ownership of the kingdom or inheritance in his or her own name. The younger child manages it well to start, but with increasing self-interestedness born of the fatal flaw, and the people suffer. But finally the older child, mature and with new-found confidence to match virtue, returns to claim the throne or family responsibility to which he or she was rightfully entitled. And the people rejoice.

With perhaps a touch of poetic license, this fable tells the story of democracy and capitalism in the United States. Democracy was the first-born, but capitalism soon began to steal the show. Both were shaped by the values and the society already in place, and they could endure for quite a while in uneasy accommodation. This first stage ended in about 1860. Not long after the Civil War, the dynamism inherent in capitalism demanded assertion, and in the transformation of 1877 to 1920 it consolidated its triumph. Democracy was never completely absent, and indeed its nagging presence achieved enough results to keep its memory fresh. But it was redefined so as to narrow the range of its virtues, and it was declared relevant only to certain matters. This second stage of the relationship endured to about 1967.

But conditions changed, and the very practices that once led to capitalism's ascendancy now threaten to undermine its hold. The question posed by our four alternative economic renewal programs is whether capitalism can return to its early accomplishments, or devise another way to hold the throne, or will finally yield to the return of the older child. The answer is shaped in powerful ways by the enduring legacies of the first two periods.

Capitalism Versus Democracy I: Early Childhood

SHARED VALUES, COMPETING DEFINITIONS

The basic values and beliefs dominant in the American constitutional period were those first asserted by the new merchant class in chaotic seventeenth-century England: individualism, property, and contract. The first meant putting the satisfaction-seeking individual at the center of thinking about social life instead of starting with the nature and needs of society as a whole. The second meant protecting that individual's property against all threats—including particularly those from kings and lords—except those mounted through the established legal procedures. The last meant finding the origins of obligations between people, businesses, and governments in the voluntary (and usually written) agreements of those parties, instead of in some divine, "natural," or traditional source.

Probably these values really were self-evident, as Jefferson alleged in the Declaration of Independence. They were nevertheless charged with vitality from their success in subverting and partially transforming English society. They were fighting concepts, weapons in the wars waged by traders, merchants, and financiers to wedge their way into political power. Still more forceful versions had been used by Puritans, republicans, and their allies against royal absolutism. Not coincidentally, the American continent was settled by many of these same people after they had been repulsed in England. The three values served them well in the economic development and social arrangements of the new continent. When the descendants of these groups sought independence from England nearly a century later, they had only to sharpen these by now everyday tools for another round.

The notion of the free market gained some of the unique strength it enjoys in American beliefs from its origins and role in this period. Adam Smith's *Wealth of Nations*[1] was not the only vigorous call for replacing the (British) mercantilist system with freedom for all enterprises to compete in a free market to be issued in 1776. The Declaration of Independence of 1776 was reluctantly sponsored by American commercial, financial, and landholding groups precisely because they saw no other way to get free of the systematic British preferences for homeland businesses. Monopolies and franchises, trade and navigation provisions, monetary policy and land titles—all were purposefully manipulated from London for the advantage of royal favorites and the royal treasury. To disadvantaged American business interests, a government of their own seemed essential. For the moment, the idea of a free market could rally support against the British system. Later, with the British excluded and both manufactured goods and foodstuffs scarce, the same appeal would lead to greater profits for American entrepreneurs and merchants.

The key American values of freedom and equality also took on decisive form in this period. To many, freedom naturally meant freedom from (British) government management of economic affairs. It also meant freedom from arbitrary government actions against individuals (including those actively opposing British enforcement of the oppressive economic policies). Equality meant equal status before the law and an equal right to take part in an open contest for economic rewards.

Both rights had special importance for American merchants and developers chafing under British policy. With these definitions, moreover, freedom and equality were compatible. They could be seen as two sides of the same widely shared goal and not as the mutually conflicting claims that they have become in the twentieth century. It surely helped that conditions of life in the colonies at the time were roughly equal and quite fluid. Few people held possessions so vast as to overawe, and others could reasonably aspire to achieve parity from the plentiful resources available. Freedom from restraints genuinely implied the prospect of gain for all.

But many other Americans, not part of the merchant or entrepreneurial groups, held distinctive forms of these values and beliefs. Britain was their target partly for wielding the heavy hand of distant authority as it did. But their real goal was an internal as opposed to external revolution, the elimination of vestiges of antiegalitarianism and social hierarchies rather than mere separation from England. Their version of freedom certainly endorsed readier means of achieving material gains. But it also had more images of a better community and fuller future, in which personal freedoms would enable people to take part in politics and grow and develop as people.

Their version of equality called for greater reality in opportunities to advance in the contest for material things, with fewer burdens from usurious interest rates and creditors' claims. It also included the notion that people should be equal in the less formal but perhaps more meaningful terms of status and dignity as people. They were by no means so committed to the free market as a principle limiting government action as they were to different kinds of government actions, ones that benefited broad public interests. For example, many of them supported price controls during the Revolutionary War and tariffs against British manufactured goods afterward.

Those architects of revolution Sam Adams and Tom Paine were prominent in the latter group. The precedents and arguments they used were not finely drawn lessons from the revered British constitution but ringing assertions of natural rights that echoed from seventeenth-century battlefields. They called their goals republicanism at first because "democracy" was still in disrepute as the equivalent of mob rule. But their notion of republicanism involved far more social reconstruction than did that of the "better people," and was a true model for the French Revolution that followed two decades later.

The Declaration of Independence represented many of the ideals of these early democrats. The egalitarianism that it helped set loose lasted through the Revolutionary War and into the aftermath under the Articles of Confederation. Perhaps the best illustration of this democratic tradition is the Pennsylvania constitution of 1776, drafted by Philadelphia radicals right after the Declaration of Independence was promulgated. At a time when most states limited the franchise to men with substantial amounts of property, it granted voting rights to all free men who paid any public taxes whatsoever—a move that greatly expanded the electorate. The document began with a stirring declaration of individual rights and included the principle that all men possessed the right of "acquiring, possessing, and protecting property and pursuing *and obtaining* happiness and safety."[2]

These egalitarian principles were further translated into the structure of Pennsylvania government. A one-house Assembly whose members were elected annually was made the seat of almost all power. The Assembly was required to function in open public sessions, and to keep full records. Legislation had to indicate its purpose clearly in the preamble, and except in emergencies had to be published and distributed publicly by the Assembly before it could be considered for enactment—but only by the *next* session of that body, after another election had been held.

The office of governor and its veto power were eliminated in favor of a weak Supreme Executive Council of 12 members, four of whom were elected each year for three-year terms. Judges were elected for seven-year terms, but were made removable for cause by the Assembly. A Council of Censors was to be elected every seven years to review the government's performance and recommend a new constitutional convention if changes in its structure or powers were required. The extent of popular control involved in such a system exceeds that of any American government before or since. Indeed, opponents at the time referred to it as "mob government."

Against this background, the Constitution has been seen as a counterrevolutionary document. The question posed for any self-governing population is deceptively simple. How can at least some large proportion of the people take part in the process of governing and still have a government that does the right thing in timely ways? Answers go aground, of course, on the issue of what *is* the right thing. For the early democrats, the answer was that people should be completely equal in their opportunity to take part in, and exercise effective control over, what government did. With such participation and control, which were the essence of their definition of democracy, government's actions would be acceptable to the majority and minority alike. Guarantees of natural rights, contained in formal Bills of Rights, were a vital part of this design.

But their opponents were not at all confident that the minority, whom they understood as the property-holding "better people," would be so well protected. The Constitution as it was written, therefore, included a number of antimajoritarian provisions designed to prevent majorities from what were assumed to be their likely goals—redistributing property to the "have nots." The democrats always denied such goals and saw instead a determination by people of power to exercise dominion over them in one way or another. In particular, they protested bitterly the lack of any Bill of Rights in the Constitution as it was submitted for ratification.

TENSIONS IN THE MAINSTREAM

This was the context in which the celebrated conflict between Hamilton and Jefferson arose—a clash between contending visions of a future nation that carried unequaled importance and has continuing implications. For 20 years, Hamilton laid major accomplishments on top of one another until he built a tower of achievements so compelling that not even Jefferson the President could fundamentally change the course of history. Hamilton's first triumph lay in organizing the call for the constitutional convention and framing it so that economic goals were foremost. His second was in selling the counterrevolutionary product to a querulous country. Through the persuasiveness of his pen in the *Federalist Papers,* and the power of his practical politics everywhere, he was surely the leading force behind ratification.

But perhaps his greatest triumph was in setting the country on course to an independent, powerful economy from his position as secretary of the treasury in Washington's early administrations. Hamilton's model was always the Bank of England and British economic policy, now adapted to serve American interests. In a succession of major state papers, Hamilton inspired creative use of the national debt and public lands to restore the country's credit, draw capital into the new national bank, and be ready to defend the value of the nation's money. (One major proposal, not implemented until later, would have provided incentives for entrepreneurs to develop manufacturing capabilities, and an elaborate transportation system competent to support truly national commerce—perhaps still the most ambitious "industrial policy" in American history.) The accompanying tax programs articulated excises and tariffs to put the burden of supporting his program disproportionately on small back-country farmers and urban consumers. Throughout, he argued for the supremacy of national power, to be confirmed by a supreme constitution-interpreting power located in the hands of leading lawyers, particularly in the (national) Supreme Court.

Hamilton's programs pleased the commercial and financial interests in the country, but antagonized all but the most dedicated anglophiles among other sectors. James Madison, his colleague in the writing of the *Federalist Papers* only months before and now Speaker of the House, split with him over the issue of how the debt was to be repaid. Hamilton insisted that repayment be made only to current holders, well known to be the financial houses and speculators who had acquired the formerly worthless bonds and currency of the Revolutionary period in a frenzied orgy of speculation that began when the Constitution was first offered for ratification. Madison urged that the original purchasers, often ordinary farmers and other patriots whose sacrifices had helped finance the war, be permitted at least some share of the unexpected bonanza of redemption at full value. But Hamilton would have none of it, and carried the day in both houses of Congress. From this early conflict began the systematic argument that led to the development of contending political parties before the nation was six years old.

Hamilton and Jefferson clashed essentially over the model of economic development to be applied in the new nation. But associated with their economic visions were crucial preferences about the role of government, built from premises about human nature. Hamilton's goal was a strong economy, grounded in manufacturing, commerce, and finance. A powerful government would purposefully guide and promote national prosperity. To assure the vital "business confidence," the government had to be capable of maintaining order and stability against the likely self-seeking and redistributive tendencies of propertyless majorities.

To Jefferson, the proper model for economic development was something like the land-based economy he knew in Virginia. He began with the conviction that people were rational and fully capable of self-government, provided certain conditions were met. Personal independence was essential, and was most likely to come from the ownership of at least a small farm from which the necessities for survival could be drawn. Next was the opportunity for education and discussion of issues, and a government close at hand to respond to their wishes and give people practice in exercising responsible judgment. What Jefferson most feared was the detachment of people from their land base so that they would have to work in factories in urban settings, like those of Europe. There they would be subject to the pressures of their employers or the persuasion of demagogues, both of which would destroy free and stable government.

Moreover, real value in the sense of the goods that made life possible—food, clothing, shelter—came from the work of people with and on the land. The wealth of a nation was grounded in such production, not in the paper titles or chains of repeated profit takings by speculators that produced nothing of value. Finally, Jefferson might be said to have trusted the people so much because he trusted elites in government so little. He was sure that temptations to corruption would grow as distance from the people increased. While he never thought people were angels, neither did he fear their intentions with the dread of Hamilton.

Jefferson was therefore repelled by practically everything that Hamilton stood for and did. The credit and debt measures were tricks to enrich speculators by impoverishing farmers. The bank project would pile up paper titles and manipulate money to enrich the same groups, with the ultimate burdens to be borne by the real producers on those same farms. The proposals for government aid to manufacturing entrepreneurs were efforts to force workers into low-wage jobs in factories and cities. The insistence on broad national powers including national power to interpret the meaning of what the people had said in their constitution was a direct road to insulating a self-appointed elite from accountability. Far from a wild-eyed radical, Jefferson nevertheless named his budding political party the Democratic-Republicans to make clear the difference beween his thinking and that of those he saw as retreating from the true spirit of republicanism. His sympathy for the French revolutionists and Hamilton's distaste for the same movement were perfectly consistent with their domestic views.

EARLY RELATIONS OF DEMOCRACY AND CAPITALISM

This is the point (say, the 1790s) at which first democracy and then capitalism were born. Neither had to struggle for life because both of them were thoroughly grounded in the heritage of the Revolutionary period. Democracy finally became a term acceptable to many people, and now stood for those beliefs that stretched from Sam Adams and Tom Paine on the left to Jefferson and his new political party on the right. (Of course, there was plenty of room for Hamilton and true conservatives to the right of Jefferson.) While Jefferson generally endorsed a free market approach to government, other democrats saw the need for purposeful government action in their behalf. They emphatically did not support Hamilton's bank or his tax program or his repayment plan. But they were attracted to the idea of protective tariffs so that the artisans among them might compete more effectively with British manufactures.

Democrats were ardent supporters of the French Revolution, viewing it correctly as modeled on what they had accomplished earlier. With enthusiasm, most democrats supported Jefferson in the election of 1800. Within a few years, many were disillusioned. Jefferson was too acquiescent, too concerned with maintaining continuity and national power, too little interested in undoing Hamilton's work. Indeed, the long-term effect of Jefferson's Presidency was to affix the label democratic (as in Democratic-Republican) on the institutions and policies of the government in Washington that seemed to many to be Hamiltonian in character. Jefferson left many democrats bitter and resentful, with goals and needs unfulfilled.

Capitalism arrived on the scene in the early decades of the nineteenth century, often under the protective umbrella of national and state government franchises and other encouragement. The legal system began to change the substance of tort, contract, and property law to protect entrepreneurs who took risks and engaged in development. New inventions and improving transportation seemed to promise progress and further development of the continent. It was difficult for anyone to resist excitement at the accomplishments of science, technology, and industrialization. Capitalism *was* exciting.

Hamiltonian uses of government, familiar at first, became less necessary as time went on and virtually disappeared by mid-century. With the basic infrastructure in place, capital increasingly available, and popular support assured, the free market principle was more than adequate. For most of this era, capitalism and democracy seemed compatible enough. The society still had a relatively high degree of practical equality to it and offered tangible opportunities to the "have nots" to work hard, rise, and become one of the "haves." Democracy seemed vigorous. Ironically, it was thought to be at a peak during the Jacksonian period—just when capitalism was gathering momentum to send it into comparative decline and eventual eclipse. Only a few were worried about the working conditions and dependence of the factory workers or the assimilation of the immigrants arriving to work in factories, mines, and railroads. Fewer still were concerned about the wealth and power being amassed by the more successful entrepreneurs and financiers. As industrialization moved forward, however, the seeds of inequality began to grow and the idea of democracy to be meaningful chiefly with respect to politics.

Capitalism vs. Democracy II: Sibling Rivalry and Separation

After a brief return to Hamiltonian practices in order to fight the Civil War, the national government settled back into free-market laissez-faire principles in economic affairs. The basic industries of the country—railroads, steel, manufacturing, mining—had been spurred to new levels by the war. But bankers and other policy makers were convinced that hard-money discipline was required to cure wartime inflation, increase the real value of repayments of government debts, and prevent excessive speculation or expansion (except for their favored projects). There followed a sustained period of effective contraction of the supply of money and credit, with frequent panics and depressions lasting almost to the end of the century. Workers and farmers bore the brunt of the hardships brought about by these policies. Business might have experienced cycles from booms to busts, but workers and farmers bumped from one bust to another.

In all our history, the period from 1877 to 1920 is most like circumstances today. Economic crises and transformation made for 40 years of profound social upheaval. The United States entered the era as a predominantly rural, agricultural society and emerged as an urban, industrial one. National government institutions and practices were reconstructed and given both new forms and functions and a new justifying ideology. And the United States moved from insularity into prominence as a world power as it acquired colonial possessions and entrance into new world markets.

Workers erupted first, and in the great railroad strike of 1877 established the formal beginning date of the era of transformation. Thereafter, bloody and destructive strikes continued through 1894 as workers sought decent wages and working hours, often by means of unions, and employers fought back viciously. Farmers also bitterly protested low prices, lack of credit, and the systematic forfeiture of their land to banks and merchant-creditors. Pressure began to build for reforms that would limit workers' hours, put a lid on railroads' charges for transporting farmers' products, and make money and credit available.

Workers and farmers experimented with associations such as the guilds, unions, grange, and various alliances. Both groups ventured tentatively into electoral politics as well. Some state legislatures, and in limited ways even the national Congress, enacted new legislation in response to these demands. But the Supreme Court resourcefully wrote laissez-faire principles into the words of the Constitution and triumphantly declared several of the new statutes unconstitutional in 1894 and 1895.

If ever class lines were drawn in American politics, it was as the election of 1896 approached. The depression of 1893 still had the country in its grip. Farmers had gained political experience in 1892 as the Populist party and seemed likely to improve their showing. Alternatively, they were ready (some would say too ready) to add their strength to a Democratic candidate who would really represent their goals. Workers were organized broadly, both within and outside the Democratic party. Potential agreements existed about the need to nationalize the railroads, construct a new banking system, regulate the big corporations, curb the Supreme Court's adventurism, institute a progressive income tax, and many other radical goals. The "better people" were genuinely alarmed at the prospect of social and economic reconstruction, more so than at any time since Jefferson's first election.

But the potential class alignment fell apart, and despite a high voter turnout, the Republicans won a relatively close election. The nomination of William Jennings Bryan, who had been the congressional sponsor of the progressive income tax law voided by the Court in 1894, might have cemented a worker-farmer coalition. But Bryan was nominated because of his famous oration in behalf of the coinage of silver, and he chose to campaign almost exclusively on that issue.

Unfortunately, it was the one issue most likely to deflect large numbers of his potential constituents and allow the Republicans to paint him as a dangerous radical. Many true Populists knew that silver coinage was an illusory cause and were committed to their own creative banking proposals. Workers saw damaging inflationary reductions in their wages in prospect with silver coinage, and as urbanites (and often of immigrant origins) felt little identity with the Nebraskan's style. Other factors entered also. Race issues were used to split southern farmers. Civil War memories were invoked again in the North. William McKinley's campaign was particularly well organized and funded. And the press was nearly unanimous in its attacks on Bryan.

The bottom line is that a major democratic opportunity was lost, and capitalism gained a 20-year period to consolidate itself. After this election, the economy picked up. The "splendid little war" of 1898 called forth patriotic fervor, notions of manifest destiny, and imperialist pride for many. The Democrats cooperated by renominating Bryan, who lost to McKinley by a larger margin in 1900. Various "good government" groups instituted tougher residency and language requirements that cleaned up machine politics in some cities by purging immigrants from the voting rolls. Turnout dropped in subsequent elections for these and other reasons. Jim Crow laws multiplied and were enforced throughout the South, encouraged by the Supreme Court's endorsement of racial segregation laws in 1896. In short, conditions changed, and the winners of 1896 effectively blocked further democratic thrusts by changing several of the rules of participation in politics.

By the time that the vestiges of the Populist and workers' movements tried to regroup after Bryan's third unsuccessful try in 1908, a new formation of political and economic forces was taking shape. Dominating the center was an alliance of farsighted larger corporations and middle-class professionals whose causes were rationalizing the nation's economy and promoting efficiency in government. At the national level, they established a business-government partnership that gave the appearance and some of the substance of reform. But the new statutes, commissions, and agencies primarily served the needs of corporations and banks for a more stable, predictable, and less destructively competitive national economy. The period has come to be known as the Progressive era after the third party of that name, though only a minority of this center alliance actually supported it when Theodore Roosevelt was not involved.

To the right of the new corporate-government partnership were smaller businesses and the more rock-ribbed conservatives, still locked into the antigovernment stance of their triumphant 1890s. To the left were some mavericks from the major parties, banded briefly in the Progressive party. Then came the Socialists and the unions. The International Workers of the World on the far left served as a kind of symbol, far greater in notoriety than their numbers could ever justify, but useful to the center and right as a threat justifying broad repression. With Theodore Roosevelt and Woodrow Wilson endorsing essentially the same government role in the economy, there was solid political support for the centrist business-government partnership. It was free to build a new Hamiltonian structure and call it by various democratic-sounding names.

There were repeated demands from Socialists, workers, and farmers for larger shares of the economic pie and a larger voice in control of the economy. But their effect was primarily to enable the new partnership to gain grudging business and conservative support for its own prior intentions, and to present the results as a progressive reform. The Federal Reserve System is a good example. The basic statute was drafted by bankers, and the system itself is set up to be run by banks and bankers, all in good Hamiltonian style. But it had the appearance of the banking reform that the Populists had called for as early as 1892, and was presented as embodying similar goals.

This process was repeated with statute after statute, from the Progressive era through the New Deal, until it became practically a hallmark of the new business-government ruling style. On occasion, as with the Social Security Act or the Wagner Act (establishing enforceable rights to collective bargaining) in 1935, the reforms had real substantive importance. Such achievements are proof that mobilized popular power can gain vital ends in a crisis context. But they were products wrested out of a continuing system of power, not a significant change toward popular control of that system.

SEPARATION OF THE SIBLINGS

How could Americans from the Progressive era to the present be induced to accept Hamilton's system, with its frank priority for government promotion of capitalist inequality and resistance to a significant role for people, as the embodiment of *democracy*? There are many reasons. War, patriotism, and fear of enemies makes whatever we have, capitalism *and* democracy, merge into one indivisible unit recognizable only as ours and good. Systematic indoctrination, backed up by repeated war-justified coercion, makes many people unwilling if not unable to look critically at what we have. General affluence makes the issue relatively unimportant, or other matters such as racial tensions take precedence.

But perhaps the most powerful reason is to be found in our American way of thinking about economics, politics, and society as separate spheres of life. In this respect too, we Americans are distinct among people of the world. We militantly refuse even to notice that there is a profound conflict between the multiple inequalities of capitalist society and the claim to have a democratic political system. This occurs because we mentally compartmentalize each and erect an impenetrable barrier between them. This phenomenon is neither quirk nor coincidence, but a cultural characteristic that began in the period of capitalism's surge to domination. It grew, paralleling capitalism's consolidation, until it now seems "natural." How it managed to do so requires some consideration.

In the first stage of accommodation between democracy and capitalism, people thought and talked of "political economy" and other integrated and simultaneous ways of referring to social life as a whole. They worried explicitly about whether industrialization would subvert republican values. But the lure of science, technology, and progress was very strong. Everybody's life seemed likely to benefit from the new inventions, and economic development seemed to promise so much to all. What the new machinery required was apparently neutral, as mechanical and scientific as the machines themselves.

And so the door was opened; in came "efficiency" and a package of imperatives that led to new hierarchical organization and comprehensive social control systems. Bureaucracy followed increasing scale, and the need for efficiency legitimated the whole process. Efficiency dominated the sphere of production, and equity was posed in apparently inevitable conflict and relegated to some other, less important sphere of life. The notion of efficiency, grounded in impersonal imperatives flowing from the technology used in production, served as a convenient cover for the crucial need to control and manage workers. Economics had to be a separate sphere of life where neither rights nor equity were relevant and only the supposedly neutral needs of the machines applied.

And so the idea developed and took hold. One set of rules for economic life, another for politics. In the 1890s and early 1900s, separate and specialized academic disciplines developed to apply distinctive and increasingly scientific methods to the understanding of each area in isolation. In this and many similar ways, boundaries became real and rigid.

There is a positive side to this separation. The same government that is kept away from the economy is kept away from interference with social matters as well. A private sphere is kept free for individuals to pursue their interests as they wish. This is the original meaning of the concept of "liberal democracy."

By now, most of us grow up reading, learning, and thinking about our society, economy, and politics as if they really were three distinct spheres of activity. We can accept the idea (perhaps reluctantly) that there is vast inequality in both of the former, and at the same time believe that, in the political world where each person has the same single vote, all are truly equal. Thus democracy is made into a partial version of what it used to be, a term applicable to politics only, not to the social status or influence people have, nor to the wealth or power they can wield.

Rather than its full, comprehensive older meaning, democracy now signifies only the formal rights one has in the political-legal side of life: rights to vote, to be heard in court, and so on. It has been redefined, in effect, to take away all the social and economic preconditions that make democracy *real*. It is as if the older child never left home, but was forced to speak only words written by the younger child—and then celebrated as a thoughtful and wise guardian!

Capitalism vs. Democracy III: The Return of the Dispossessed?

The first two decades after World War II were a time of rising affluence shared by a clear majority of Americans. The U.S. economy literally dominated the world, and the modern capitalist system—Hamilton tempered by the welfare state—seemed to be one of humankind's great achievements. But its very success sowed the seeds of a new crisis. Competitors rebuilt their economies with more advanced technology and modern productive capacities than the United States had in place, and began a steady march toward parity. Formerly quiescent colonies demanded both independence and a better price for their raw materials. The burden of the U.S. role as world policeman was an economic drag and, increasingly, a nagging moral contradiction.

The first signs of the coming crisis in the early 1960s were not overtly economic but seemingly political and cultural in character. Fundamental sea changes occur first below the surface; their first visible ripples may seem mere aberrations. Their economic linkages and implications, however, soon became clear enough. By the early 1970s, all major factors had converged to reveal once again the basic features of another period of crisis and transformation, right on its 50-year schedule.

The civil rights movement and its governmental response, the Great Society package of social legislation, focused attention on the long-established distributional inequities of the capitalist economic and social system. Two decades of unparalleled affluence had left millions still locked in abject poverty, including the great bulk of the nation's minority population. The Vietnam war drained billions from the strained economy and started it on the path to persistent inflation. The results shook the world trade and monetary system in ways from which they have yet to recover. Perhaps most important, the image of omnicompetence and impregnability that had been a major ingredient of American economic success was lost, possibly forever, in the eyes of Americans *and* the rest of the world.

CHANGES IN VALUES AND BELIEFS

The basic values identified earlier have been through some significant changes in these years. Because they remain the building blocks for any future change, we need an update on both the changes and their implications.

The first trio of values (individualism, property, and contract) has shown some movement over the years toward the views of the early democrats. Our notion of individualism has lost some of its "rugged" nature, trading in utter self-reliance for a recognition of the interdependence of modern society. While the idea lives on as a symbol, few people really aspire to full and complete self-sufficiency; fewer still could ever actually attain it. Most people recognize the collective nature of contemporary life, the extent to which risks and opportunities are shared and indivisible, even if these thoughts have not yet fused into an articulable concept of community.

Our current idea of property has also lost some of its exclusiveness. We still are strongly drawn to the idea of private ownership of houses, cars, stocks, and other material things; and we often define ourselves in terms of the life styles that such possessions allow. But we are also attentive to the things that can only be owned in common and that can be threatened by thoughtless action that will damage everybody. The environment is a good example; toxic waste, destructive pesticides, acid rain, pollution, and many other side effects of profit-maximizing or other private-regarding behavior are no longer accepted. They are recognized as impinging upon others' tangible property rights and also some intangible but propertylike rights to good health and the opportunity to enjoy attractive views.

Our sense of the importance of contracts as the basis for establishing rights and responsibilities has been and remains a pervasive fact of life. Indeed, we have developed a truly distinctive national faith in the efficacy of formally specified rules to govern complex future situations. In so doing, we have raised the role of litigation, courts, and lawyers generally to the point where vast areas of private and public life are utterly dependent on their sometimes whimsical and always backward-looking principles and procedures.

We are now coming to the recognition that this route is leaving us paralyzed and that litigation represents the failure of politics. It is not only the delays involved, in which the sheer volume of litigation in the courts means potentially infinite postponement of vital actions, but inherent limitations in the law itself that define this problem. Of course law is not merely the mechanical projection of the past into the present. History has shown that there is more than ample opportunity for judges and lawyers to insert their personal values and preferences into the meaning of key words and phrases.

But that is just the point. The law gives us, first, a range of the possible fixed in terms of past preferences and relationships. Then it turns us over to the guidance of lawyer-technicians whose habits of thought are firmly constrained by the same assumptions. As we fully grasp the unprecedented nature of our current situation, impatience with the inability to think and act in similarly unprecedented and creative ways may well make for further change in our notion of what the principle of contract should mean for us today.

The great value attached to the ideas of the free market and laissez faire has recently been proved again. Defying all laws of gravity and corporeal propriety, the free market has leaped from its grave in the 1890s into the White House. It was always an enduring symbol with broad appeal, but one that in most houses was hung on the wall like an honored ancestor. It was effectively embalmed by the discipline of neoclassical economics, however, and enshrined by the power of ideology and the wealth of new millionaires. But most observers were still unprepared for its resurrection and skeptically insisted that it must be only a facade for a new round of rapacity by the rich. While its appearance today certainly has that effect, the notion of the free market seems to have an independent existence, and we are probably well advised to avoid underestimating it again. Its appeal has little relationship to its performance, and it seems determined to play the role of a better-forgotten relative who insists on turning up unexpectedly at family picnics.

Of all the basic values and beliefs, perhaps the greatest and most significant change has occurred in regard to freedom and equality. Many Americans now understand each concept in ways different from their early meanings. Freedom no longer means merely freedom from various governmental constraints, but freedom to achieve something or become somebody—in both cases implying a change for which government assistance is necessary.

Equality no longer means merely formal equality of rights, but a genuinely equal opportunity to compete fairly for all the goals of life. And the more one thinks about what conditions and prerequisites are required to have *real* equal opportunity to compete, the more the definition of equality becomes equality of condition, or social and economic equality. For the many people who hold these new definitions, there is no conflict between freedom and equality now any more than there was earlier. Such people have bridged the boundary that separates the political from the economic and social in American minds.

But for those, probably still a majority, who think of freedom as freedom from government limits on what they can do with their property, there is clear conflict with the idea of equality as something that government has an obligation to promote. Even equality of opportunity in its most limited forms implies some need for government to aid some people in ways that cannot help but constrain others' "freedom," if only by requiring them to pay taxes. If government is to do more to make equality of opportunity real, it will surely have as one of its effects further limitation on the freedom of others to do as they wish with their property. Such people have not only not bridged the boundary between politics and the economic-social worlds, they have every reason to want to defend those boundaries as immutable walls given by the framers of the Constitution. That many people *see* this conflict, however, is clear testimony that the process of change is running—in deep underground currents, if not in explicit and publicly articulated ways.

This movement toward widening the concept of equality was first generated by civil rights and other minority activists of the 1960s and received its strongest expression in the form of the welfare rights movement of those years. The latter was a coalition of white and minority welfare recipients and their supporters, including social service workers, who pressed claims for expanded government assistance with particular vigor. The cause of expanding the idea of equality got further impetus from the feminists of the 1970s, and new dimensions of the notion are being urged regularly. For many people, equality is coming to mean at least some right to a minimal standard of living, and for some it means the right to a job.

All this expansion in the notion of equality insistently raised the question of democracy again. Shouldn't a truly democratic society deliver equality in these terms? Doesn't a broad understanding of equality and a full version of democracy amount to the same thing? And so, even before the great economic changes that are still coming to a head, the question of a full versus a partial definition of democracy was coming back on the American political agenda. The issue has been made more urgent, and not created, by the current focus on economic renewal alternatives.

3. The Stalemate in American Politics

Since the early 1960s, the American political system has been steadily congealing into what is today a dangerous stalemate. The primary form this takes is an almost complete lack of effective linkage between governing elites and broad electoral coalitions. Without sustained political support, elites can undertake new policy directions (if at all) only through gross assertions of power that are likely to generate substantial resentment if not resistance. Without an effective vehicle to organize their strength and apply it to the control of officeholders, people cannot make democratic policy choices or see that they are implemented.

The fragmentation of the electorate is part of this problem. But in a participatory system on the scale of the United States, there is a vital need for organization within the electorate and a linkage mechanism through which popular priorities can be translated into a governmental program. These can be vehicles managed from the top down or ones in which active participation by rank-and-file voters gives reality to initiatives and preferences that arise from below. Without broadly inclusive organizations capable of mobilizing voters and building something like a consensus, there is likely to be only sporadic protest, continuing frustration, a rising tide of complaints about "special interests"—and massive nonvoting.

The secondary form that this stalemate takes is an institutional impasse in which the national government has great difficulty acting at all. Our eighteenth-century institutions were designed to promote opportunity for many different interests to block legislation they considered undesirable. They have never served this end with greater fidelity or success. Battalions of lobbyists, Washington lawyers, ex-senators and congressmen—to say nothing of the multitude of Political Action Committees and other special-interest groups—have learned the means of applying pressure to block action very well. Auxiliary institutions created to provide continuing oversight or carry out specific functions have become very nearly independent of representative institutions, except when scandals materialize. Control by elected officeholders over the vast federal bureaucracy, or clear direction of the activities of even a single major agency, increasingly seems impossible.

This has meant at best government by fits and starts, with coherent action evident only in emergencies. Most of the time, the national government fulfills the image suggested by a leading political scientist's book published in the 1960s, *The Deadlock of Democracy*.[1] At worst, it means presidential action to fill a vacuum left by delay and deliberate paralysis. Many observers see no alternatives in prospect except unilateral action by "the imperial presidency" or no action at all.

The institutional impasse might be less significant if the political linkage were strong and effective. Broad agreement on purposeful policy directions would empower officeholders to find a way through the balky institutional system, despite its multiple veto points. But in combination with the lack of an organized electorate and active vehicles for enforcing its will, the institutional stalemate is paralyzing. A government that cannot act in timely and decisive fashion will be in trouble when the problems it faces cumulate sufficiently—and so will the people whom it is intended to serve.

The obvious possibilities are dramatic "government of national emergency" actions by elites in power, continued stalemate until decline and growing chaos force matters to a resolution of some kind, or the restoration of democratic responsiveness through changes in which an organized electorate plays a major role. The choice of an economic renewal program is a basic question that, once decided, is likely to speed our movement in one of these directions. I briefly explore this situation, first at the separate elite and electoral levels of American politics and then in somewhat greater depth at the level of organization-linkage and institutional problems.

The Two Power Systems of American Politics

Two connected systems of power are at work in the United States today. One is the power system rooted in the great aggregations of wealth represented by the corporate economy and the financial community. Some descendants of long-wealthy families may be participants at this level, but for the most part such elites are based in major institutions—banks, corporations, law firms, universities, foundations, and a few key research institutes. The needs of the institutions they represent simply must be served, and these elites go about that task night and day. One of the primary ways to serve those ends is through shaping and executing the policies of the national government. Indeed, the purposes and goals of this structure of power and those of the national government become one and the same. Day-to-day uses of power in the American system thus mirror the needs and the preferences that developed within this first power system.

But there is a second, nonroutine power system at work. Regularly scheduled elections mean that some grouping of voters periodically serves to confirm a particular set of policies or elites in government, or to reject or replace them with others. Voters do not necessarily divide in interest or goals in the same way that elites do, and so issues that are important at the higher levels may not be the ones that determine the outcome of elections. But elites must always pursue their goals in office with concern for what the electorate will do on the next occasion they have to intervene in the process.

How the electorate understands what the issues and problems of the day are can be shaped to some extent, but not completely, by contending elites. Often the electorate acts in gross reaction to basic trends of the year or so preceding an election, and elites from the basic power system are obliged to make the best of the new mix of interests and officeholders thereby installed. There is a major opening here for popular impact on public policy directions, if an aroused electorate makes use of it. Obviously, it is highly desirable for elites faced with the opportunity/responsibility of everyday management of the basic directions of government policy to have some continuing link to a supportive mass base. It is just that, under present conditions, such automatic support is hard to mobilize except in moments perceived as national emergencies.

The present situation in American politics is that elites of the basic power system are divided, and under considerable pressure from the declining American economic position in the world. Neither of the two leading groups within that structure has a very strong link to an electoral coalition, primarily because political parties have lost the capacity to provide that connection. Many factors are at work in the electorate, resulting in high volatility and unpredictability.

THE ELITE LEVEL

The longest-lived component of American elites is essentially the eastern establishment, based principally in old families and multinational corporations and banks, which I have associated with Yankee capitalism. Yankees are principally concerned about cooperative international relationships, monetary matters, and international trade. While they believe in the need for military strength, such power is primarily to maintain American leverage in the complex international setting of shifting Third World alliances, nationalist movements, resource availability, and the vitally necessary debt repayment. Military strength is needed to balance the Soviet Union, although Yankee capitalism's long-term preference is a search for limitations in costly strategic weapons and other accommodations of mutual benefit, particularly involving trade relations.

Organizationally, Yankee capitalism is represented by the Council on Foreign Relations and the Trilateral Commission. Politically, it is (or was) reflected in the moderate wing of the Republican party and centrist northern Democrats. Its popular base is limited to the middle class and professional sectors, but it is overrepresented in the national media. In the 1980s, Yankees joined with cowboys and other leading elements of the corporate-banking sector of the economy in a general effort to roll back the welfare state, reduce the power of the unions, and reduce the burden of government taxes and regulations. But in priorities and style, Yankee capitalism is distinctive. And it is profoundly worried about the international debt and monetary structures and the prospect of interruptions in international trade. Serious troubles in either would damage the American economic system, perhaps beyond repair.

The other grouping within the basic power system is the one I have termed cowboy capitalism, with the proviso entered earlier about using that term to suggest nostalgic and individualistic entrepreneurialism as well as geographic and military connections. It is grounded in sunbelt newer wealth and the industries of that area, particularly military contractors; high technology, construction, and energy firms; and some southwestern oil companies. It is much more free market oriented than the more "socially responsible" and international corporations allied with the Yankees. Cowboy capitalism addresses the rest of the world primarily in cold-war terms, taking a hard line against the Soviet Union and seeing that country as singlemindedly engaged in worldwide subversion and attempted conquest.

Organizationally, it is represented by the Committee on the Present Danger, the American Enterprise Institute, and the Hoover Institution. Politically, its strength lies in the conservative wing of the Republican party, particularly its New Right component, and some southern Democrats. Its popular base is primarily among small businesspeople, southeastern fundamentalist religious groups, and "populist conservatives"—people the New Deal helped to affluence and who now seek affirmation of older social values and a greater sense of national strength in the world.

The issues between these two sets of elites are clearly subordinate to their shared goals of maintaining business predominance and supportive government priorities. But they are also real. They center on the needs of international finance and international trade. Simplifying vastly, Yankees want to make money from money. They want a world open to investment in which all countries accept the American influence that comes with American capital—and all governing elites in such countries see to it that their debts are faithfully repaid. That requires a stable world system with growing international trade and steady prices so that debtor countries can earn the dollars needed to make payments and the banks can profit from financing multiple transactions in all directions. If imports flood the United States and ruin small businesses and cripple older industries, that is an unfortunate by-product but a tolerable one under the circumstances.

Conversely, cowboys want to make money from selling things. Often such things are made or extracted at low cost and sold at high prices under conditions of much lower risk than the cowboys' chorus of praise for free enterprise would suggest. For the most part, these producers sell to American markets, particularly the military arms of the U.S. government. There is considerable need for government assistance in realizing profitable opportunities at home and providing military or other support abroad. If government could be counted on to do the right thing with appropriate discretion, it could be very useful indeed. But because it often fails on both counts, cowboys believe it is better to invoke the free market principle and go it alone. Cowboys are thoroughgoing nationalists, and protectionist help to U.S. industries is a good way to bolster profit margins. Banks and other countries should worry about any by-products that arise. Under conditions of economic decline, American industries come first and the free market should work its impersonal will.

THE ELECTORAL LEVEL

We have already noted the low and declining turnout of voters that distinguishes American elections from those in other advanced industrialized countries. Population shifts of various kinds were also noted as helping to generate an unpredictability and volatility that is quite new. Contributing to this same sense is another fundamental trend, that of the breaking up of the "New Deal coalition" that came together in the 1930s behind Franklin Roosevelt's programs and continued to support the Democratic party well into the 1960s. The basic ingredients of this coalition were white southerners; urban working-class northerners, particularly recent immigrants and Catholic ethnic groups; and industrial workers and populist farmers across the Midwest. Blacks began to join this coalition in the 1940s and then more rapidly in the 1950s as the Democratic party started to become the party of civil rights. At the same time, white southerners began to leave by the other door.

In the 1960s, there developed what analysts variously call the "new class," "new politics," or "new liberalism." By these terms they meant an activist component made up of middle-class northern whites whose concerns were left-wing and life-style issues instead of the bread-and-butter liberalism of the older coalition. The result of all these developments, combined with the rising affluence of most Americans and changing basic issues of politics, led to the fragmenting of this basic coalition. There came a point at which these elements were opposed to each other on most issues of the day, and there was little that national candidates could do to hold the disparate pieces together.

The disintegration of the New Deal coalition was visible in electoral data by the late 1950s. One of John F. Kennedy's arguments for a place on the Democratic ticket in 1956 was that as a Catholic he could restore the waning Catholic component of the old coalition. By the late 1960s, a number of political scientists were talking about the transformation of the party system and potential realignments.

The conservative columnist Kevin Phillips probably did more than any other observer to characterize what was happening. His first book was an expansion of a strategy paper written for the Republican campaign of 1968 and was titled, *The Emerging Republican Majority.*[2] Coining the phrase "sunbelt," he essentially declared the New Deal coalition dead. In its place, he stressed the population and power shifts commonly recognized and showed how an appeal to the interests in that quadrant of the country could lead to a winning (and permanent) Republican coalition. The Goldwater candidacy and attempted coalition of 1964 might have been rejected by the voters and mocked by the commentators, but it was a preview of the long-term future.

In his most recent book, *Post-Conservative America,*[3] Phillips assesses the coalition that formed in the mid-1970s and gave rise to the Reagan candidacy in 1980. He argues that Reagan benefited from a constituency best understood as "populist conservatives." These people are not really conservatives, he says, except in the way that they yearn for past American glories. Nostalgia, nationalism, and resentment of the social and life-style changes of the 1960s and 1970s are the emotions that are common to them, and these fuse with fundamentalist Protestant religious beliefs to generate a powerful political movement. Phillips views this constituency as leaping beyond conservatism, into the past. One of his terms for this phenomenon is "1980s Restorationism"; "the politics of cultural despair" is another. The title of the book is intended to suggest that a new politics is taking shape in this new postindustrial era.

But these are also people who once supported the old New Deal coalition on economic welfare grounds, Phillips argues, and if Reagan's economic policies do not result in a tolerable combination of inflation and unemployment, they might revert to their old habits. The Reagan coalition is fragile, in other words, and utterly dependent on economic conditions. This populist constituency is also "radical," in the sense of wanting to participate in politics on a mass basis and take whatever measures might be necessary to "set things straight." What this all adds up to, in Phillips's eyes, is a highly volatile situation in which the established political order ultimately might be at stake. Nor is Phillips uniquely alarmist in this respect. His concerns are shared by several leading political scientists who specialize in the implications of voting trends; at least one regularly refers to these prospects as "a crisis of the regime."[4]

One intense and purposeful component of the Reagan constituency certainly was the white fundamentalist Protestants, primarily southerners, who swung behind his candidacy with special fervor. Organized by New Right leaders with both religious and secular goals, these elements gave Reagan decisive majorities throughout the South and Midwest. They had first come together around the Panama Canal Treaty issue in the mid-1970s and now focused on family-related issues that expressed their traditionalist reaction against changes of the 1960s and 1970s.

I characterized the 1980 election earlier as *not* a realigning election but an expression of rejection of Jimmy Carter. This tendency to vote against incumbents or circumstances is an increasingly characteristic feature of American elections. It can be seen in 1980 not only from the poll results cited earlier but also from the way that Reagan drew almost equally from all major social groups in the population. Normally, relatively low-income and less-educated people vote disproportionately Democratic, while higher income and education levels go Republican by equally large ratios. The ratios among such groups, however, and between regions, religions, and occupations were remarkably similar in 1980. Only blacks stayed with the Democrats in their usual high proportions. Jewish voters and working-class Catholics were still Democratic by good margins, but not the usual ones.

In 1982, some of the old ratios began to return, which led some analysts to think that there was life in the New Deal coalition or something like it after all. When economic welfare issues are paramount, in other words, a crude socioeconomic alliance forms to defend public services and promote social welfare. Electoral coalitions form and reshape themselves, at least in the present period, according to issues that are prominent. What happens if the issues seem to be ones involving national security and the threat of communist expansion we do not yet know, but probably such issues would take precedence over all else.

The 1982 elections also gave some hints that economic problems might inspire greater turnout. There was clear evidence that the unemployed were turning out in larger than usual proportions. Black voters also turned out in larger than normal ratios, as did women. Only an unusually well organized and funded campaign enabled the Republicans to hold their losses in the House to modest levels for a midterm election.

The Organizational Linkage Problem

There is an obvious and substantial gulf between the clarity of goals and uses for government among elites and the electorate's inability to organize and express itself as favoring one or another policy direction. The tensions generated from conflicting styles and interests at the elite level find little or no counterparts in the electorate. The latter is either discouraged from participating or unable to get itself together so as to play a continuing role in shaping the basic directions of public policy. And yet each side at the elite level knows that coming elections can reorder their relationships and opportunities. Elections *matter.* Consequently, elites are concerned with finding ways to mobilize popular support in anticipation of those moments when the electorate has the capacity to intervene and disrupt things.

As loyalties to political parties have declined, it is becoming more difficult to "find" voters through organizations. Unions, which once helped make voters available for labor-related issues, have declined precipitously in membership and political consequence. Indeed, given the American lack of any social democratic movement or party such as exists in European countries, there is now in the United States no readily available, organized popular support for social welfare causes. Elites are under less pressure to make concessions to popular social needs than they have been for some time.

Along with the decline in political party and union significance has come a parallel rise in the importance of the mass media and single-issue mobilizations within the electorate. Candidacies are created, shaped, or destroyed by media presentations in a matter of months or sometimes days. Issues rise quickly and disappear even faster. At the same time, well-financed efforts to organize voters around special causes can produce powerful impacts in very short order. The most salient of such efforts recently was the highly effective direct-mail system of organizing New Right groups in the late 1970s.

American elections today are decided first by which voters actually turn out to vote and then by some very gross choices that they make. Appeals are designed in part to tap the emotions of atomized individual voters, but also to shape the definition of what the election is about. In the absence of other organizing vehicles, the atomized voter is likely to respond to his or her reactions to immediate past events or continuing problems as they can be fitted into some very fundamental boxes or categories in people's minds. There are only about four such categories. Elections are "about" economic welfare; foreign policy; race relations; or the "social issues" of sex, crime, family, and religion. Sometimes an election can involve more than one such definition, but in a clear priority order. The election of 1980, for example, was one in which Carter was rejected because of the twin failures in foreign policy (Iran) and economic welfare (inflation and unemployment). There was neither a mandate for a Reagan program nor even a clear choice for the conservative alternative.

Incumbents are not just prisoners of events, of course, because their actions in office shape the way that the electorate is likely to categorize the coming election. For example, high unemployment might normally define the election as one in which economic welfare was paramount—and the Democrats would have an important edge. But an incumbent administration faced with such a prospect might well try to make the election instead a referendum on "standing up to the Soviet Union" in Central America—with devastating effects on Democratic hopes.

ORGANIZATIONS: OLDER FORMS

Certain long-established forms of voter organization remain significant as ways of linking the first and second power systems, in part because there are no real alternatives. Political parties and unions are good examples.

Although they are clearly weaker than ever before, the two major political parties are still the first symbols with which people identify politically, and are the best set of cues about how to vote. Cowboy and Yankee elements in the first power system are strong in the Republican and Democratic parties respectively. These major parties thus represent the organizing vehicles most likely to provide a means for them to gain the electoral coalition necessary to implement their programs. But in the confused and volatile context of American politics today, they are very uncertain vehicles indeed.

Table 3.1 presents some recent data on the way people identify with and feel about the two major parties. Different measures of identification and "feeling" are included, and the growing differences between men and women are

TABLE 3.1
PARTY IN THE ELECTORATE, 1982 AND 1983
(in percent)

	Men	Women	Total
Call themselves (June 1983)			
Democrats	32	43	38
Republicans	25	21	23
Other (Ind. and "don't know")	43	36	39
Vote in 1982			
Democratic	53	57	55
Republican	44	40	42
Believe Reagan deserves reelection (June 1983)	52	33	42
Party best able to ensure economic recovery			
Democratic	32	39	36
Republican	49	32	40

SOURCE: *New York Times,* 10 July 1983, reporting CBS/New York Times poll data from June 1983.

highlighted as a way of indicating that new fissures are opening up all the time in the electorate. Democrats are clearly the "majority party," but it is uncertain what if anything that means. More people, and many more women than men, identify with the Democrats; the margin, however, has been shrinking in the past few years. But even when the election involves only the Congress, the level at which party ties have been strongest in recent years, the final vote is closer than party identifications might suggest. As we have noted, the ratio reverses in most presidential elections, and the same electorate supports the Republican candidate.

The contrast between men and women is a new one in American politics, and apparently is generated by Ronald Reagan. Men are apparently attracted toward Reagan's military and rugged individualist images and believe that the Republican party can solve the economic recovery problem better than Democrats. (These are the same men who say by a good margin that they are Democrats.) Women show sharply contrasting levels of confidence in the parties with respect to economic recovery and end up far less supportive of Reagan than men. Part of this difference lies in the difference between men and women in expectation that Reagan will engage us in war, but that is not as sharp as differences with respect to economic recovery.

Both major parties certainly have the essential negative strength that makes them eternally attractive. If the other party holds the White House and can be blamed for economic troubles, foreign policy embarrassments, or other bad things, voters' vengeance is likely to bring them into office. But these are not only negative attributes; they are probably indicative of only a temporary hold on the offices obtained. Our recent history has been too full of rejections of incumbents and choices of lesser evils to require further comment. The lesson for economic renewal purposes is that initiating a program requires more. It requires either a positive and continuing support for that program or a continuing alternative focus that *permits* institutional change and redirection of policy needed to accomplish the program.

The condition of the major political parties has drawn much attention from political scientists and others. Their decline is regretted because it implies a less organized, more chaotic electorate in which support for necessary new policy directions is difficult to achieve. One of the most insightful of these specialists is political scientist John Petrocik, who likens the party system to "a hibernating mammal; not quite dead, not even moribund, but not very lively either, neither exerting much influence on its immediate environment, nor being very affected by it."[5] Petrocik is one of the relative few to argue that what the parties need is a program, and (by implication) that a party cannot be rebuilt except around a coherent and specific program. Writing in 1981 he said:

> What is needed for a dramatic rebuilding of the parties is an agenda which will galvanize voters and office-seekers. It seems very unlikely that any of the issues of recent years have such potential. . . . The missing element in the contemporary electorate is a public agenda sufficiently compelling to overcome popular indifference to the parties.

The economic renewal agenda, including as it does both institutional reconstruction and redistribution of wealth and power in the society, would appear to be one—perhaps the best—example of the kind of revitalizing element for the current political parties.

The Republican party today is a party of the right. Its strength lies in elections defined generally as national security elections, when it can appeal to patriotic symbols and keep the New Right by its side, or in times of economic prosperity, when social issues or national security issues can be used to handle the New Right. It is likely to have constant difficulty with the actual conditions of an interdependent economy and with the rightful claims of minorities, the poor, and many others.

The Democratic party is a party of the center. Its strength is much less identifiable, although greater in the abstract than that of the Republicans. Currently, it seems to depend on a relatively low level of international conflict and a concurrent need for some degree of social services. Under such conditions, an inoffensive candidate has a good chance to win—all other things being equal, which they seldom are. But there is no program at its center, and no particular purpose that it seeks to serve, except what is becoming the memory of the New Deal.

There is no American political party of the left. Elsewhere, trade unions and social democrats have combined to make viable alternatives known, and sometimes to govern. This void is part of the problem for full-employment advocates and economic democrats. Lacking a powerful and purposeful labor movement, there has not appeared to be a base from which to start.

The decline of the political parties has a parallel in some important respects in the current state of American unions. Where unions once represented about 35 percent of the American work force, they have slipped steadily to the point where they now represent less than 20 percent. Several factors have contributed to this decline. One is the shift from manufacturing, where unions have traditionally been strongest, to services and the public sector. The ratio went from 41-59 percent in 1950 to 27-73 percent in 1982.

Another factor is the resistance to unionization in the sunbelt, where many states have "right-to-work" laws and employers in newer (particularly high-technology) industries campaign vigorously to prevent unionization. Sunbelt states' proportions of manufacturing workers who are unionized are roughly one-third that of the older industrial states. This resistance has spread nationwide, with a new specialty developing among law firms and management consultants in the field of destroying unions and preventing their formation. The new influx of women into the workforce has also reduced the share of workers who are unionized. The jobs that women get tend to be clerical and nonunion, and organizing is very difficult; even where men and women have similar salaried positions, women are unionized at about two-thirds the proportion that men are.

All these trends have added up to some dark days for traditional unions. The recession and their own weakness have led to a series of concessions in newer collective bargaining agreements so that it is increasingly difficult for unions to point to positive achievements that might justify the costs of membership. Employers have undercut some unions by instituting worker-participation arrangements and quality-of-work-life programs that similarly make unions seem unnecessary. Workers in high-technology fields, reflecting their greater educational backgrounds and skill levels, have acted as individuals in high-demand circumstances often do. They have proved uninterested, at least for the present, in unionization.

Not surprisingly, membership in some of the country's biggest industrial unions dropped precipitously between the mid-1970s and 1982. The United Automobile Workers dropped from 1.358 million to 1.037 million, a loss of almost 25 percent. The United Steelworkers of America dropped from 1.3 million to 685,000, almost a 50 percent fall. The International Association of Machinists went from 918,000 to 590,000, a drop of about one-third. Paralleling these membership losses was a sharply increasing number of decertification elections, in which unions were losing at higher ratios than ever before.

When the AFL-CIO declared its intent to endorse a presidential candidate before the Democratic primaries began in 1984, national opinion polls promptly asked samples of the country's voters how they would react to a candidate that carried such an endorsement from organized labor. The reply was stark and direct: More people said they would be *less* likely to vote for such a candidate than *more* likely—*and by a ratio of almost* 3 *to* 1! Even Democrats were more likely to be negatively influenced by such an endorsement. Only union members or their families were positively moved by such a prospect, but 47 percent of them said it would not matter and 18 percent said they would be "less likely" to vote for a labor-endorsed candidate. When Walter Mondale was finally endorsed by the AFL-CIO Council, surveys showed considerable rank-and-file disagreement with the choice.

The loss of identification with political parties is clearly paralleled by a loss of identification with unions' political positions. This is borne out by the increasing similarities between union members' voting and that of other people at the same educational and income levels. In 1980, union members were indistinguishable from others in the extent of their support for Reagan except at the lowest income levels.

ORGANIZATIONS: NEWER FORMS

The prototype of new political organization is the New Right. It is essentially a group of four organizations headed by leaders who successfully consulted and worked together in the late 1970s and early 1980s. These are the Conservative Caucus (Howard Phillips), the Committee for the Survival of a Free Congress (Paul Weyrich), the National Conservative Political Action Committee (Terry Dolan), and the *Conservative Digest* (Richard Viguerie). Viguerie's activities include both publishing the *Conservative Digest* and managing the direct-mail system of communicating to (and raising money from) conservatives of every kind that he pioneered. These groups and leaders are united around religious, moral, and cultural rather than primarily economic positions. In 1980 they worked very closely with the Moral Majority (Jerry Falwell). They are "populist conservatives" in their antielitism and advocacy of mass-based action to recapture the past. Kevin Phillips incorporates all their features in a single sweeping characterization.

> I submit that the New Right combines three powerful trend patterns that recur in American history and politics. First, to some measure it is an extension of the Wallace movement, and as such represents a current expression of the ongoing populism of the white lower middle classes, principally in the South and West. All the right symbols are present: antimetropolitanism, antielitism, cultural fundamentalism. Second, the New Right is closely allied with the sometimes potent right-to-life or antiabortion movement, the current version, perhaps, of the great one-issue moral crusades of the American past—the pre-Civil War abolitionists and the early-twentieth century prohibitionists. And this one-issue element, in turn, folds into the third phenomenon—the possible fourth occurrence of the religious revivals or "Great Awakenings" that have swept across the land since the middle of the eighteenth century. If so, the *religious* wing of the New Right may be the *political* wing of a major national "awakening."[7]

These nonconservative "conservative" groups have their own agenda—one that includes the overthrow of the Big Business-Big Labor-Big Government structure that they see destroying the country. Phillips refers to them as "neopuritans" and estimates that they might amount to as much as 20 to 30 percent of the electorate. These and other factors make them an indigestible and unreliable component of a larger coalition, as cowboy capitalism may be on the verge of learning.

The one major commitment that they share with the cowboys is toward a powerful military role for the United States in the world. They favor a faster and more drastic reduction of the size and scope of the national government than cowboys want or can produce. They want the government to restore the status quo ante of social and cultural values and practices—something *no* government can accomplish. But they also want to preserve the economic security built by the New Deal, which the free market side of cowboy capitalism disdains.

The New Right has repeatedly declared its dissatisfaction with Reagan administration staff appointments, compromises with Yankees and moderates, and delays in implementing its promises. Leaders have publicly threatened to form a separate party. But the core groups committed themselves in 1983 to make the 1984 elections into a referendum on "defending America in its own backyard"—the presence of Soviet influence in Central America and the need for use of American covert or military power to root it out. This is certainly a powerful, unifying focus. It should enable the Reagan administration and the New Right to hold together at least through 1984, and to jointly seek to find ways to satisfy enough demands from each side so that open conflict is avoided.

The New Right is the most salient, but far from the only, new organization or linkage mechanism seeking to bring voters together in American politics. There has also been a widely noted proliferation of Political Action Committees, organizations of contributors that maintain lobbying headquarters in Washington and funnel campaign funds toward their preferred candidates. Not all of them are run by trade associations, businesses, or wealthy individuals; some are also funded by many small individual contributions and serve specialized ideological or public-interest causes. Many local coalitions have formed around specific issues or problems, usually with a reform-oriented perspective. In some cases, these groups have been explicitly "populist" or "progressive," with the intent of building upon initial electoral successes toward state or national significance.

Perhaps the most significant new organizations are those emerging from the women's and minority movements. These groups made their initial gains through appeals to the nation's sense of fairness and justice toward fellow citizens, and supplemented these claims with victories in court and the Congress. Women and minorities began to run for office and get elected in increasing proportions. But in both cases, the process of movement toward full citizenship and genuinely equal opportunities seemed to stall amid some mistakes, widespread misunderstanding and resistance, and the apparent general swing to the right represented by the election of 1980. Subsequently, there seems to be a regrouping and new urgency toward broad electoral engagement on the part of both women and minorities—in organizations and as individual voters. If this trend should mature as present evidence indicates, it would have potentially dramatic effects on American politics; we explore this possibility in greater detail in later chapters.

The Institutional Impasse

As I suggested earlier, our existing institutional structure was clearly designed to have conflict *within* the government—but not too much conflict. Parties were discouraged as "factions," and the hope was that most conflict could be contained within governmental institutions where it could be resolved by the best minds in the nation in relative calm, apart from popular pressures. The separated power system, with its accompanying checks and balances, seems to us to be self-evident and essential. But it is distinctive among nations of the world, and is actually an eighteenth-century recipe for paralysis. It has created stalemate and incapacity to respond in a coherent and sustained manner to any number of problems that confront modern governments. It has spawned often dangerous auxiliary means that have arisen in order to get the job done. These include the "imperial Presidency," an excessive and discretion-laden judicial role in certain areas, and monotonous efforts at depoliticizing issues and mobilizing support for "bipartisan" solutions through the use of presidential commissions.

Meanwhile, whole new systems of governing have grown up around this older structure, unsanctioned by the Constitution but nevertheless powerful policy-shaping entities in their own right. The bureaucracy created in the Progressive era and expanded in the New Deal is only the most visible of these. An elaborate special-interest complex has surrounded the Congress, deploying lobbyists (including those for foreign countries), Political Action Committees, and Washington lawyers in what amounts to a supplementary governing system.

More recently, the media have come to play a decisive yet inconsistent and unaccountable role in affecting politicians' images of one another and the understanding that the public has of officeholders and issues. In one period, an outraged and moralistic press plays up the implications of a relatively minor incident into a sequence that drives a President from office, and in the next accedes supinely to another President's perspective on communist "takeovers" in Central America. Important national policies were in the first case blocked, in the second furthered, with neither apparent cause, explanation, or accountability.

Modest changes have been attempted, with little effect on the basic problem. Efforts to gain greater presidential control of the bureaucracy through such centralized agencies as the Office of Management and Budget or other units in the Executive Office of the President have not been notably successful. Congress has loosened its rules considerably, giving more opportunities to junior members but losing leadership capacity in the process. Larger staffs have not enabled the Congress to reach informed consensus positions and articulate them clearly. The new budget process has been a modest improvement in an area of much greater need and potential. Fragmentation, frustration, and mutual cancellation seem to be more characteristic of the Congress than ever, and it shows in members' retirement rates.

Political parties, particularly the Democrats, have over the past few years instituted several rules changes in an effort to "democratize" the party and give more representation to women and minorities. Primaries have been emphasized in order to provide more popular impact on the choice of delegates to presidential nominating conventions. Paradoxically, the latter changes may have made it possible for small but very active minorities to obtain numbers of convention delegates for their candidates and leave much larger but relatively inert majorities without many delegates at all. None of the institutional changes of recent years has attempted more than patching, and most have not been successful even in their own terms.

PARLIAMENTARY SYSTEM PROPOSALS

Frustration with the fragmented and parochial character of American political parties and the separation of powers and other obstacles to coherent action in the American national government has led to repeated calls for adoption of some version of the parliamentary system. These proposals have surfaced before, but are doing so now with increasing frequency if limited hope. They take two principal forms: proposals for reform of the parties, and proposals for integrating the legislative and executive branches. Both seek to enable the government to act more decisively in behalf of programs that the winning political party has effectively promised the voters to implement, and to make it possible for voters to hold the party accountable for its actions in power.

Proposals for party reform are no longer either frequent or hopeful, but their history is instructive. The intent of these proposals was to move American parties in the direction of British models, by encouraging them to take issue positions more strongly and giving them some powers to enforce such issue stands on their elected officeholders. Nothing as bold as control of nominations was included, in deference to the tradition of independent districts; nevertheless, the proposals met with either blank incomprehension or outright hostility.

The best-known proposal came in 1950 from a study undertaken by the American Political Science Association. Its tentative nature was underscored by its title, *Toward a More Responsible Two-Party System.*[8] The report served principally as a target for the hard-bitten "realists" of the political science profession. They argued that the independence and parochialism of state and local party components fit well with (their image of) the interest-group character of American politics.

The report deserved better of the political science profession. Its foresight may be illustrated by a passage in which the authors warned of dangers that they saw as possible if the then-visible decline of the parties continued:

> The first danger is that the inadequacy of the party system in sustaining well-considered programs and providing broad public support for them may lead to grave consequences in an explosive era. The second danger is that the American people may go too far for the safety of constitutional government in compensating for this inadequacy by shifting excessive responsibility to the President. The third danger is that with growing public cynicism and continuing proof of the ineffectiveness of the party system the nation may eventually witness the disintegration of the two major parties. The fourth danger is that the incapacity of the two parties for consistent action based on meaningful programs may rally support for extremist parties poles apart, each fanatically bent on imposing on the country its particular panacea.[9]

Allowing for the authors' understandable postwar preoccupation with events prior to the war in Europe, this is a rather accurate forecast of exactly what has come to pass 30 years later. We are still, despite Watergate, in the age of the imperial Presidency, particularly whenever anything needs to get done. The disintegration of the parties is common knowledge, and several leading political analysts are already talking of the long-term implications of today's splinter parties. We have the explosive era, and all that remains is to learn the specifics of the grave consequences.

Future historians may well understand why it seemed impossible or undesirable to modify the party system in the 1950s, but they are likely to mark the failure as one in a series that led to the convulsive transformation that has yet to occur. Given the state of major parties today, if no other factor, it is impossible to imagine reforms of this kind in the future. There might have been a time during the 1940s and 1950s when the Hamiltonian system could have been effectively democratized through parliamentary-style reforms, but that moment has passed.

Proposals for integrating the legislative and executive branches continue to be made, however, and can still be taken seriously. The goal is to reduce conflict between the branches and make their operations more coordinated, coherent, and decisive. One proposal is to encourage the President to appoint leading members of Congress to be "shadow" heads or otherwise represent Cabinet departments while they hold their seats in Congress. Although members are constitutionally prohibited from holding "offices under the United States," the failure to mention Cabinet positions in the Constitution would permit them to serve simultaneously in informal roles with the various departments.

Proponents hope that this would give Congress greater knowledge, closer oversight, and a fuller sense of responsibility for the operations and legislative needs of various departments. One of the merits of this proposal is the opportunity that it would provide for other members of Congress to question the Cabinet representative on the floor of the legislative chamber. It has not been possible to accomplish this in other ways because only members have floor privileges.

Another proposal along parliamentary lines would give the President, or perhaps both the President and the Congress separately, the power to call for elections under specified circumstances. This would require a constitutional amendment, perhaps creating more trouble than it is really worth. The goal is to enable either branch to break stalemates when they arise, and to add to their respective leverage over each other in such a way as to increase the prospects of compromise agreements. It might elevate certain issues to more of a focal role than they would otherwise have in the ensuing election, a goal well worth seeking. The problem is that this procedure would probably not be used very often. The two- and four-year cycles of elections contain a beginning dynamic of "wait-and-see, give-them-a-chance," which soon enough becomes the early maneuvering for the forthcoming election.

The fact of fixed dates for elections *is* a significant drag on policy-making momentum, foreign policy negotiations, or both. It takes time to get either process moving, and American efforts are regularly undermined by having to stop and have an election. Nor can foreign governments count on much continuity in American positions, which as far as they can know may vary sharply almost from one year to the next.

A proposal that responds to the latter concerns, though not necessarily part of the parliamentary package, is for a single six-year term for the President. The idea is that a President with a longer term could provide consistent policy positions, benefit from experience gained in foreign policy and congressional relations, and not have to face the organizational task or the political temptations of a second-term election. The President would also lose the leverage that the prospect of a future winning candidacy gives today, but it is argued that this is an acceptable tradeoff. Some depoliticizing is apparently also hoped for, although it seems likely that this would only substitute some more personal basis for intragovernmental loyalties for that of political party that now helps to tie people in government together.

Many proposals for increasing national government efficiency along parliamentary lines emanate from frustrated former government officials. The American system *is* cumbersome, in many ways obsolete, and almost always slow to respond. But some of the complaints seem traceable to an impatience with the failure of the government to act in a particular way, not with the process itself. Conflict is often unwelcome to those whose goals are frustrated thereby. The urge to depoliticize, and to promote efficiency, can easily turn into a "government of national emergency" to accomplish ends otherwise unacceptable to many people. Classic questions of governmental organization have a way of resurfacing in different forms all the time.

SOME SUMMARY IMPLICATIONS

The combination of political stalemate and institutional impasse may be generally unrecognized, but it is at least as portentous as the economic transformation with which it is so fully integrated. This is not an idiosyncratic judgment. Seasoned observers from all across the American political spectrum have warned of the dangers we face from our current political incapacity. Some are concerned about the intentions and capabilities of impatient elites, others about the readiness of a frustrated electorate to institute a demagogue's solution, and still others about institutional breakdown.

Bertram Gross, a leading political scientist with long experience in government, published a book in 1981 with the self-explanatory title *Friendly Fascism: The New Face of Power in America*.[10] His concern was that the growing urgency of a wide range of problems combined with new technological capabilities would tempt elites to ever-greater manipulation of the electorate. Gross argued that the United States was well on the road to a new and wholly American brand of fascism in which bureaucracy and apparent rationality would mask the role of corporate elites in managing the system in their interest.

The conservative columnist Kevin Phillips regularly warned in 1982 that the conditions of pre-Hitler Germany were ominously converging among ordinary people in the United States:

> I would . . . suggest four rough parallels between the United States of the late 1970s and early 1980s and Weimar Germany in the late Twenties. The first is the impact of inflation and the resulting frustration of the middle classes; the second is the trauma of a nation's first defeat in war—World War I for Germany, Vietnam for the United States; the third is the antipathy of the German *Volk* and much of Middle America to the ensuing postwar "liberation" of moral, cultural, and sexual standards; and fourth is the pervasive erosion of popular faith in the fair-

> ness, responsiveness, and effectiveness of government and other political institutions. Within a nation, such frustrations accumulate only slowly—and rarely.[11]

The careful language of a 1983 study of the sources and nature of institutional change in the American national government carries a similar message about the prospect of institutional breakdown:

> The magnitude of the governing problems at hand, the press of time, and popular outrage aimed at bureaucratic bungling may ultimately work to complete the Progressives' break with the past. The search for control and direction may yet persuade us to move beyond our unwieldy Constitution. It hardly need be said that this path toward a regeneration of American government requires the utmost caution, lest in disgust with bureaucracy we stumble upon a sense of the state far more threatening than any we have yet known.[12]

This consensus among informed observers is broad and encompassing. Even though there is vigorous disagreement about which of the major elements in the system should exercise the greatest leverage—one or another elite grouping, one or another version of electoral majorities—there is no dispute about the existence of the present stalemate or its dangerous implications. Our economic problems and the current economic renewal programs are only one stimulant toward a multidimensional transformation that has been gathering momentum for decades.

4. U.S. Decline and Transformation in the New World Economy

As always, informed observers differ about how to characterize what is happening to the American economy. There is a core of consensus, the scope and depth of which may be quickly summarized in the words of two leading experts. Leonard Silk, the economics columnist of the *New York Times,* says, "The world economic system is suffering the most acute stress it has known in half a century"; he goes on to ask rhetorically if it can be saved without abandoning democratic institutions.[1] Harvard's Robert Reich, a prominent advocate of aggressive new industrial policies, adds a historical dimension: "Since the 1960s, the U.S. economy has been slowly unraveling."[2] Once past this consensus, characterization depends on one's perspective. Those most impressed by future profit potential prefer "The Molting of America"[3] or "Industrial Renaissance."[4] Those most concerned with the plight of working people and their communities are more likely to use terms like "disinvestment," "deindustrialization," or "capital flight."[5]

If economists and other analysts did not differ so dramatically about both causes and cures for our economic problems, I might not be bold enough to attempt even this limited synthesis of current interpretations. Economists, like lawyers, are often most intimidating when they are dead wrong. But their very differences may be put to constructive use. Each statement and characterization above has captured an important dimension of what is happening. These insights can be combined into one coherent general interpretation. It is vital to stress, first, a world historical context, as suggested in the above consensus. Within that context, two major trends incorporate all other characterizations. One is comparative decline in American economic performance, occurring simultaneously with a basic economic transformation. The other is the specially rapid and increasingly dangerous swings in the inflation-recession-recovery roller coaster.

The notion of *context* is crucial. What has happened over the years since World War II, but particularly since the 1960s, is that nonsocialist world economies have progressively integrated. They are now delicately intermingled. Profit and wage levels are dependent on similar conditions elsewhere. Inflation and recession occur everywhere and simultaneously, rather than as national phenomena. Many individual histories have merged into one new network that is rapidly making its own history as an integrated unit. Tensions and differences remain, of course, but risks and opportunities are increasingly shared. Nearly all recognize, for example, that the question posed today is whether capitalist recovery can be achieved in a manner that preserves democracy. It might be added that few ask the next question: If we must choose between them, who will decide—and for which option?

The new world economy reflects neither a choice nor a coincidence, and it is irreversible. It should come as no surprise that it was built by the very driving forces that are the defining characteristics of a viable capitalist economy: growth and profit. Silently, inexorably, these basic factors reconstruct an economy according to the nature of new opportunities for profit and the pressures of competition. Once the process of change develops momentum, it cannot be arrested or reversed. Decline and transformation define our times.

The two trends usually occur independently, and are alone viewed as major social problems. But today all these distinctive components have converged to create an unprecedented situation, a modern megaproblem. Separately, each involves powerful forces hard at work to reconstruct American economic and social life. But it is their cumulative effects that create capitalist crisis and accompanying democratic danger—and opportunity. No danger without opportunity, no opportunity without danger. No wonder the symbols or words for these two concepts are the same in several languages.

The *decline* we are experiencing is both absolute and comparative. The U.S. economy has declined from its own former levels in profitability, and in its rate of increase in productivity (units produced per hours of work), since the 1960s. Real wages dropped in the latter years of the 1970s, even before the recession of 1981. But it is in comparison with other industrialized countries that the U.S. decline is most evident. The American economy is still by far the largest in the world, but it no longer has the edge on others that it once did. Several countries have passed us in per capita production, income, and many other categories. They are increasingly able to compete with American producers in both domestic and foreign markets. American companies are losing profits, and American workers are losing jobs, as a result.

The *transformation* that is under way also has deep historical roots, ranging from the electronic revolution and other technological developments of the space age to the energy crisis of 1973. What is changing is what we produce and where and how we produce it. Products and their ingredients, processes and the people who run them are all changing, with potentially profound impact on our quality of life and employment. Dramatic forecasts from sober observers now crowd a field once left to professional futurists, with terms like "the knowledge society" and "high technology" becoming commonplace. A relatively sedate version is offered by John Naisbitt, author of the best-seller *Megatrends:*[6]

> The United States is rapidly shifting from a mass industrial society to an information society, and the final impact will be more profound than the nineteenth century shift from an agricultural to an industrial society.

But it is often difficult to distinguish the characteristics and effects of either decline or transformation from the more familiar workings of the business cycle. The *inflation-recession-recovery* roller coaster is simply more immediately visible to most people than (long-term) decline or transformation. It currently involves a cycle in which inflation and unemployment trade positions as the principal source of suffering with increasing rapidity. In the past decade, for example, we have had both the highest unemployment rate since the Great Depression of the 1930s and the highest inflation rate in modern American history. The causes of inflation are hotly debated. But nobody seems to doubt (certainly not after the experience of the early 1980s) that inflation can be controlled if policy makers impose a deep and prolonged recession. The key question for the future is whether the current economy can be brought to a level of activity that will restore profits and jobs and stability without also renewing a destructive level of inflation.

The Process of Decline

Economic decline is said to occur when a nation's economy, by certain measures, does not perform as well as it did at some previous time. Measures used include profitability, gross national product (GNP, the total of goods and services produced), per capita productivity, personal income, and the like. The standard of comparison may be its own prior performance or that of other countries in relation to it. The current U.S. decline is visible in both ways.

Decline in comparison with prior U.S. performance is readily traceable from about 1967. Table 4.1 on page 60 presents the movements of the leading components of "stagflation," the term coined in the early 1970s to suggest the combination of low growth, unemployment, and inflation that characterized those times. It focuses on distinct periods. The first is the time prior to 1967, after which it is clear that "something happened." The critical period of change is 1968-72, and after that the oil shocks helped spur decline.

Inflation had been relatively low throughout the 1960s, until given a boost by rapidly rising government spending for the Vietnam war. It has risen steadily ever since, except for brief drops during recessions, until the mini-depression

TABLE 4.1
U.S. ECONOMIC PERFORMANCE, 1960-83
(in percent)

Indicator	Averages 1960-67	1968-72	1973-80	1981	1982	1983
Inflation	1.6	4.6	8.9	10.4	6.2	4.5
Unemployment	5.1	4.7	6.6	7.6	9.6	9.6
Rate of growth in GNP	4.3	3.3	2.8	2.0	−1.8	5.5
Rate of growth in productivity	3.8	2.3	1.1	1.8	.4	4.5

SOURCE: *Economic Report of the President, 1983,* table B.41.
Calculations by the author.

of 1981-82. Unemployment started to rise in about 1969; it climbed steadily, except for brief periods, until its peak in that same mini-depression. Growth as measured by the gross national product was modest by earlier postwar standards and declined over the last years. (Corporate profits, except for the oil industry, were below prior levels also throughout the period, but changes in reporting criteria make comparisons unworkable.)

Productivity growth also shows remarkable slowing during the same time. There is a lively controversy over the meaning of productivity data, however, which must be taken into account so that future arguments will be understood. Some analysts deny that many different industries, with their different kinds of economic activity and necessarily idiosyncratic measures of output per labor input, can be lumped together to make up a meaningful total. Others deny that "productivity" measures anything, except perhaps an attempt to justify some preferred solution to be advanced later. My detached judgment is that some measures used are weak indeed and comparisons between different kinds of industries probably are not worth much. But it seems to me that a certain general insight can be found in comparisons of large aggregate totals using the same measures over an extended time. *Something* is changing when ratios of this sort show sustained trends in the United States (and, as we later see, between the United States and other countries).

In any event, table 4.1 shows a remarkable combination of the indicia of decline—indeed, a long-term slide downhill. This may have been masked by brief reversals or by interpretation as mere short-term fluctuations of the business cycle. More detailed analysis would support such views: the brief boom of the war, the short recession of 1970, and the equally brief preelection boom of 1971-72 are evident. But the most striking contrasts lie in the before-and-after averages; in every case, the 1973-80 period was one of much poorer performance than the early 1960s. The data point to the early stages of a cumulating problem with which we have yet to come to grips.

With the help of hindsight, the start of economic decline in comparison with other countries can be dated from the moment the new world economy began to take shape in the mid-to-late 1960s. A key factor was sluggish profitability in the United States, stemming from a variety of still-disputed causes ranging from unions, taxes, and regulation to the end of postwar dominance, massive waste, and poor management. What is "new" about the current economy is primarily its integrated world context. Opportunities for profitable investment, production, and sales now beckon compellingly from all corners of the world, and competitive pressures flow from foreign corporations once far distant from the American marketplace.

The first effects of such higher-profit opportunities occurred when American corporations began to invest heavily in new plants in Europe to be able to sell in that reviving market. Some companies licensed their advanced technologies to foreign manufacturers as a means of improving short-term profits. Others shifted production intended for American markets to lower-wage areas of the United States, and later to Third World countries. The process quickened as improving transportation made it possible to ship goods quickly and inexpensively all over the world. Technology made the exchange of information (and thus central managerial control) possible on a worldwide basis. Facilities could therefore be located wherever wages or other costs were lowest. Satellites and computers made capital instantly mobile, able to seek out and respond to any good opportunity. Banks joined the search for higher-profit investments, and found them in development loans to Third World countries.

Hundreds of billions of dollars were lured out from one region to another in the United States, into mergers or short-term markets and/or out of the country in the 1960s and 1970s.[7] Some went into productive investment in the United States, but much did not. The higher profit ratios available elsewhere were simply irresistible. Another irresistible opportunity was that of escaping from American trade unions, whose considerable powers were deployed in defense of the gains made in wages and working conditions during the postwar years. By the end of the 1970s, one-third of all profits of the largest American corporations and banks were derived from foreign investments. The productive capacity of American-owned plants overseas, if calculated separately, would be the equivalent of the world's third or fourth largest economy.

U.S. government policies helped encourage the movement of capital abroad by providing deductions for taxes paid to other countries plus other inducements and guarantees against loss from such investments. Government tax policies also encouraged the acquisition of other U.S. companies in order to offset their losses (or other deductions) against profits already earned. Such mergers were useful in addition as ways of increasing short-term profits, when the acquired company could be operated for a time without new investment and then closed for additional tax benefits.

Just how lacking in needed new capital investment the U.S. economy was in this period is a matter of dispute among reputable analysts. Some argue that investment was adequate, or that it would have been if the American economy had not been operating so far below capacity. Why invest in new productive capacity when you are not using what you have? But it seems clear that, as the new world economy took shape, one of its first major consequences was the diversion of much of the capital generated in the U.S. economy to overseas and nonproductive uses. "Disinvestment" and "deindustrialization" are not too strong as characterizations of this process.

Some stark comparisons may help convey the scope of the changes that have resulted. In 1960, the United States led the world in per capita gross domestic product (GNP less income from abroad) by a comfortable margin.[8] In 1980, the United States stood eleventh among nonsocialist industrial countries, and the leader outpaced the United States by 39 percent. U.S. steel production accounted for 26 percent of the world's total output in 1960, while Japan's was just over 6 percent. By 1980, Japan was at 15.5 percent and the United States at only 14.0 percent. In 1967, the United States built more cars and trucks than the rest of the nonsocialist world combined. By 1982, the United States was third behind Japan and Europe.

The volume of international trade was rising rapidly in this period as countries sought to find export markets for their new products. In 1969, Japan exported about 600,000 cars per year. In 1981, Japanese exports totaled more than 6 million. In the case of the United States, exports rose steadily to the point where, in 1982, 20 percent of industrial production and almost double that of agricultural production were exported. The United States took in about $210 billion from exports in 1982, or about 7 percent of GNP.

But the most dramatic consequence of the new world economy—and a nagging measure of the extent of the American decline—lay in the shares of American markets achieved by imported manufactured products and semi-finished materials such as steel. Americans suddenly found themselves surrounded by a wide variety of foreign-made products, from cars to radios, televisions, and computers. Moreover, they were quality products at lower prices than comparable American-made goods, and so American consumers bought them in ever-increasing numbers. In some industries, foreign companies made sharp inroads on the sales and profitability of domestic producers. In others, it was not so much an inability to keep up with foreign competition as that American corporations *were* the "foreign competition." Goods manufactured overseas by American corporations, often in Third World countries, were capturing markets once supplied by American domestic production—and American workers. Payments for all such imports were estimated to exceed earnings from exports by $60 billion per year in the mid-1980s, imposing another substantial drain on American capital.

Once again, the 20 years from 1962 to 1982 offer instructive contrasts.[9] Predictably, the import share of the U.S. automobile market soared, from 1.9 percent in 1962 to 22.8 percent in 1982. But so did the import shares in such other areas as consumer electronics (18.5 to 42.1 percent), communication and electronic equipment (1.3 to 13 percent), and metalworking machinery (1.9 to 14.9 percent). Less predictable perhaps were fields such as textiles (4 to 15.4 percent), shoes and leather (5.3 to 43.5 percent), and engines and turbines (1.2 to 18.9 percent). The point is that the impact of imports was widespread and general, not limited to one or two industries.

What accounted for the apparently sudden spurt in imports? To some extent, it was production in low-wage settings such as South Korea, Taiwan, Singapore, and the Phillipines. But it was also the fact that new plants in other countries used recently developed technological capabilities to produce at much more efficient levels than those of the older American factories. Productivity in American plants, long the magic factor assuring American predominance in world markets despite (previously) higher labor costs, grew more and more slowly while it leaped ahead in other countries.

Another source of expansion in imports came from the vigorous efforts of many countries to increase their exports in order to pay their rising bills for imported oil. The managed shortages and rapid price increases of oil after 1973 put a heavy burden on most industrial economies, but some responded more effectively than others. Japan and the continental European nations, all heavily dependent on imported oil, were able to conserve energy and expand their exports so as to cover most of the outflow of cash involved. The United States, starting from a position of lower dependence on foreign oil, also used energy more efficiently as prices rose. But it still suffered a net loss of about $90 billion a year during the mid and late 1970s, higher than any other country.

One of the first results from the rise of import competition is pressure for government action to limit the entry or raise the price of such goods. The rhetoric of "free trade" can be heard almost as often as that of the free market, and as a principle of action is violated nearly as frequently. Free trade is an idea that assumes international competition, slow-changing technology, and open markets with plenty of time for them to adjust to new products, suppliers, and conditions. It does not address a world of government subsidies, rapid transfer of technology, private cartels, and government-managed terms of trade. The wonder is not that governments act inconsistently with the free trade model but that so many people continue to talk as if it were still applicable. A real and increasingly dangerous problem, however, is the multiplication of protectionist measures by national governments around the world. If international trade is seriously inhibited in the new world economy, profits and employment are reduced, and depression looms.

In any event, U.S. practice has been to respond to calls for protection by seeking to negotiate "voluntary" restrictions or quotas on other countries' exports to the United States. Sometimes the introduction of protective legislation has been part of this process, or tariffs have been increased to discourage shipments of low-priced goods. The "domestic content" route has been followed recently with respect to steel and automobiles. This proposal calls for a specific proportion (90 percent) of certain final products (cars) to be made in the United States, and, if enacted, it would have the effect of encouraging other manufacturers to either set up new plants in the United States or buy components from American suppliers. Many countries employ such legislation as part of an overall trade strategy, particularly when they are seeking to protect a new industry while it is developing.

The consequence of protecting established domestic industries against foreign competition is that a declining industry is propped up artificially. We do that now in steel and other areas. Instead of modernizing the declining industry, or shifting its capital and labor to new industries where they might be more successful, the old industry is effectively subsidized by the taxpayers, or by consumers' payment of higher prices for its products. Adaptation is slowed. Eventually, with this practice in force for several industries over a period of time, the entire economy is slowed and inflationary pressure generated. Sometimes the ramifications of a major company's collapse are so great that a federal "bailout" is essential, as in the cases of Chrysler Corporation and others. Established industries often have well-entrenched unions. Together their political strength in Washington may be great—certainly greater than industries as yet unborn or their potential workers.

The Search for Explanations

It has not been easy for Americans to come to terms with the fact that, for a period of years, the American economy has been outperformed by that of several industrial nations. Once far inferior by the standard measures, these countries have caught up and passed us in many respects. Overwhelming U.S.

advantages in fields of historic dominance, such as productivity and technology, have melted away so that head-to-head competition for new markets today can result in German or Japanese victories.

Recognition of the successes of foreign countries set off a search for explanations. One possibility was that the others had an easy time catching up because they had so far to go and that once they neared our level of performance they would slow and fall into line behind us. Another major explanation was that the U.S. government was the problem; it took too much in taxes, spent too much (particularly for social insurance and social welfare programs), was too concerned about the equity of income distribution, or regulated too much (particularly on behalf of labor). A version of the tax explanation held that incentives for savings and investment were so inadequate, particularly for corporations and the wealthy, that the United States had a very low rate of capital formation and hence the widely recognized decline in productivity. Finally, some analysts simply blamed the people: Americans had lost the work ethic that had made the country great, were too ready to live off a too generous government, or were just generally enjoying too lush a standard of living.

Most of these "explanations" are completely false. Those that have some partial validity are far from adequate to explain the loss of American leadership in economic performance. Cutting through the fog of ideology has not been easy either, particularly as some distracting events like the oil shocks or recessions hit all countries in the new world economy. But at least some are starting to see the outlines of a better explanation: (1) a singleminded focus on international competitiveness, in Japan and Germany particularly, especially in newly developing product areas; and (2) implementation by cooperative business-government planning and multiple government support systems.

ECONOMIC PERFORMANCE

Once the immediate postwar reconstruction period was over, the capitalist world economies passed through three periods. The first lasted through the 1960s to the first oil shock of 1973. It was marked by continuing high economic growth and strenuous government efforts to make the most efficient use of expanding plants, raw materials, and labor. Japan, for example, maintained a truly phenomenal average annual economic growth rate of more than 10 percent for a 20-year period. No other country compared with that level, but most exceeded the United States by comfortable margins. In the case of Japan, a good share of its early momentum seems to have come from centralized efficiency-promoting measures first instituted by U.S. Occupation forces to rebuild its war-devastated economy. The same is true of Marshall Plan developmental efforts in Germany.

It should be recognized that the major European countries and Japan all have long-established traditions of centralized state support for economic development. Indeed, administrative capabilities were improved and expanded in order to promote business more knowledgeably and effectively in all these countries before the twentieth century was well under way. In rebuilding from the war's destruction, therefore, it was only natural that there be a major role for the state in maximizing cooperation and efficiency in use of resources. Close relations existed between governments, finance, and industry in France, Germany, and Japan. The first two countries were major factors in the development of the European Common Market, with its new institutions for international public-private cooperation. Only Great Britain has had anything like the American romance with the free market and laissez faire. Great Britain employed none of the purposeful development banking of the other countries, was the last to join the Common Market, and has had the lowest growth and highest unemployment rates of all these major countries since the war.

The second period, from 1973 to about 1980, was one of slower growth and continuing efforts to adjust to rapid escalations in oil prices. Older and more energy-intensive industries experienced difficulties, and inflation/recession concerns came to the fore. All the major countries had lower growth rates, but in the same comparative relationship as before. That is, Japan, Germany, and France led the way; Great Britain and the United States trailed. The first two stepped up their efforts to shift capital and labor away from declining industries to areas of future expansion. Great Britain, on the other hand, followed the same general policy as the United States, instituting general protections and quotas to preserve older industries and undertaking various supportive measures for them. Japan, Germany, and to a lesser extent France made substantial gains in key new export markets, particularly the high-technology fields.

In the current period, from 1980 to the present, the new world economy was fully in place, and first inflation and then recession became worldwide facts of life everywhere and at once. For the most part, however, the same comparative relationships between major countries obtained, although France was suddenly in difficulty. For all its dependence on external sources of raw materials, particularly oil, Japan was still in better shape than most. Following Japan in most categories was Germany, and finally Great Britain and the United States. Table 4.2 summarizes the contrasts between the United States and its two primary competitors in key categories.

EXPLAINING THE CONTRASTS

That others had an understandable catch-up period with a clear end to it is refuted by the fact that they are not only catching up but steadily passing us.

TABLE 4.2
THE UNITED STATES AND MAJOR COMPETITORS,
KEY INDICATORS

Indicator	United States	Japan	West Germany
GNP per capita, 1981	$12,783	$9,578	$11,132
Annual % change, GNP per capita			
1975-80	2.6	4.2	3.7
1981	.9	2.1	−.5
GDP per capita as % of U.S.			
1960	100	30	85
1980	100	68	101
Inflation, average per year			
1977-81	9.9	5.7	4.4
1982	6.2	2.6	5.3
Unemployment, average per year			
1977-81	6.7	2.1	3.4
1982	9.6	2.4	7.7

SOURCE: *Statistical Abstract of the U.S., 1983,* tables 1526, 1527, 1532, 1536.

New countries surpass us each year. It *is* true that the rate of growth of *all* countries has slowed. But the reasons do not have to do with maximum levels set by standards of American performance. They have to do with the integrated nature of the new world economy and its inflation/recession problems.

The notion that the American government is to blame deserves burial with full ceremonial honors. It is undoubtedly to blame for many things, some of which have to do with sluggish economic performance. But excessive levels of taxation and spending, or overzealous regulation and redistribution of income, do not seem to be the culprits here. In regard to taxation, Germany, France, and Great Britain all exceed the United States by wide margins when total government revenue is compared to GDP. Only Japan has lower shares of GDP going to governments in the form of taxes than the United States, but Japan has the highest *corporate tax* of all the major countries. Corporate taxes in Japan provided nearly half of all government revenues, as compared to about 10 percent in the United States in the years before the U.S. corporate tax was effectively eliminated in 1981.

When the nonmilitary spending of national governments is compared with total GDPs, Germany, France, and Great Britain lead again, with the United States in last place among the major countries.[10] Sweden, a country with better all-around economic performance than the United States, spends at the rate of 56 percent of GDP; the United States is below 30 percent. The United States spends more for military purposes than any other nonsocialist country, and so when military expenditures are added for all countries, the American ratio of national government spending to GDP rises. It still trails all the other countries with the exception of Japan. When the totals of all spending for social insurance and social welfare programs are compared with GNP, moreover, Japan once again exceeds the United States. The United States again spends the lowest proportional amount of all major countries for these purposes, less than half as much as does Germany. The conclusion is inescapable that the United States taxes at lower levels, spends at lower levels, and provides less in the way of social programs than its major competitors.

Similarly, the United States does less to "coddle" its workers than any of the other major countries.[11] A lower proportion of workers are covered by unemployment insurance in the United States than in any of these countries, for example. For workers who *are* covered, the United States pays the lowest share of previous earnings of any of these same countries. American workers have the shortest annual entitlements to paid vacations, and (not surprisingly, perhaps) the highest proportions of person-hours lost through strikes, of all these countries. In every major category of assistance to workers and their families, the U.S. government does less than its major competitors. Clearly, the life of the American worker has not been rendered so comfortable by government that the United States has suffered competitive disadvantage thereby.

Finally, the excessive redistribution and failure to promote capital formation explanations may be addressed together because both argue for reducing taxes on corporations and the wealthy. In proportions of after-tax income received by the lowest 10 percent of families (or the lowest 20 percent, it does not matter), the United States is lowest of all the major countries.[12] This means that the poorest people in the United States are receiving, *after taxes,* lower shares of the total national income than in any of the other countries. The country in which the lowest 15 percent, and the lowest 20 percent, of all families receive the *highest* share of income produced is Japan. Next, the United States *leads* all these countries in the share of total wealth held by the top 1 percent of all households, and the top 2 percent. In other words, while all countries have wealth and income patterns that are skewed toward the top (a relatively few people having the most, most peple having little), the United States is more skewed than the others—and *after* taxes.

These data suggest that there is ample capital in the hands of individuals for investment purposes. Inasmuch as capital gains taxes and the corporate share of total taxes have both been declining for the past decade—and both were sharply further cut in the tax "reform" of 1981—the problem of capital formation must be restated. It is not a problem of the availability of capital or of a lack of savings. It is a problem of what choices are made by the wealthy concerning the uses of their discretionary income, and more generally about how capital is invested: in mergers, money market certificates, speculation, Third World adventures—or in new plants and products in the United States.

Lest it be thought that the other countries must have reduced their land areas to smoky industrial wastelands dominated by wizened efficiency experts, I shall add just a few quality-of-life measures.[13] Mortality rates for infants are one standard indicator, and here the United States ranks eighteenth in the world. In 1950, the United States was fifth, but since then, even some much less developed countries have passed us (e.g., Hong Kong, Singapore, and East Germany). Fourteen countries are ahead in male life expectancy at birth, and seven in female life expectancy. Only Canada compared with the United States in pollution levels among Western countries; the others were well below in measures of various pollutants.

Meanwhile, the United States leads in some negative statistics, particularly those related to crime. More Americans per 100,000 of population are in prisons at any given time than in any other country except the Soviet Union and South Africa. The death rate per 100,000 population from homicide and other purposeful injuries inflicted by other people in the United States is about triple that of any other country in the world and nearly seven times that of any of our major economic competitors. It is not a matter of economic growth *versus* quality of life; comparatively, we are losing on both counts.

I want to be clear about what all these comparisons *say* and *do not say*. They do *not* say either that the United States is a bad place to live or that Americans generally have failed. Most of us would not live anywhere else; we are glad to be Americans. The data *do* say that our economy—like our political system—has fallen far short of its capabilities, and both are in danger of falling very far behind both their capabilities and the performance levels of others.

The Nature of the Transformation

An economic transformation may seem to share some of the characteristics of general decline in that some industries may be starved for investment capital and particularly vulnerable to foreign competition. But the reasons that lie behind the decline of certain industries during a transformation are rooted in some revolutionary technological development and other changes associated with it. And the latter simultaneously lead to the rise of new industries to replace the older ones in a nation's economy. In other words, *structural* change in the nature of the economy itself is involved.

The U.S. economy is undergoing just such structural change today, in three basic ways. *What* we produce is shifting from heavy industry and primary metals to high technology and services. *How* we produce is shifting from labor-intensive and high-volume practices to highly automated and more flexible methods. *Who* does the work is changing also, with many assembly tasks shifted to Third World countries. In the United States, more people are needed in service and technical jobs and fewer in the familiar blue-collar mass production occupations. If not entirely irresistible, the forces making for this structural change are at least very powerful. If the United States does not make changes necessary to keep up with foreign competition, it risks losing the profits and jobs it needs to sustain its economy. We must run very fast, in effect, in order to stay where we are.

It is easy to exaggerate the role of a single factor in this transformation, and to end with dire predictions about the eclipse of the role of human intelligence in production or other work. But it is probably true that among the many new materials and applications involved, the microprocessor or semiconductor chip—a tiny silicon wafer with a myriad of electronic circuits printed on it—lies at the heart of our economic revolution. One Nobel Prize-winning economist was quoted in 1982 as ranking the chip just behind the wheel and equal to the steam engine among history's technological thresholds.[14] It is at once the replacement for giant computers and cadres of scientists and engineers, making possible both manufacturing and other tasks with less material, lower energy consumption, greater reliability, higher productivity—and far fewer workers. We shall someday produce many new products and be able to *do* much more, much of it at lower costs. But along the way there will be profound upheaval for millions of people.

The so-called sunset industries are often actually chains of industries, from producers of raw materials to fabricators of components to manufacturers of finished products. Steel, whose precipitous decline in share of the world's market was cited earlier, is a good example.[15] The U.S. steel industry in 1982 had a production capacity 10 percent lower than it did in 1975, and was still operating at only 38 percent of that capacity. A total of 200,000 jobs, both blue and white collar, had been eliminated since 1965, mostly in the late 1970s and early 1980s. Steel companies were rapidly diversifying out of steel production instead of modernizing their plants. Bethlehem Steel, for example, was only acting in ways typical of many of the older industries when it declared its intent to sell still-profitable plants as a way to consolidate its operations and free capital for new and more profitable ventures.

The problem facing the steel industry was partly intense pressure from the automated competition of Japanese and German companies. This pressure was so heavy that the industry and its principal union went together to the national government in search of protective legislation. A good share of the industry's problems, however, stemmed from the sharp decline in automobile sales experienced by American manufacturers in the late 1970s and early 1980s. Even more came from the fact that the materials going into cars were changing in character. The "downsizing" of American-made cars and trucks came relatively late, but it arrived with a vengeance. The steel content of the average Ford car, for example, was cut by 31 percent between the years 1977 and 1982. In 1976, the U.S. steel industry sent about 25 percent of its total output into automobile production, but by 1981 this figure was 15 percent of a much lower total. Much of the impetus for this change came from the national government's efforts to deal with the oil shortages of the mid-1970s. In the words of a leading business journal:

> Congress, in legislating fuel-consumption standards for American cars, committed itself to a radically different industrial structure. You downsized the American car to save gas, and you wound up downsizing not only the U.S. auto industry itself but a substantial part of the industrial base that supported it. You saved gasoline. And you destroyed blue-collar jobs.[16]

Other industries also were affected by the downsizing of American cars, as well as by the sharp inroads made by foreign imports in total sales. Table 4.3 gives some idea of the scope and economic meaning of weight reductions

TABLE 4.3

THE CHANGING INGREDIENTS OF THE AVERAGE FORD CAR

	Pounds (dry weight)		
Material	1977	1982	1985
Plastics	165	224	225
Aluminum	110	133	135
High strength steel	105	252	270
Cold rolled steel	820	510	490
Hot rolled steel	1419	864	760
Cast iron	620	352	315
Glass	93	74	67
Rubber (synthetic, natural)	180	129	120
Sound deadeners	85	46	42
Copper and brass	35	32	25
Lead	29	28	25
Zinc die castings	34	10	10
Other	65	50	49
TOTAL WEIGHT	3760	2704	2533

SOURCE: *Forbes,* 22 November 1982, 165.

accomplished by Ford as it moved to meet fuel efficiency standards set for 1985 models. Not only steel but also iron (and behind them both, coal) and rubber were seriously affected by the changes, as attested by a wave of plant closings in the Midwest.

These data make clear that the unemployment and borderline bankruptcy problems of the industries centered on automobile production will not go away with economic recovery. Indeed, recovery is likely to make the sunset nature of these industries (and the jobs they used to provide) even more obvious. A good proportion of the remaining American automobile production is likely to be accomplished through fewer plants but much more fully automated methods than ever before.

This combination of energy-induced downsizing, the substitution of newly developed materials, and automated production processes is evident in other industries as well. Housing, for example, has turned toward construction of smaller residences and increased use of lighter, prebuilt materials. Some of this was intended to improve fuel consumption, and some was the result of changes in interest rates and the multiplication of investment opportunities alternative to the traditional home mortgage. But the effect on the lumber, construction, cement, glass, and copper industries was likely to be substantial.

The "sunrise" industries that many hope will replace these long-established building blocks of the American economy, at least in the value of their products and sales, are nearly all in the high-technology and services fields. In manufacturing, the leading candidate is of course the electronics industry: computers, communication equipment, medical instruments, fiberoptics, bioengineering, and robots. In each area, most of the inventions, ideas, and innovations that made the industry possible were American in origin. But much of the actual development and many current innovations are in fact Japanese accomplishments.

What once was a clear American edge is now much less certain. In a study conducted in 1982 by Japan's Society of Science, Technology and Economics, Japan was found to be inferior to the United States in 56 key technologies but superior in 51. Given the intensity of Japanese government organization, planning, and support for industrial improvement, this does not bode well for a continued American edge. The U.S. share of world trade in high-technology products, in fact, has already dropped from 30 percent in 1962 to 22 percent in 1982, Japan's rose from 4 percent to 12 percent in the same period.

The robotics industry neatly sums up the problems and prospects in the future high-technology world. The first patents were those of an American inventor, but only Japanese companies would undertake development. Currently, robots are in greater use in Japan and the Japanese robot-producing industry has a significant edge on American producers. Americans are, however, investing heavily to catch up and perhaps hold on to much of the growing U.S. market for robots. Currently only about 5000 robots are in use in the United States, mostly in the automobile industry. But anywhere from 100,000 to 150,000 are expected by 1990. When a variety of "smarter" robots are available, of course, hundreds of thousands of current jobs will be eliminated. Experts disagree sharply about the net employment effects of the imminent arrival of widespread robotization, but few expect the people displaced to become the makers or servicers of the complex electronic robots. At best, their children might.

The other major area of employment expansion expected as part of our economic transformation is in services, a category that includes more than half of all current workers. Some of this increase is expected to occur as the new technological capabilities are brought to bear on current practices, such as in reorganizing manufacturing procedures and much increased data processing. The "knowledge society" will in effect develop many new jobs by eliminating many more existing jobs. A good share of the increase in services, however, is expected to occur in fast-food restaurants, hospitals, and other areas of traditionally low pay and marginal job security.

Enthusiasm for an "information society" booming with new service occupations has been tempered by critics who argue that long-term prosperity depends on a healthy manufacturing sector. Acknowledging that the service sector has grown rapidly in recent years, they still insist that no economy can sustain itself simply by passing papers, talking, and eating. One such critic sardonically comments:

> Perhaps unemployed steel workers (or their children) can sit at computer terminals making American Express travel arrangements for a convention of paralegal personnel, systems analysts, and economists with a taste for McDonald's hamburgers.[17]

Other second thoughts about the ongoing transformation have come from observers who argue that "smokestack" industries are needed to provide at least a residue of jobs and productive capacity in those fields. Giving up on such industries would place an unsustainable burden on other sectors and perhaps endanger national security. The romantic appeal of high-technology occupations far exceeds the real prospect of employment in those fields, and most people will have to hope for jobs in more familiar areas. The problem will be to find such jobs as industries' demand for labor declines. Not only are massive redistributions of job opportunities among middle- and lower-class workers involved, but also the question of maintaining an acceptable level of employment and some balance among industrial capabilities.

The Inflation-Recession-Recovery Roller Coaster

Decline and transformation are long-term processes with cumulating effects leading in a single direction. The business cycle, however, involves short-term changes in alternating directions. Its consequences are likely to be more visible to people because inflation and unemployment have an immediate personal impact that is recognizable—and because the media are attentive to the familiar government measures. Both the President and Congress try to see that the cycle appears to be headed up as elections approach, as the inflation-unemployment ratio is likely to be translated into votes for one or the other party. But it is probably less important than the more basic factors that lead to long-term decline or transformation.

Inflation refers to a rise in the general price level such that the dollar buys less, or in effect shrinks in value. It is usually measured by the government's "consumer price index" and expressed as the percentage or rate by which prices now exceed those of the previous year. Inflation is destructive for several reasons. It usually proceeds unevenly, with some prices or wages or rates of return on investment rising more rapidly than the average and some more slowly. Some people gain, more lose ground, and nobody can predict confidently what the future will bring. A psychic anxiety or "inflation psychology" is created, one consequence of which is that people buy now in expectation of higher prices later. This adds to current demand, keeps prices going up, and actually contributes to fulfillment of the original expectations by thus spurring inflation.

Another important reason is that long-term investment and plans for future construction or product development are inhibited. When people cannot be sure of future profits from transactions, they avoid them—and needed capital investment is sacrificed for short-term profits in money markets, speculation, or mergers. Finally, uneven national rates of inflation set off currency fluctuations and exchange problems, inhibiting trade and encouraging speculation. One measure of the extent of inflation-induced troubles for the U.S. economy is the fact that the inflation rate during the 1970s ranged from a low of less than 4 percent to a high of nearly 14 percent.[18] Cumulatively, inflation totaled 120 percent from 1967 to 1982. In other words, a person who earned $10,000 per year in 1967 would have to have earned $22,000 in 1982 just to stay even! And a person who retired on a fixed income of $10,000 in 1967 would have been reduced to an effective purchasing power of $4000 in 1967 dollars by 1982. No wonder that many people feel cheated by inflation or that sustained inflation has explosive political potential.

The technical meaning of recession is that the nation's GNP declines for two consecutive quarters. The practical meaning is that unemployment is on the rise. Unemployment dipped as low as 3.4 percent of the labor force in the early 1970s, but reached 10.8 percent, the highest since the Great Depression of the 1930s, at its recessionary height in 1982. The latter total meant that some 12 million people were involuntarily out of work, many of them for long periods. Indeed, one measure of the depth of the 1981-82 recession was that it set a postwar record for the total weeks of unemployment people experienced. By multiplying the number of unemployed people by the number of weeks they had been out of work, analysts produced the figure of 220 million weeks of unemployment represented by people without jobs in May 1983. But no measures can really capture the meaning of sustained unemployment for workers and their families. If nations experience unrest and protest during periods of inflation, they are likely to face much more serious problems with sustained unemployment.

There *are* other indicia of recession, of course. Prices may drop, and production slows. Some businesses may be driven into bankruptcy, and perhaps even some banks may require government rescue. Foreclosures of mortgages on farms and homes become common. The severity of a recession can be measured by how many of these things occur and to what extent. By all such measures, the recession of 1981-82 was clearly the most severe since the 1930s. More businesses went bankrupt, plant utilization was lower, foreclosures were more numerous, and so forth, than in any other postwar recession.

The recovery stage of this cycle is identified by the return of economic growth. The nation's GNP begins to rise again, often quite rapidly at first because inventories are down and plant capacity is underutilized. Productivity increases, in part because workers remaining on the job are eager to prove themselves and are less concerned about wages or working conditions than about keeping their jobs. Typically, business activity (measured by housing starts, levels of production, etc.) picks up first, followed by consumer spending for automobiles, appliances, and retail goods. At some later point, when employers are convinced the future looks promising, workers are recalled and unemployment begins to drop. The issue then becomes how long growth can be sustained before inflation reaches intolerable levels and the cycle is renewed.

The recession accomplished by the severe monetary restrictions of 1981 was, as noted, the most severe since the 1930s. Monetarists believe this is the only way to wring inflation out of the economy. But many others argue that it is unnecessarily punishing to workers and their families, intended as much to "discipline" labor into lower wages and other concessions as to cure inflation. Indeed, the classic principle that the recession was "necessary" was challenged by economists who advocated price and wage controls or other means of controlling inflation.

Such a deep recession could not fail to slow inflation. By 1983, the inflation rate was down to about 4 percent, the lowest in more than a decade. As recovery began, the vital question was whether the *causes* of inflation had been eliminated. How long would growth continue before inflation threatened, and the Fed resorted to its money supply and interest rate remedies to choke off both inflation *and* recovery? Hardly any informed observer would have doubted that such a massive recession could stop inflation, at least for a while. But it might also have done serious damage to prospects of future growth, to the maintenance of transportation systems and educational opportunities, for example, such that competitors would gain a new edge. And it might have missed its inflationary target by so wide a margin that inflation would soon return anyhow.

The early signs were mixed. Productivity was up and efficiency greater than in recent years. Wages were still depressed, and so business profit margins seemed likely to rise. The oil glut would probably endure for some time, and so price pressures from that source would be minimal. All these encouraging factors were balanced by the fact that the unprecedented federal deficit seemed likely to force interest rates up again and/or otherwise rekindle inflation.

The New World Economy

The window provided by the international financial system is surely one of the best ways in which to see how fully integrated and mutually dependent the new world economy really is. American investment abroad totaled well over $700 billion in 1982, for example, and at the same time there was more than $550 billion in foreign money invested in the United States.[19] The top ten U.S. corporations derived half their revenues, or about $250 billion, from foreign operations in the same year. The five biggest banks in the United States held $233 billion in foreign investments, and derived 58 percent of their revenues and 64 percent of their profits from abroad as well.

But the most compelling facts about the interdependent world financial structure in 1983 were the inability of Third World countries to pay their vast debts to the developed countries and the international exchange effects of high interest rates in the United States. Normally sober sources such as Federal Reserve Board Chair Paul Volcker declared that the financial and social stability of the United States for years to come would depend upon continuing efforts to enable debtor countries to make their payments.

The debt crisis began routinely enough with major banks in the industrialized world making high-profit loans to developing countries in the 1960s. Repayment was expected to be accomplished through the sale of raw materials and other export products in an active world economy. In 1973, these banks extended another series of even larger loans, necessitated by the leap in oil prices. Oil-importing developing countries had to borrow to pay the much higher prices, and oil-exporting countries effectively provided the capital for the loans by depositing their new receipts in the same banks. The banks served as "recycling" agents under near-emergency conditions. But repayment still seemed practical as long as exports were earning the necessary dollars.

By 1982, not just the lending banks but the whole world financial system was in deep trouble. The transformation began things by reducing the markets for oil and certain other raw materials. The recession of 1981-82 completed the job by reducing demand for all exports, and in many cases reducing the prices offered as well. Suffering the same or higher inflation as the industrialized countries, and losing their export earnings, many Third World countries simply could not pay their debts. A total of 34 countries formally asked to have interest and/or principal payments "rescheduled" or postponed.[20]

The International Monetary Fund (IMF), an international agency dominated by the wealthy countries, sought solutions that would prevent outright default on loans and preserve the prospect of repayment at some point when times improved. Repudiation had to be avoided, even if that meant making new loans in order to pay the old ones, because so much of the assets of the capitalist nations' banks were so deeply sunk into Third World countries. The IMF settled in most cases for agreements with the debtor governments to impose stricter limits on the share of national income that was available to the general population so that they would be better able to pay their debts.

It would be difficult to overstate the seriousness of these problems. The IMF estimated in 1982 that the 115 countries it calls "non-oil developing nations" had $612 billion in outstanding debts. Many of these loans had been made by governments or international agencies, leaving a bit over $300 billion in debts to private creditors such as the big banks of the developed countries. About 80 percent of the total private debt outstanding in countries that had asked for rescheduling was owed by only seven countries: Brazil, Mexico, Argentina, Venezuela, Poland, Yugoslavia, and Chile.

The total debt service owed by these countries in 1982 exceeded their export earnings by substantial margins. In order to repay the loans as scheduled they would have to find the resources within their own borders—with almost certain protests and perhaps more from the people being asked to undergo new hardships. These are the worst cases, but they are far from the only countries in trouble.

The problem was also acute for creditors. Large proportions of the capital of major U.S. banks are riding on their repayment. The largest of the American banks involved is Citicorp of New York, which earned $153 million in profits from Brazil in 1982, or 20 percent of the bank's profits.

The loans that are in jeopardy represent very substantial shares of the banks' total capital and come to more than 110 percent of the banks' stockholders' equity. Many of the loans are already overdue, and interest payments are not likely to resume until new loans are made. In all probability, failure to arrange such new loans would lead to default, which is tempting to some Third World countries (a "debtors' OPEC") as a step in their continuing efforts to get industrialized countries to grant them more help in development. In the case of default, the U.S. government would probably have to intervene to save the endangered banks—assuming that was possible.

The other half of the world financial crisis comes from the high value recently attained by the U.S. dollar against other world currencies. U.S. anti-inflation policy in 1982 drove interest rates to record highs and reduced inflation to ten-year lows. The United States became an attractive place in which to invest capital and the U.S. dollar a relatively strong currency. Interest rates are staying relatively high in the United States in part because the Fed appears determined to prevent renewed inflation and in part because federal deficits create the impression that they will stay there. Foreign capital is being drawn to the U.S. stock market and to U.S. Treasury securities, much to the annoyance of their governments and the detriment of their own internal development goals. This happens not only because interest rates are attractive but also because the United States promises political stability in an uncertain world. Thus the dollar stays high, "overvalued" in comparison to other currencies, and American tourists overseas enjoy expanded spending power.

But the consequences for the American economy and the world are very damaging. American exports cost more and therefore lose to Japanese or German competitors. Imports flood the United States and undersell American products. American corporations lose markets both ways, and American workers lose jobs. The United States ends up with a record trade deficit of about $60 billion per year. *Business Week* estimated in 1983 that the overvalued dollar was costing the U.S. economy $100 billion in lost production and 1.6 million jobs per year.[21] It also means the Third World countries have an even harder time paying their debts, most of which are payable in dollars. And it encourages U.S. companies to invest overseas rather than in the United States. The longer this condition lasts, and the deficits imply that it may be long-lived, the more competitors enjoy advantages in export markets—to the point where some American companies worry that they may never recover.

These two sets of conditions carry major public policy implications. They make the policy or the fact of high interest rates very much a double-edged sword. They may serve to curb inflation, but at the cost of export markets and perhaps the U.S. industrial base itself. The management of debt rescheduling and new loans through the vehicle of the IMF becomes a crucial process, requiring the utmost care and delicate cooperation between governments of industrialized nations.

The fact that the most crucial countries are Central or South American nations adds another dimension to the U.S. foreign policy posture in that area. Governing elites in those countries must be encouraged to continue their payments. But doing so may require that stricter austerity measures be imposed on their populations, which may in turn lead to social upheavals, chaos, and further inability or unwillingness to pay. The great weight of the history of U.S. intervention in Latin American affairs stands in the way of any government supinely doing American bidding in these respects. Finally, in order for the IMF to help arrange new loans and continued payments, it needs larger contributions from its leading member countries. But cowboy capitalists and free market conservatives often see such contributions as "bailouts for the banks" and refuse to go along.

The interdependencies involved in the two situations just reviewed almost defy itemization. But they serve to illustrate the nature of the new world economy, the last major component of our current economic context. Decline, transformation, the business cycle, and the new interdependence together create an economic situation that is at once unparalleled in American experience, acute, and dangerous. Within that context, and despite its political stalemate, the United States is at the point where it must soon do *something*. It is always possible, and often easier, to do nothing. But if we do something, it is very likely to be one of the four economic renewal programs to which we now turn.

PART TWO

The Economic Renewal Programs

5. Cowboy Capitalism: A "Free Market" Solution?

The Reagan administration programs serve as the basis for my analysis of cowboy capitalism's free market solution. Some blurring of principles are introduced, of course, by making use of those actually in office for illustrations. But the Reagan administration is about as "pure" in its commitment to cowboy capitalism as any American government is ever likely to be. The apparent contradictions of Reagan administration policies may be in part a necessary accommodation to reality.

The part played by these contradictions is actually an intriguing problem. To what extent would *any* free market solution be forced to embody contrasting policy components? How much do today's specific economic problems require or encourage such inconsistencies? The contradictions I examine go well beyond mutually conflicting supply-side and monetarist policies and the fact that budget deficits in this conservative administration are the highest in history. They focus particularly on the role of military spending, where cowboy capitalism's free market administration is injecting a vast economic stimulant into the economy in a fully planned manner. Is this just a coincidental ideological accompaniment to conservative free market thinking? Or does it amount to a fundamental ingredient, such that we must reunderstand cowboy capitalism's "free market" prescriptions as just a different form of targeted industrial policies? Carried a step further, we might even see "corporatist" tendencies among some cowboy capitalists that would rival anything that Yankee capitalists seek.

The Cowboy Capitalist-Free Market Program

SUPPLY-SIDE THEORY AND PRACTICE

I first summarize the key elements of the Reagan administration programs, moving from premises to practices with particular attention to the economic implications of military spending and the social consequences generated by the entire package. Then I review some major critiques made by advocates of other economic renewal policy directions and the free market responses to them.

There can be little doubt that supply-siders are the free market purists in the Reagan camp. They claim that their prescribed tax cuts would have worked faster and better if they had not been accompanied by restrictive monetary policy and new government spending. But they say that the eventual recovery was generated by the stimulus to investment and growth produced by the tax cuts and that sustained high growth without inflation will ensue if their principles are followed consistently.

The basic principle of supply-side theory is that productivity increases are the key to economic growth without inflation. With greater productivity, more goods can be produced at lower unit costs and thus sold without increasing prices. Sluggish productivity growth in the United States is due to the burdens of government taxation and regulation. The increases in production costs and paperwork resulting from regulation can be eliminated by simply abandoning or vastly simplifying all regulations. But there are more subtleties to a new tax policy.

Tax reduction should be accomplished with several principles in mind. First and foremost is the need to cut taxes so that new investment is possible. This means cutting taxes drastically for corporations and the wealthy, who are the ones most likely to be able to save and invest. But cutting everybody's marginal rates and the "progressivity" of rates in general will help because it shifts incentives from leisure to work and from consumption to production. Current tax policy discourages work in a variety of ways. It also provides revenue for other government activities that simultaneously discourage work and promote consumer demand. All of these provisions should be adjusted to encourage work and shift funds into new investment.

For example, the "safety net" of income support for the poorest people means that they suffer a tax penalty and net income loss when they do find work at the wages they are likely to command. Income transfer programs of all kinds, such as unemployment compensation, welfare, and disability, have the same work-discouraging effects. Moreover, all these programs contribute to consumer demand instead of capital investment. A better overall tax program would be one focused on consumption rather than on income, with credits for investment made.

Supply-siders are unconcerned about the deficits in the federal budget produced by tax cuts. They argue that the new investment accomplished by such cuts will increase productivity so much that inflation will actually be reduced thereby. And they point out that deficits are inflationary only when they contribute to greater consumer demand. By keeping the capital released by the tax cuts out of the hands of consumers, inflation is avoided. Supply-siders insist that they do not lack compassion for the poor or jobless, but that they have a better route toward a more lasting improvement in everybody's lives—which cannot be accomplished in any other way.

Finally, supply-siders claim credit for the prospect of sustained high growth because of the 25 percent tax cuts of 1981-83. If the monetarists would just keep their hands off—let the money supply and interest rates find their own levels—there would be a sustained boom for years to come. At some point, a standard for the value of money might be reestablished as a means of enforcing spending discipline on future governments. This should be a link to gold in some form. But that is all that is needed in the way of monetary controls in a supply-side boom period where new productivity is preventing inflation.

MONETARIST THEORY AND PRACTICE

Monetarists yield to none in their commitment to letting the free market fulfill its economy-regulating role. Market inefficiencies are created by government taxing and spending, and the overall size of the government sector is therefore crucial. Obviously, it should be kept as small as possible. One paramount danger justifies policy intervention, however, and that is inflation. The key to controlling inflation lies in careful management of the supply of money in the economy.

This management is accomplished in the United States by the Federal Reserve Board (the Fed). This seven-member board has the capacity to increase or decrease the supply of money or raise or lower the level of interest rates (and thus the availability of credit) in the country. In theory, a steady rate of increase of about 4 percent a year would allow for stable growth without inflation. But it can be very difficult to control the supply of money in a complex modern economy, even if the Fed is not under pressure from various sources to purposefully inflate or deflate the economy. Inflation *can* be caused by a large number of factors, and the fact of inflation may confront monetarists with the necessity to act. In such situations, their remedy is to choke off the money supply, raise interest rates, and limit the availability of credit. With inflation roaring in 1979 and again in 1981, the Fed did exactly that, with the drastic results that we have seen.

What monetarists hope to accomplish is an atmosphere of stability that will permit long-range plans and investments that will spur new growth. With such a climate, new output and employment will more than make up for what was lost during the deliberate slowdown. The key in monetarists' eyes is popular expectations. If people are convinced that inflation will not return, or that if it does, it will be resolutely controlled, they will invest, spend, and otherwise act in ways that will assure growth and prosperity.

"REAGANOMICS"

President Reagan came into office with campaign commitments to a supply-side tax cut and controlling inflation. His free market ideology had surrounded him with both supply-siders and monetarists. The problem was that, just as momentum for the tax cuts was being generated, inflation was rising at what seemed dangerous rates. The Federal Reserve Board is an agency independent of both Congress and the President, and the Chairperson was Paul Volcker, a Carter appointee and a thoroughgoing monetarist conservative. The Chair of the Fed is sometimes referred to as the second most powerful person in the government, and Volcker acted decisively. He implemented every inflation-controlling policy known to monetarist theory, and accomplished the intended recession.

For the most part, his goal had Reagan administration support, although there were complaints about the severity and length of the Fed's efforts to finally rid the economy of both inflation and inflationary expectations. Supply-siders, however, were vocal in their opposition. Everything the Fed did to raise interest rates and restrict credit worked to prevent the investment that was the whole point of the tax cuts. The two sets of policies were fundamentally at odds. Monetary policies are very powerful when wielded in this grim manner, and they won out.

One clear result of implementing both polices at once showed up quickly in the form of the huge deficits that began in 1981. A severe recession cuts deeply into government tax revenues and increases government outlays for such programs as unemployment compensation, welfare, health care, and other income transfers. Moreover, the Reagan adminstration was also committed to major increases in military spending. It was simply not possible to find enough other places to reduce government spending to make up for the size of these increases.

Some perspective on these deficits is in order so that we do not become stampeded with traditional concerns. First, the imbalance has much to do with the unemployment rate. For each percentage point of unemployment, the deficit is increased (by additional expenses and lost revenue) a net of $30 billion.[1] The fiscal 1983 deficit would be about $120 billion lower at 6 percent unemployment, the Reagan administration's definition of "full" employment. Second, the current deficits are very large in current dollars, but only about 5 to 6 percent of today's GNP. In World War II, deficits amounted to 22 percent of GNP. Similarly, the national debt is now about 35 percent of GNP; at the end of World War II it was 119 percent.

The combination of tax cuts, monetary restrictions, and huge deficits came to be known somewhat derisively as "Reaganomics." Part of the disparagement involved was thoroughly justified because Reagan had campaigned on the fanciful claim ("voodoo economics") that he could simultaneously cut taxes, add to military spending, and control inflation. But some share of the blame lay with longer-term factors already in place in 1981 when Reagan came into office and only worsened by his policies. Let us take up some specific components of the rest of his program in somewhat greater detail.

THE MILITARY BUILDUP

Central to Reagan fiscal policies, at once the cause of the giant deficits and of increased pressure to reduce social spending, is the amount and duration of the military buildup. It is essential to try to grasp the extent of this unprecedented (in peacetime) shift in federal budgetary priorities. To begin, the totals are staggering. The President's requested budget authority for fiscal year 1984 was more than $280 billion in 1983 dollars, and his projections for subsequent years rose steadily to more than $333 billion in the same dollars in 1988.[2] By contrast, the leading welfare category, about which there is so much hand-wringing (Aid to Families with Dependent Children, or AFDC), runs at about $8 billion a year.

Next, military spending is also rising as a proportion of the national budget, from less than a quarter in 1980 to roughly 35 percent in 1988. Most of the national budget represents fixed costs, or spending for previously obligated purposes about which the government has little choice unless it is to retreat from legal commitments. Examples include interest on the national debt and pensions to veterans and retired civil service workers. With the military share (which is, by contrast, part of the "discretionary" budget) increasing this much, there will be heavy pressure for more reductions in areas that have the weakest political support. If the military share were to be expressed as a proportion of the "discretionary" part of the budget, it would be between 75 and 80 percent.

The military budget expressed as a share of the nation's GNP is also rising in a similar fashion, from 5.5 to almost 8.0 percent in the same period. Of considerable economic importance is the fact that the composition of military spending is also changing. It is being shifted away from operating expenses, such as salaries and maintenance, and toward research and development and heavy capital investment, such as new weapons procurement and construction. In the Reagan administration's own words, the buildup in weapons procurement and research is more rapid than occurred during the fastest-expanding years of the Vietnam war.

One implication is that the effect of the economic stimulus involved will be lower in terms of new jobs, particularly among the less skilled workers whose unemployment rates are highest. Another is that this buildup is more likely to be competitive with civilian capital needs than others. As an economic stimulus then, the military buildup leaves something to be desired. I return to the problem of understanding this remarkable spending pattern on the part of free market advocates later, but for now these comparisons are summarized below.

TABLE 5.1
THE MILITARY BUILDUP, 1980-86

	1980	1981	1982	1983	1984	1985	1986
Military outlay ($ billions 1983)	135.9	159.8	187.4	214.8	245.3	285.3	323.0
Military outlay as % of total budget	23.5	24.3	25.7	26.7	28.9	31.0	32.6
Military outlay as % of GNP	5.5	5.6	6.2	6.7	7.0	7.5	7.8
Composition of military budget authority:							
Operating	63.8%	60.7%	56.7%	53.6%	52.4%	49.3%	48.9%
Investment	36.2	39.3	43.3	46.4	47.6	50.7	51.1

NOTE: Data are based on actual military outlays in 1983 dollars, except composition data based on budget authorizations. The years 1984 and later years are estimates.

SOURCE: Calculated from Office of Management and Budget, *The U.S. Budget in Brief, 1984*, and Congressional Budget Office estimates.

THE REDUCTION IN NONMILITARY PROGRAMS

In addition to the tax cuts, free market principles have had their greatest effect in easing regulations on business and in cutting back on social services and the transfer programs that aid the poor and less advantaged. In the case of regulations, changes in attitudes or number of inspections may be as important as the actual language of safety or health requirements. Much can be accomplished within the bureaucracy without surfacing publicly in the form of requests for new or changed legislation. Moreover, the effect of a steady stream of appointments to governing boards or commissions is felt only over time. Former Interior Secretary Watt was thus unusual in his visibility, but not in the substance or direction of his efforts. The pattern is general. Public lands and ocean beds have been opened for oil and gas drilling or other development, pollution control standards relaxed, new safety requirements postponed, nuclear licensing standards eased, and so on.

But most attention has focused on the administration's efforts to change the level of government assistance to lower-income people. In the first two years of his tenure, President Reagan proposed the reduction or elimination of some 84 federal programs. Roughly 60 percent of these proposals were adopted by Congress in some form, and estimates are that about $40 billion might have been saved under what would otherwise have been spent.[3]

Changes in GNP, inflation, and unemployment rates make comparisons between assumed and actual totals between budget years very shaky, but some basic directions come through clearly enough. What the Reagan administration accomplished in the first two years was substantial, particularly in the light of past history. The rate of increase of social program spending was sharply curtailed, and many programs were slated for further reduction or elimination. Spending reductions were accomplished, for example, in disability benefits, welfare, Medicaid, food stamps, social security, unemployment insurance, and employment and training programs. The largest reductions achieved were in federal housing programs, and the greatest gap between proposed cuts and actual congressional appropriations occurred in the area of education.

With the proposal of his fiscal 1984 budget, Mr. Reagan began to bite deeper. Military spending proposals were up 9 percent in real terms, while nonmilitary outlays were reduced 3 percent in the same after-inflation terms. Not just the growth, but now the actual costs, of education, job training and employment, welfare, food stamps, and legal services for the poor would be reduced. Spending reductions included, for example: employment and training, 8 percent; food stamps, 9 percent; child nutrition programs, 8 percent; all forms of education, 6 percent; low-income heating-cost assistance, 30 percent; and housing assistance, 84 percent. A variety of other programs were slated for elimination, such as the Legal Services Corporation, Economic Development Administration, and Community Services Block Grant.

Even with these reductions, the proposed budget was sharply unbalanced, with the greatest deficits in history stretching into the foreseeable future. Presidents notoriously underestimate expenditures and overestimate revenues, so actual deficits exceed original estimates by great margins. Estimates made at the start of the fiscal year 1983 for the budget deficit of that year were off by more than 100 percent. Estimates of future conditions are difficult if not impossible, and the natural tendency is to make optimistic assessments now and worry later.

In the case of the 1984 budget projections, for example, the Reagan administration assumed congressional compliance with all his proposed spending cuts in nonmilitary areas. It *also* assumed enactment of so-called contingency tax increases and spending cuts intended to go into effect in the event of budget deficits in excess of 2.5 percent of the GNP at the time. Table 5.2 shows how important such assumptions were to the estimates made, and com-

TABLE 5.2

PRESIDENTIAL ESTIMATES OF BUDGET DEFICITS, 1980-88

(in billions of current $)

	Fiscal Years			
	1980	1981	1982	1983
First estimate	- 29.0	- 16.0	- 27.5	- 91.5
Actual year-end deficit	- 59.6	- 57.9	- 110.7	- 195.0

	Fiscal Years				
	1984	1985	1986	1987	1988
1983 estimate	- 82.9	- 71.9	- 66.0	- 53.2	NA
1984 estimate	- 189.0	- 194.0	- 148.0	- 142.0	- 117.0
1984 estimate without social cuts proposed (or contingency taxes after 1986)	- 231.0	- 253.0	- 271.0	- 292.0	- 300.0

SOURCE: Office of Management and Budget, *The Budget in Brief, 1984.*

pares first estimates in other years to actual totals where available. The basic pattern of budgetary change is for a leveling of payments to individuals, a sharp expansion in the military share, and a compensating squeeze on all other programs.

Critiques of the Cowboy Capitalist-Free Market Solutions

The Reagan programs have attracted much criticism, often for conflicting reasons. The deficits have drawn the most complaints because they offend traditional conservative *and* a wide band of conventional economic thinking. The military buildup is next. In both cases, critics come from all sides of the political spectrum. The social consequences of program reductions are of concern chiefly to people on the left-liberal side, however, and the failure to address international financial problems is the concern of bankers and others tuned to a multinational world.

DEFICITS

Two things happen when the federal government runs a very high deficit, according to most analysts (or do not, according to others). Skeptics doubt that deficits matter much when the economy is so depressed, and point to deficits in other countries that represent higher proportions of their GNPs. But the majority believes that heavy federal government borrowing in the nation's capital markets to finance the deficit means that the price of capital (i.e., interest rates) will be forced up as the supply of capital decreases. In other words, big deficits mean rising interest rates and another recession. The majority also believes that such an excess of spending over revenue taken out of the economy will mean inflationary pressures. This will require stringent monetary policy measures again, and thus another recession. Either way, the majority says, deficits are bad because they prevent long-term growth with stable prices.

The truly radical nature of the supply-side gamble can be grasped by listening to the shock and horror of the authors of the "Bipartisan Appeal" addressed to the President and Congress in early 1983. Organized by five former secretaries of the treasury and one former secretary of commerce (three Republicans, three Democrats), the appeal attracted more than 500 signatures from leading business executives, economists, and university presidents. Their statement, published in the *New York Times* and other leading newspapers, began this way:

> The Federal budget is now out of control. It is primed to generate immense deficits, year after year, for decades ahead, deficits far larger than any in our history. This fiscal course is senseless. It threatens to lock the economy in stagnation for the remainder of this century.
>
> Massive deficits would absorb savings urgently needed for investment in plant and equipment, infrastructure and R & D. Productivity would sag and inflation resurface. Interest-sensitive industries would be smothered and exports would dwindle. The result would be a period of gradual decline, punctuated by high unemployment and social conflict and culminating in an America that is permanently poorer and weaker.[4]

These are strong words, from distinguished and presumably knowledgeable people. Clearly, not just the causes of inflation are in dispute; the argument extends to the effects of remedies as well. Uncertainty about the future direction of the business cycle did not end with the welcome recovery of 1983. If anything, it increased. A major factor promoting both uncertainty and concern was that continued unemployment for millions of people was widely anticipated. The appeal goes on to analyze the budget "disaster" as unrelated to the recession and built into existing policy even if the GNP growth rate should rise to a "buoyant" 5 percent annual rate.

But the remedies proposed by this appeal are as revealing as the anxiety expressed. What the Reagan budget proposals of 1984 tried to do was to use the ballooning deficits to increase the pressure on Congress to accept the President's cuts in nonmilitary expenditures. Reagan's acceptance of the contingent tax increases for 1986 and beyond, for example, is conditioned upon freezing those nonmilitary programs not actually cut, with both the freezing and cutting calculated in constant dollar terms.

The bipartisan appeal focuses on the long-term "out-year" budget deficits, insisting that the 1985 deficit should be cut by $175 billion. The approach urged for doing so *basically accepts Reagan's priorities,* merely scaling down the military buildup a bit. There are three parts to their program for "regaining mastery over our economic destiny." The first involves freezing most of the social entitlement programs (social security, pensions, veterans' benefits, etc.) and then putting limits on their protections against inflation so that in real terms they will fall behind all but the most minimal inflation.

Second is thinning the military buildup by $25 billion, to an overall increase of 7 percent per year. Third is raising taxes by $60 billion per year by means of *consumption-based* taxes and user fees for government services. These steps are thought likely to cut the FY 1985 deficit by $145 billion, and that reduction would save another $30 billion in interest on the national debt to make the $175 billion total. (The appeal leaves unstated the apparent total of an additional $60 billion to be squeezed out of the budget by the first step of freezing and cutting social entitlements.)

The most vocal complaint about the size of the coming deficits is thus essentially that Reagan and the supply-siders have gone too far. There is nothing really wrong with their free market principles or priorities, but only with the vigor they have shown in slashing taxes. This can be compensated for by imposing new (and regressive) taxes on consumption while reducing the incomes of many of those same consumers—and by slowing the military buildup a bit.

Clearly, the traditional notion of the desirability of a balanced budget has wide and deep support in both major parties and in the nation generally. It endures in spite of the experience of the post-Depression years and is triggered anew when deficits loom. To be sure, the deficits in store *are* staggering. No one but a dedicated free market purist could possibly survive in office with deficits of that size in store. But what then does the free market solution really stand for if it comes so deeply compromised by massive military spending and huge budget deficits?

To some observers, the problem is not necessarily the fact or even the size of the deficits, although few knowledgeable analysts other than the dedicated supply-siders are *not* impressed by the deficits in store. The issue instead is what the deficits are accomplishing. If they were a giant economic stimulant in the form of broadly spread investment in new bridges, sewer and water systems, highways, mass transit, railroads, terminals, hospitals, or other "infrastructure," many liberal economists would welcome them as useful job-producing renewal of our economic base. New consumer demand would help to pull manufacturing industries up from their currently slack levels toward full capacity output.

In other words, the government would be providing a good dose of classical Keynesian stimulation to a slack and stagnating economy. The effects could rival World War II's impact on the 1930s' Depression.

Other observers all across the political spectrum ask whether the deficits are accomplishing what the supply-siders said they would. Where is the new investment in plants and facilities that will provide a prolonged spurt for United States productivity? Some capital was going into new high-technology ventures, and some into job-eliminating automation of present forms of production. But these totals were modest in 1983. Corporate capital investment was distinctly low, and future intentions were reported to be low as well. Instead, money was flowing into the stock market. Corporations used their new capital to merge with or fight off acquisitions by other corporations. If the newly released funds do not find their way into new productive capital investment somehow, a colossal failure is in store for the supply-side Reagan gamble. And the price is not likely to be paid by those who have received most of the benefits of the tax cuts.

THE MILITARY BUILDUP

Opposition to the Reagan military program spans the political spectrum. It embodies two different dimensions corresponding to the ideological and practical justifications regularly offered in support of increased military spending. The ideological rationale is of course that the United States is falling behind the Soviet Union and every dollar of investment is crucial to national security. Some critics accept this argument, others respond with varying degrees of disagreement ending in complete rejection. The practical rationale used to mobilize support for military spending has always been that it creates jobs. Lately this has been expanded to include the argument that research and development leads to new high-technology applications in civilian industries. Critics have begun to assert, however, that more jobs and new industrial applications would flow from any number of other ways of allocating the same government funds. Some find considerable economic harm emanating from the new military expenditures.

One set of critics accepts the necessity of the current buildup and questions only its extent or rapidity. Waste, cost overruns, inefficient management, and the like lead such critics to oppose giving so much and so fast. They question, for example, whether the Defense Department has the practical capacity to spend so much money all at once. Conservatives and Republicans are well represented within the ranks of such critics.

Another set presents itself as neutral on the question of the necessity of the current buildup and concentrates instead on the economic justifications offered. Only a few such critics worry about possible inflationary consequences. Their concern is with the documentable difference in the number of jobs that might be produced by equivalent investments in other areas. Military production involves high value-added industries with much capital investment per worker, and new investment produces relatively few jobs per dollar of capital. Even then, the jobs are tilted toward engineers, scientists, and technicians rather than the currently unemployed less skilled workers.

Another concern is for the effects of the new mix of military spending in which expensive new hardware is a larger and larger share of total spending. One cost of such "star wars" emphases may be that civilian high-technology industries will lose out in the competition for scarce capital and highly skilled workers. Existing impressions that high-technology industries have benefited from previous military research and development have also been challenged on the ground of recent investigations.

Some of the data developed in connection with these arguments deserve notice. The general calculation is, for example, that $1 billion in military spending creates about 28,000 jobs.[5] The same $1 billion might create 57,000 jobs if left in consumers' hands to function as additional demand, or 71,000 jobs if directly invested in education. New military industry jobs will go so fully to skilled workers that they will leave the nation's unemployed practically untouched. Scientists, engineers, and other professionals make up more than half the military weapons workforce, but had a combined unemployment rate in 1983 of only 3.3 percent.

Finally, opponents cite the recurring comparisons that find an inverse relationship between countries with large military expenditures and those with the highest growth rates. The United States has spent an average of 7.3 percent of its GDP for military purposes over the 1960-80 period, and had an annual rate of growth over that span of 2.6 percent.[6] West Germany, on the other hand, invested only 3.8 percent of its GDP in military spending over that same period, and had growth averaging 5.3 percent. But Japan invested only 0.9 percent in military expenditures, and had a growth rate averaging 9.2 percent for those twenty years.

A final category of critics denies the military necessity for the buildup, arguing that a better definition of national security would call for arms limitations and various alternative uses for the funds saved thereby. The economic dimensions of these arguments include the massive waste involved in spending such sums for weapons that can at best (or worst) only be used once, and then to our mutual destruction. The military budgets planned for 1981 through 1988 alone amount to about $2,000,000,000,000, two trillion dollars. Such an allocation of scarce capital means that massive needs for new infrastructure, civilian capital investment, human resources development, and the like must be ignored or essentially starved. Some critics assert that this level of military spending is necessary to prop up the contemporary capitalist system and argue that it cannot be reduced until equivalent other public investment is made.

The three sets of critics occasionally join forces to attack particularly egregious examples of waste or mismanagement. For the most part, however, military spending decisions are made on the basis of the ideological dimension. Very few elected officials are willing to expose themselves to the charge that they have acted against national security interests by denying the military new weapons. The Reagan administration succeeded in 1982 and 1983 in getting practically all the military appropriations it requested. The concept of military parity with the Soviet Union is almost infinitely manipulable, so advocates with credible portraits of Soviet power or intentions can justify new expenditures with relative ease. The notion that military supremacy might be possible is always available if further arguments are needed. By comparison with national security arguments, economic considerations usually reduce to the question of whether the jobs or subcontracts are going to be in one congressional district or another.

THE POLICY OMISSIONS

There is one broad and vital area where the Reagan free market approach has little or no policy at all: international economic affairs. Critics seem limited to international bankers and other Yankee capitalists, but the policy gap is nonetheless important and revealing. The Reagan administration came late to a recognition of the need to allay fears that Third World debts would be allowed to go unpaid except when gunboat diplomacy is congenial for other reasons.

Some administration members encouraged congressional resistance to new appropriations for the International Monetary Fund (IMF), at least until the President himself endorsed the proposal. Their opposition to the IMF's frantic efforts to avoid Third World collapse or repudiation of debts to the capitalist world's biggest banks was based on the belief that this would be a "bailout for the banks." Of course it *was,* just as it was essential to keep the banks afloat. Very little understanding has been shown about the impact of U.S. economic policies, such as high interest rates, on other countries. Little or no real cooperation has been attempted with other countries in matters such as exchange rates or currency valuations.

With respect to imports and exports, no systematic approach has been evident. The rising tide of imports has been met with many complaints but little action. What actions have been taken have been protectionist in character, in direct contrast to the volume of free market rhetoric with which they are surrounded. Almost nothing has been done to promote American exports. Instead, the administration at first attempted to cut appropriations for the Export-Import Bank, which finances purchases of American products by foreign buyers. Major American companies such as the nation's leading exporter, the Boeing Company, were thus left at a competitive disadvantage and lost sales worth more than a billion dollars in 1982.

It is not unfair to say that the United States is the acknowledged world leader in at least two categories: volume of free trade rhetoric and incoherence of economic policies. The patchwork pattern of existing policy owes much more to political power than to economic purpose. But what seem like glaring failures to act on the part of the free market position may in fact be quite intentional. Indeed, there appears to be more to the Reagan approach than at first is evident—a substantive vision inherent in the free market rhetoric and visible in its actual practice. What looks irrational and uncoordinated may nevertheless be purposeful. Pared to fundamentals, the Reagan version of economic renewal policy employs the free market flag to seek to install cowboy capitalism as the modern version of American capitalism's halcyon days of growth, profit, and power.

The Social Consequences of Reagan Administration Policies

Many of the social costs of the reductions in transfer programs and regulatory protections are not yet known. Tracing the causes of disease or injury back to renewed pesticide usage, toleration of acid rain, relaxed pollution standards, or lack of health and safety inspections may prove ultimately impossible. The impact of what is now regularly termed "the Reagan Revolution" by many observers (and "the new class war" by critics) can be seen readily, however, in the consequences of the first round of reductions in taxes and social programs.

Tax cuts were enacted in 1981 to take effect over three years. Reductions in social programs were also enacted to take effect at various future times. These took two forms. One was reductions in cash transfers, such as unemployment compensation, disability insurance, and welfare. The other was reduction or elimination of some in-kind benefits, which are services or commodities provided by the government, such as Medicaid, food stamps, or housing assistance. The net results of the tax cuts and social program reductions are shown in table 5.3, along with data that show the part played by federal social programs of this kind in American income distribution.

The table follows the long-established Census Bureau practice of ranking all U.S. families by the income they earn in a given year and then dividing them

TABLE 5.3

NET IMPACT OF FEDERAL TRANSFER PROGRAM AND TAX REDUCTIONS, 1983

	U.S. families grouped by fifths of total U.S. income received (12 million families per fifth)				
	Poorest Fifth	Next Poorest Fifth	Middle Fifth	Next Highest Fifth	Highest Fifth
Threshold between fifths	$7,168	$13,709	$21,573	$32,730	
Reductions in cash transfers, in dollars	80	90	50	40	50
Reductions in in-kind benefits, in dollars	178	106	67	40	12
Additions to income from tax reductions, in dollars	10	110	330	690	2,080
Total net impact, average family	– $248	– $86	+ $213	+ $610	+ $2,018
Total cash income of average family after all changes	$3,760	$9,450	$15,370	$22,680	$39,200
Share of that income derived from cash transfers from federal government (in percent)	56	26	13	6	3
Resulting shares of total U.S. income (in percent)	4.2	10.4	17.0	25.1	43.4

ASSUMPTIONS: Spending and tax reductions enacted for 1983 applied to actual 1981 income.

SOURCE: Reconstructed by the author from data reported in *National Journal,* 23 October 1982, 1788-95. Original sources include U.S. Census, Congressional Budget Office, and Joint Economic Committee. For comparison, see Marilyn Moon and Isabel V. Sawhill, "Family Incomes: Gainers and Losers," in *The Reagan Record: An Assessment of America's Changing Domestic Priorities,* ed. John L. Palmer and Isabel V. Sawhill (Cambridge, Mass.: Ballinger, 1984), 317-46.

into five groups of equal size. The highest fifth consists of the roughly 12 million families at the top of this rank order, and the poorest fifth of the 12 million with the lowest incomes. These "income fifths" are arrayed across the table with the poorest at the left and the highest at the right. The first row of data in table 5.3 shows the cutting points between these 20 percent segments of U.S. families. The poorest fifth, for example, consists of all families earning less than $7168 in 1981, and the highest of all those earning over $32,730.

The next three rows show the changes in dollars per year that the cuts in social programs and taxes will mean for average families in each income fifth. These sums are computed by applying the reductions in force in 1983 to income actually earned in 1981, because the latter figures were the only accurate ones available to the researchers from the Congressional Budget Office and congressional committee staffs who conducted the study. Notice that the reductions in cash transfers affect the two poorest fifths somewhat more than the higher-earning families. The reductions in in-kind benefits, however, hit the lower fifths much harder than they do the upper ones. But it is in the effects of the tax cuts that the greatest disparities show up. Tax cuts do not affect lower-earning groups much because these people do not pay much in taxes, but for the highest fifths they are a major source of new income.

The total net impact of just these changes is shown with plus and minus signs in the next row of the table. It establishes very clearly that the Reagan program reduces the income of families in the poorest fifth while greatly increasing that of families in the highest fifth. In other words, these Reagan administration programs amount to a substantial redistribution of income from the poor to the rich. Reactions to this finding vary, of course, according to ideology, income, and other factors. Reagan administration supporters see this redistribution as necessary to encourage new investment and ultimately more jobs; others see it as an example of Reagan's bias toward the rich.

Table 5.3 also serves to set these changes in context. One approach is to compare the total cash income of average families in each income fifth. In this row, notice that the *average* family in the highest fifth earns more than ten times as much as the average poorest-fifth family. Next, notice the difference in what federal government transfers mean to families in different fifths. For the average family in the lowest fifth, fully 56 percent of cash income comes from the federal government. Looking back at the average family's income, the enormity of dependence on the federal government begins to come through. Finally, the last row shows the shares of all U.S. income received by each fifth of families. This may be the most significant figure in the table. The highest fifth receives well over 40 percent of all income, while the lower 40 percent of families must find a way to survive with only 15 percent of the nation's income. And Reagan administration policy is shifting a larger share toward the highest fifths every day.

The people targeted for this sort of redistribution are disproportionately the elderly, the poor (both categories are also made up disproportionately of women), and minorities. But they also include normally employed people who are victims of the ongoing economic changes.

Take the case of a hypothetical worker laid off from a declining industry during the height of the 1982 recession. Extended unemployment insurance benefits are no longer available unless his or her state meets certain new criteria of eligibility, which only 13 states met in 1982. He or she might meet the newly tightened standards for aid under the Trade Adjustment Act, assuming the job had been lost in part because of import competition—but only a very few workers were able to do so in 1982. The worker might be able to meet the newly raised standards for food stamps, but new limits would apply if there was a second earner or part-time work was found by a family member.

There would be no retraining possible under the Comprehensive Employment and Training Act, which used to provide more than 300,000 public service jobs, because that has been eliminated. Job training will become even more difficult in the future, because the administration made an 8 percent actual spending cut in these programs in 1984, as part of a 20 percent overall reduction in Department of Labor services.

New barriers to receiving welfare assistance may have their greatest effect in keeping the worker off Medicaid (which is tied to welfare eligibility). Thus an illness or injury to a family member during this period when work-related health insurance is unavailable could be catastrophic.

These are circumstances likely to be encountered by an ordinary American worker who has normally earned an adequate living until caught in an economic recession and transformation. The government proposes to help by cutting taxes for the rich while reducing or eliminating programs that might have sustained the worker and his or her family through hard times.

The cutbacks that have been accomplished so far and those yet in store will have the effect not only of imposing hardships in the present but the strong likelihood of additional costs well into the future. Consider the probably unmeasurable effects of recent and proposed cuts in school lunch and other nutrition programs. More than 3 million children lost their opportunities for decent lunches in 1982 because reduced federal contributions forced many schools to raise prices or abandon their low-income lunch programs entirely. Other nutrition cutbacks will probably mean higher infant mortality in the future, more premature babies, a higher incidence of births of retarded children, and the like.

Each of these cutbacks carries implications for long-term social costs, such as care for retarded persons. Proposals for reductions in disease control, public health, food and drug inspections, and so forth make a long list of potential future costs. What seems clear is that a very large sector of the American population has been put at risk, in both the short and the long term, in what we are fond of calling the richest country in the world. These appear to be some of the costs, and apparently necessary costs, of the cowboy capitalist-free market solution to the economic renewal problem.

Deflecting the Critics

President Reagan has been the chief defender of his administration's policies, but an ample corps of neoconservative writers and conservative think-tank employees has joined in mounting a spirited defense of cowboy capitalism. This defense consists of three arguments. The first is a denial that any of the policy changes have had, or will have, significant damaging impact on any deserving people. What is damaging, whether it stems from policy changes, and who is deserving are all matters about which vigorous disagreement is likely. While the argument is going on, presumably, there will be time for the investment encouraged by this redistribution to work its magic and restore jobs for all.

The second argument is an appeal to the traditional symbol of the free market, with the image of unparalleled economic and social achievement by the American economic system that it calls forth. The free market is held up not only as what the administration is really practicing but also as the means to a renewal of the work ethic, rugged individualism, the pioneering spirit, and the old American character with its optimistic approach to the future. This is the appeal that brings together skeptical or fainthearted business leaders, writers who unite religion, democracy, and capitalism in a single celebratory explosion, and many ordinary Americans, in hopeful support for the administration. Failure of the current policies will be a serious blow to the symbol of the market, though probably (given recent experience) not a fatal one.

The last major argument is simply that "industrial policy," the only alternative the cowboys recognize, will not work—and if it did work, it would be highly undesirable. No "government bureaucrats" know enough to make the choices involved or carry them out without serious damage to the economy. "Industrial policy" is viewed as massive government intervention in the economy on the scale of the socialist countries. The Japanese and German experiences are considered inconclusive if not downright demonstrative of the failure of industrial policies elsewhere. In any event such approaches are inapplicable to American experience, institutional capabilities, or popular preferences. Meanwhile, the Reagan administration has implemented proposals for commissions or study groups to look into particular aspects of the "competitiveness problem"—as if to undercut business interest in industrial policy proposals.

Both President Reagan and his corps of eager defenders have emphasized, probably correctly, that the real proof of the administration's economic renewal program will lie in whether it seems to be working when the time comes for it to be judged. Any incumbent, and the media, would probably celebrate a cyclical recovery, however partial it might be, as permanent and stable economic renewal. History suggests that it would be very unwise indeed to discount the resiliency and flexibility of American capitalism, particularly when it has enjoyed sharp reductions in real wage levels, taxes, regulations, and the power of unions. There seems to be a real chance that the American economy could enjoy at least a temporary surge, one more than adequate to postponing the peak of crisis for a few years.

The Reagan administration has, after all, delivered essentially what the combined business elites sought in the way of agreed-upon rollback of the welfare state. It is a bit unfair for some segment of such elites to seek now to distance themselves from what they once encouraged. Such business critics are indeed vulnerable to the Reaganite charge of faintheartedness. Critics on the left can be dismissed as "bleeding hearts" whose excessive concern for the undeserving got us into economic difficulties to begin with.

So far, this defense has succeeded in turning back much potential opposition. How far even this spirited effort can carry the principles of cowboy capitalism once the results are fairly clear will make a very interesting case study in the contrast between rhetoric and reality. Nostalgia and a revived cold war will not conceal real failure except for the duration of a crisis, and sooner or later the basic character of cowboy capitalism will become visible. But this makes the issue of that "basic character" of cowboy capitalism even more pressing.

There are two nagging contradictions inherent in cowboy capitalism's connection with Ronald Reagan's administration and its rhetoric of "free market" principles and practices. One has to do with the real nature of cowboy capitalism, the other with the diversionary focus on Ronald Reagan as a politician. In both cases, it is as if we were being encouraged to think of this economic renewal program as *less* than it really is—less purposeful, less competent, less dangerous.

It is essential to see that some components of cowboy capitalism are by no means completely or even mostly committed to the notion of the free market as an *operating* principle of government. As an abstract or symbolic principle, or as a compelling requirement for other people, yes. But for these cowboys, no. Too many cowboys sell only to the government, or depend on government to get cheap resources or exclusive franchises or inside information. And many cowboys are ready and willing to use the legitimate power of government to control any opposition that might get in their way, no matter how much expansion of institutions or powers that might require. There is a real corporatist tendency within cowboy capitalism that demands continued attention.

It is also essential to view Ronald Reagan as more than an empty-headed Great Communicator—unless we are prepared to see him rehabilitated in a decade as an Eisenhower-type political genius. It is tempting to focus on his considerable political skills, including the apparent warmth and credibility he generates in many people, even opponents, and on his effective use of television. But there is more systematic substance and coherent purpose to all the efforts of the Reagan administration than might be suggested by the latter focus. It is as if somebody read the history of 1877-1920 carefully and gave Reagan the role of McKinley to play. And the script has many more pages to go.

Behind the facade created by these two diversions, some major units of a restored capitalist economy are being set on a launching pad and prepared for takeoff. The exhaust from their launch may leave most of us covered with dirt and grease, but they will be beautiful sights in the stratosphere. A new version of Fortress America is already taking shape to protect the launching area. Its bellicose nature and real strength are even now drawing capital from all over the world into investments in the United States. Anxious wealth from politically unstable countries will finance our deficits in ways that will prevent any "crowding out" of new investment needs on the part of American corporations. This is a reasonable scenario by which cowboy capitalism could remain in the saddle in Washington for some time to come.

6. Yankee Capitalism: Business-Government Partnership

Yankee capitalism shares common origins and some basic premises with full-employment advocates, reflecting the basic Hamiltonian approach of the United States government since the Progressive era. Together, they are (or were) the mainstream of American thinking, once past the ritualistic invocation of the free market symbol. Both sets of proposals have important precedents in the New Deal years and programs. The New Deal embodied a genuine ambiguity in its commitment to modify but preserve capitalism under the emergency circumstances of the times. The Yankees, clearly the dominant of the two tendencies, have ample precedents in the New Deal's efforts to enable business to help itself while undertaking basic restoration of growth and profitability in the economy. Their economic arguments are actually a vital component of a larger, "neoliberal" perspective for many of their supporters.

Yankees put first priority on the problem of economic growth and adaptation. If businesses are enjoying expanding markets and continuing prospects of profitability, jobs and income follow. Today's problem is essentially to develop the mechanisms for achieving consultative agreements among business, labor, and government so policies can be harmonized and growth and profit assured.

Put just a bit crudely, the challenge for some Yankees is to identify the next generation of economic winners and losers (or "sunrise" and "sunset" industries). Then the task is to help prospective winners do even better, and to ease the decline of the inevitable losers so that hardships are minimized. This is a very delicate process, one that is vulnerable to disruption by political pressures. For that reason, some insulation of decision making from popular impact is needed; the exact form is very much a matter of controversy.

In effect, the Yankees put the needs of the corporate-banking sector first and thereby fit government into the role of junior partner in the enterprise. For some, it may be less a matter of deliberate policy than of "realism" in the American context, but it has the effect of yielding the initiative to business in a manner I earlier described as "corporatist." For others, the goal is precisely to assure direction by the nation's international corporations and banks; these are the true heirs and successors of Alexander Hamilton.

The Essentials of Yankee Capitalism

I introduced Yankee capitalism earlier as the program sponsored by today's version of the eastern establishment that has historically been the core of American governing elites. In the twentieth century, they constructed the first version of Hamiltonian business-government partnership, and they reconstructed the world similarly after World War II. Today they represent the American multinational and financial sectors of the new world economy. They are profoundly internationalist and financial in orientation, with continuing concern for sewing the American economy together with the rest of the world in a way that enables the American units to continue to have significant leverage.

Yankees are impatient with the fits and starts of American policy making, its parochialism, and its institutional clumsiness. Somehow, the U.S. government must be brought to do its part in the interdependent international order, or the American multinational corporations and banks will lose ground, and unnecessary strains will be added to the delicate world system. Robert Reich, a leading Yankee capitalist thinker who introduced the term "industrial policy" into the American political language, expresses a general attitude when he says:

> The United States has an irrational and uncoordinated industrial policy. . . . It is an industrial policy by default, in which government and business are inextricably intertwined but in which the goal of international competitiveness has not figured.[1]

Predictably, the first policy areas that this group turns to are trade (imports and exports) and investment, followed at a distance by the problem of designing the consultative mechanism, and then "human capital" development. An important underlying notion is that there are entrepreneurial capabilities and profitable opportunities out there in the world that are waiting to be realized through creative use of government powers. There is silence on the policy issue involved in the scope and speed of the military buildup, although the principle itself is well accepted; the buildup began, of course, under the Carter administration. And Yankees have relatively modest concern for controlling inflation. Most urge that future wage increases be linked to productivity increases, and only one or two see need for price or wage controls or incomes policies.

The international trade problem is far more complicated than might be suggested by posing the question as free trade vs. protectionism. Free trade is a notion that depended for its utility on economic conditions that no longer obtain, and that always meant distinct advantage for the stronger economies anyhow. Protectionism, if widely practiced, can mean not only barriers to trade and thus lost growth, profits, and jobs, but also a retaliatory process that can bring economic activity to a worldwide halt. Nevertheless, every major country practices a certain (and currently increasing) degree of protectionism. Older industries and their workers often have the political power to gain protection against foreign imports. Newer industries need special protection in order to develop.

The real problem is to juggle protections—quotas, tariffs, exclusions, bothersome restrictions, "voluntary" agreements, and other creative limitations—so that they achieve national goals without triggering costly reactions from other countries. The need to expand export markets must always figure in designing import policies, and frank quid pro quo bargains with other countries make sense. Industries whose interests are thus sacrificed so that others' may be advanced are not likely to be enthusiastic. But this is just another reason why the decision-making process must be insulated against parochial influences.

The proper goals for import policies are to provide a temporary cushion for declining older industries and an initial shield for new but vulnerable industries. Declining industries cannot expect indefinite shelter because that would mean taxpayer or consumer subsidizing of their inefficient operations and a costly drag on the economy as a whole. If there is a real chance that modernization could make them competitive again, then protection can be conditioned upon such investment. Otherwise, protections should be granted only for a period long enough to allow the orderly shift of capital to other ventures, retraining and relocating of workers, and transitional aid to the communities affected. Rising industries should similarly enjoy only such protection as necessary to get them on their feet and should expect to become self-sustaining on an agreed timetable.

There are a number of things an aggressive government can do to promote export markets for its national industries. One is to free prospective growth industries from antitrust or other government limitations on cooperative activities, such as pooling resources in research and development efforts. Another is to provide financing or subsidies for such joint efforts and/or for buyers of their products in other countries. But one of the most important aids is negotiation or bargaining with other governments to break down existing barriers to sales in foreign markets.

Other dimensions for consideration in export policy include limits on the overseas uses of capital or, what may be more important, the sale or other distribution of rights to technological developments. One of the most controversial current issues is the extent to which the former American leadership in high-technology industries has been dissipated by the short-term, profit-oriented sale or licensing of technology to foreign companies. In order to maintain this lead, some restrictions on the rate of diffusion of technological advances might be rational.

Trade policy, to be effective, must be articulated with policies that shape investment patterns. There must be not only a way to discourage further investments in declining industries but also a means of directing new investments toward their most productive uses. What is needed is a way of targeting certain industries for modernization or expansion and rewarding investment in increased productivity in those areas. Research and development in particular need to be encouraged.

There are at least three major ways to accomplish these goals, and all are urged by industrial policy advocates. First is a general limit to real interest rates. Keeping interest rates down makes credit more readily available for new or expanding businesses. This is the responsibility of the Federal Reserve Board and national fiscal policy. Second is a highly selective granting of tax credits for investments in areas identified as crucial. This might be as simple as establishing categories in the Internal Revenue Code or as complex as issuing certifications to particular industries or even companies at various times. Last but perhaps most important is the use of a new national development bank to make government funds directly available to rising industries or other desirable ventures. Changes in existing laws to enable pension capital to be more widely employed in development efforts, or to enable commercial banks to acquire equity in expanding corporations, are also proposed.

The scope of what would be attempted through a public decision-making body or bodies in designing and implementing this version of industrial policy makes the nature of that mechanism extremely important. The needs for information about the economy, including the workings of individual units, will alone require a major effort at data collection and much new cooperation from private business. Coordination of the vast number of federal departments and agencies whose activities have an impact on these areas will be another important necessity. Interestingly, *how* this is all to be accomplished has received much less attention than *what* is to be done. Various "advisory councils" have been proposed, usually connected in some way to the Congress—perhaps because these proposals have for the most part emanated from Democratic members of Congress.

It is generally agreed that all interested parties (usually defined as business, labor, and government) should be represented and that they should come to some shared judgment. Whether there are other parties at interest, or what the process would look like, or what would happen in the absence of agreement, is simply not discussed. It may be that advocates are so anxious to avoid the impression that they believe in the necessity of that un-American concept known as "planning" that they cannot bring themselves to speak publicly of such matters. Or perhaps the whole idea of this industrial policy effort is too new, or too exclusively the province of economists, to receive such consideration. In any event, there is a gaping hole involving major political problems left open here.

The final area of regular concern is that of jobs. Known more in rhetoric as human capital development, this concern focuses primarily on training and retraining workers to adjust to the changing needs of businesses. Both basic education and specialized professional education get support, as do training programs undertaken by corporations. Tax credits are urged to support the latter, and expanded public investments the former. There is some support for the idea that massive public investments in the restoration of infrastructure are essential to the long-term functioning of the economy. But the heart and soul of this group lies in its fascination with the future character and needs of high-technology industries and in managing the process of adaptation itself. It is as if they have to force themselves to think about such mundane matters as public works, or jobs for their own sake.

Diversity Among "Industrial Policy" Advocates

Probably no single advocate would say precisely what I have presented above or agree completely with the synthesis involved. There are important differences of emphasis within this group. Some would place higher priority than others on preserving existing industries and reducing social dislocations. The New York investment banker Felix Rohatyn, for example, believes that the forces making for change are entirely too powerful already, and that one of the priorities for national investment policy is to ease the coming transitions. Others, such as Lester Thurow of MIT, believe it is better to make inevitable changes quickly and efficiently so as to avoid bailouts and crises. But all share the basic goal of making national policy more rational, in the sense of harnessing it to the needs and prospects of contemporary capitalism. What is rational and appropriate for public policy, in other words, is what helps the capitalist economy to get wherever it is going faster and with fewer inefficiencies.

The differences among these advocates of an "industrial policy" form of economic renewal involve some issues concerning what is to be done and distinctive images of how comprehensive the new approach should be. Perhaps the most visible difference, however, is in the level of interest shown by representatives of government, labor, and business. These differences of apparent conviction and enthusiasm are in precisely the reverse order from the priorities given to the needs and goals of each. In other words, industrial policy advocates think of themselves as serving the needs of business for growth and profit, and accommodating government institutions and practices to serve those ends. Somewhat haltingly, the AFL-CIO has joined in support of these goals, seeing such policies and consultative mechanisms as the best route to preserving and expanding jobs.

But, with a few exceptions, big business has been slow to jump on the bandwagon built to serve its needs. The ideological appeal of the Reagan administration's free market rhetoric, the tangible benefits from its rollback of the welfare state, or caution in the face of something so new and untested may have prevented immediate business support for such a major shift in the government's role in the economy. Nevertheless, the core of Yankee capitalists has been committed to movement in this direction for at least a decade—and, in a sense, ever since the Hamiltonian model was established in the Progressive era. Although more than willing to accept the benefits of Reagan administration policies, they have continued to work through conferences and encouragement of other advocates toward serious business involvement in the industrial policy cause.

Part of the reason for the earlier commitment of academic economists, members of Congress, and then organized labor is simply that the Democratic party and big labor were both in need of a new program to revive their declining fortunes. But the distinctly worsening condition of the economy, the apparent failure of past policies, and the success of the Japanese and German models are also important sources of the industrial policy movement. Business, except for certain leading elements, always seems to see its own collective interests somewhat later than others who care about its long-term achievements. This was certainly true in both the Progressive era and the New Deal, and may well be the case again today. Compelling events and clear failure of Reagan administration policies may be necessary to fully energize business support for industrial policy initiatives. Experiments and demonstration projects under a new Democratic administration might be an opening in this direction also.

The idea of industrial policy is usually associated with the writings of the three leading thinkers already cited, the academics Lester Thurow and Robert Reich and the investment banker Felix Rohatyn. Thurow led off with the argument that a stagnating economy put all major interests into a "zero-sum" relationship with each other in which the gains of one were obtainable only through the losses of another.[2] He called for developing ways of targeting investment so as to promote growth where it was most feasible.

Reich's more extensive writings have focused on the shortsightedness of both government policies and corporate managers.[3] He coined the phrase "paper entrepreneurialism" to suggest the tendency of corporate managers to concentrate on financial and other paper transactions rather than increases in actual production. He has developed a comprehensive program for government aid to business modeled on the Japanese and German practices. Of all current industrial policy advocates, Reich's ideas are best represented by the synthesis in the previous section. He sees industrial policy as the long-term direction for the U.S. government: "We're building new frameworks. Administrations come and go. The frameworks can remain for generations."[4]

Rohatyn's views hinge upon the creation of an industrial development bank modeled on the Depression-era Reconstruction Finance Corporation.[5] The new bank would make loans to ease the decline or assist the modernization of American industry. It would set conditions for obtaining these loans, such as requiring certain improvements in management practice, mutual concessions or greater cooperation by both labor and management, and time limits for certain levels of achievement. Of the leading advocates, Rohatyn seems most concerned with the need for cooperative action to help disadvantaged sectors of the society, lest the whole social system be threatened with breakdown. He is also the most concerned to protect new decision-making institutions against pressures from special interests.

In the late stages of the Carter administration, these proposals began to surface in various forms. One was the general notion of "reindustrialization," and another was the proposed Economic Revitalization Board. After the 1980 election, the Democrats' need for an alternative program led to the formation of several study groups in which the potential of industrial policy was argued and converts secured. The first legislation offered in 1982 proposed only an Economic Cooperation Council in which business, labor, and government would seek agreements to be implemented through further legislation. Early in 1983, this was supplemented by proposals for a National Industrial Development Bank to provide the investment funds necessary to carry out programs of industrial development agreed upon between the representatives of business, labor, and government.

Perhaps the most comprehensive program was that announced in 1983 by 148 House Democrats led by Representative Richard Ottinger of New York and titled "A High Production Strategy to Rebuild America."[6] It was developed in conjunction with economist Gar Alperovitz of the National Center for Economic Alternatives and emphasizes promoting growth in a variety of ways. These include incentives for private investment, substantial public investment in needed infrastructure, elimination of waste in production and consumption, vigorous promotion of exports, and controlling inflation in key sectors. It goes further than any other industrial policy proposal in the substance of the measures called for, but stops short of specifying how new institutions are to be designed or in what ways democratic participation is to be assured.

Also in 1983, the AFL-CIO announced support for an industrial policy similar in content to that of the Ottinger group. Differences include greater emphasis on job creation and more concern for protecting existing jobs through import controls and "domestic content" requirements. Major advocates of industrial policies and both House and Senate supporters meet regularly in the Industrial Policy Study Group, a prototype of the business, labor, and government cooperative body envisioned. The Study Group is led by the president of the AFL-CIO jointly with a corporate president and Felix Rohatyn.

All this activity in the direction of industrial policy took place in the context of a definition of the problem of the American economy generated chiefly by representatives of big business. This definition was "lack of competitiveness," and it came from several different sources at roughly the same time. The Business-Higher Education Forum, for example, a group of 78 corporate executives and university presidents, issued a report in 1983 entitled "America's Competitive Challenge."[7] It called for a national economic policy to make the United States more competitive in world markets. Citing comparative figures regarding productivity increases between 1973 and 1980 that show the United States trailing Japan by a factor of five, the report calls for a range of national action.

One proposal, that for a National Commission on Industrial Competitiveness, was immediately implemented—perhaps as a means of undercutting the Democratic surge toward the faddish industrial policies. Another was for a national displaced-worker program like the GI Bill that would provide retraining and other benefits. Serious advocates of any of these goals would have to doubt, however, that they would ever be effectively implemented under a cowboy-free market administration.

Another report made public at about the same time came from the National Commission on Excellence in Education and was titled "A Nation at Risk." The risk, it turned out, was that of failing to measure up to the competitive capabilities of foreign countries. In addition to this concern for competitiveness, which encourages but does not necessarily require industrial policy, different business groups proposed in 1982 and 1983 several measures that amount to components of a future industrial policy. Although these various reports do not explicitly talk in terms of industrial policy, their suggestions are hard to understand or imagine in operation except in such a context.

One prestigious business organization of more than 200 corporate executives, the Committee for Economic Development, issued a report urging a wide range of national actions to encourage more rapid shifts of investment capital. The National Academy of Sciences sponsored a study advocating much more comprehensive management of the uses and diffusion of new technological developments. The Labor-Industry Coalition for International Trade, a group of ten unions and eight major corporations, issued a series of reports condemning the lack of a comprehensive program for import-export policies aimed at economic growth. There is thus a powerful convergence of thinking under way—one that enjoys wide media attention—that fits nowhere else but in the general category of probusiness industrial policy.

This is not to suggest that American corporate leadership has made a clear or full commitment to Yankee capitalist solutions to the economic renewal problem. Many businessmen remain attracted to the purer capitalism of the cowboy capitalists, and nearly all feel a deep attachment to free market principles. Only the more "progressive" executives of the larger and more internationally oriented corporations and banks are genuinely committed; others remain reluctant.

This reluctance was particularly visible in the late 1970s when the Initiative Committee for National Economic Planning was seeking to rally support for the proposed Balanced National Growth and Economic Planning Act of 1975, a pure Yankee capitalist project. The act would have set up a planning board in the Executive Office of the President to prepare biannually a six-year plan for identifying and reaching social and economic goals. The plan was to be submitted to the Joint Economic Committee of Congress for evaluation and recommendation to the Congress. Most leading businessmen were skeptical, and many were opposed to the very idea of government undertaking such a function. They saw it as simply more undesirable government intervention. Yankee capitalism clearly has a way to go to sell its message to its intended beneficiaries.

Finally, we might note another kind of difference between advocates, this time with regard to the potential threat that industrial policies might pose to democratic accountability and responsiveness. Some Yankee capitalists show much more concern for the issue of democracy than is characteristic of the others. Robert Reich has posed these issues several times.[8] For example, he urges that corporations receiving government assistance be obliged to contractually commit themselves to providing for their workers in various ways. He is one of a very few to pose the problem of structural change in the political decision-making system to ensure democratic accountability in the new economic policy making. But his concerns are the more noticeable because of the high and nearly exclusive priority given by most others to the needs of business and ways of using government to promote them.

Precedents and Models for Yankee Capitalism

Yankee capitalists have ample precedents for their proposals in American experience. Hamilton's teachings on these matters would be hard to improve upon:

> Capital is wayward and timid in lending itself to new undertakings, and the State ought to excite the confidence of capitalists, who are ever cautious and sagacious, by aiding them to overcome the obstacles that lie in the way of all experiments. . . .
>
> It is well known . . . that certain nations . . . enable their own workmen to undersell and supplant all competitors in the countries to which those commodities are sent. Hence the undertakers of a new manufacture have to contend, not only with the natural disadvantages of a new undertaking, but with the gratuities and remunerations which other governments bestow. To be able to contend with success, it is evident that the interference and aid of their own governments are indispensable.[9]

From these beginnings sprang an elaborate system for aiding the growth of manufacturing and promoting the internal improvements in roads, bridges, and canals that would make a national market possible. Later, tariffs were used continuously to protect infant industries, vast tracts of land were given to develop railroads, universities encouraged, and the sprawling agricultural potential rationalized in major ways, all through federal action. National defense often served as the basis for undertaking major projects with broad developmental impact, from building hydroelectric dams to the interstate highway system of 1954 to the present high-technology opportunities grounded in military and space developmental work of the last two decades.

More recently, the experience of New York City in the mid-1970s provides a major example of the financial side of industrial policy at work. In this case, the city was unable to meet its debt obligations to the big banks that had continued to lend it money as its budget grew larger and its tax base contracted. The possibility of the city's bankruptcy, combined with huge losses to the banks and the buyers of city bonds, seemed likely. Into the breach stepped Felix Rohatyn with a design for new institutions created first to slash and then to control the city's expenditures. The state of New York and the Congress accepted the design and the commitment to appoint bankers to manage the new institutions. They provided the guarantees that enabled New York to continue its payments to the banks.

An Emergency Financial Control Board was created by the state legislature, and the governor appointed Rohatyn as chairperson of the five-member group. Armed with final authority over budget decisions, the board stood watch over the elimination of several city services and a massive reduction in city employment. But the city made its payments and recovered from the brink of bankruptcy. This use of financial leverage over elected governments is regularly cited by Rohatyn as one of the techniques that needs to be adopted nationally.

Yankees tend to stress current Japanese and German industrial policy capabilities also, on the grounds that these are the major international competitors with whom we must keep pace. Table 4.1 (p. 60) showed why, and might be reexamined at this point. Japanese and German economic performance in several categories has exceeded that of the United States over an extended period. The differences are too great to be owed to coincidence or special conditions in one or another country. Much discussion of economic renewal policy in the United States has focused on these models, and we may as well invest a moment in a brief survey.

INSTITUTIONS AND POLICIES: JAPAN

The Japanese accomplishments must be understood against a background of Japanese culture and historical experience with the role of government in the economy. The industriousness of the average Japanese worker has probably been exaggerated, but there is a genuine concern for quality and a sense of loyalty to both employer and occupation. The oligarchic structure and conservative evolution of Japanese society lends a trace of what would in the West be recognized as the feudal notion of status or "place" to the roles of both workers and corporations. The sense of Japan as distinct from the rest of the world makes it easier to formulate global strategies and to plan for maximizing Japan's role in the light of available resources. Unimpeded by a tradition of antigovernment rhetoric, or even by a clear distinction between public and private spheres, the Japanese have long enjoyed a comfortable, genuine integration of business, government, and society that permits a gentle guiding role for government.

The primary institution exercising this guidance (chiefly in informal but nonetheless effective ways) is the Ministry of International Trade and Industry, or MITI. MITI is tiny by American standards, consisting of a mere 2500 or so professionals. Its great strength is in the fact that the whole range of government policies affecting business comes before it. The character, operations, problems, and prospects of various companies and industries define the concerns of MITI rather than a specific policy area or government function. MITI cannot act by itself, but only in conjunction with such other agencies as the Diet (Parliament) or the Ministry of Finance. But it serves as the focus of a network involving these and such other public institutions as the Japan Development Bank, plus the leading Japanese trade associations and commercial banks.

MITI's general practice is to consult with appropriate industry groups and financial interests and then decide which combinations of companies in which industries should receive assistance in order to develop along desired lines. In recent years, MITI has emphasized manufacturing industries with high "value-added" potential (i.e., the value added through manufacturing processes is substantially in excess of the total costs of materials and labor). These are the industries likely to produce high returns on investment.

MITI has also concentrated on developing new industries in entirely new fields that have high future export sales potential. Having "targeted" such industries, MITI provides financing from its related sources and encourages further private financing. Because only certain companies have been designated for this new growth, they represent safe investments for private banks; other companies are effectively discouraged from entering the new field. Import protection and tax advantages may be added to the package of inducements, and perhaps direct research and development aid as well.

In effect, the risk of undertaking expensive new product or process development is shifted from one or several private companies to the public. The government is willing to wait for the new industry to establish itself before seeking any return on its investment of public money. While these actions do not necessarily represent the difference between the success or failure of a new industry, they certainly make its success more likely and speed the process of its development.

The targeting accomplished by MITI was at first directed at shipbuilding, steel, and automobiles. It was not long, however, before shipbuilding was identified as a declining industry on a worldwide basis. MITI began to encourage the shift of capital and labor into other areas, such as machine tools. MITI also foresaw the world decline in demand for steel even as Japanese efficiency in this industry crested, and began to shift into a relatively few specialty forms of steel products.

The most recently targeted for development was the semiconductor industry, once an American near-monopoly in world markets. In the early 1970s, MITI devised a plan to develop and market a subsequent generation of larger and more valuable semiconductors. It designated the companies to pool their resources to do the research and development necessary, granted them substantial financial aid for that purpose (not to be repaid until profits were realized), and limited imports until the industry was ready. In what is sometimes known as "the chip war," Japan has now captured 30 percent of the world market. The next stage of this international competition will probably be in the field of supercomputers. American companies are already asking how they will be able to compete with the Japanese government-business partnership.

MITI operates through a combination of "visions" and "administrative guidance." "Visions" are essentially ten-year plans put together through public-private discussions with key members drawn from all major sectors of Japanese society and business. Once a consensus has been reached through these consultative mechanisms, it is communicated generally in such ways that corporations and other entities seem to *want* to make it work. "Administrative guidance" means the panoply of efforts by MITI bureaucrats to put the general standards of legislation or agreements within its decision-making system into practical effect. In Japan, statutes are much more general than is the case in the United States. Administrative departments have much greater authority to issue interpretations of their meaning. Bureaucrats regularly go beyond the precise terms of their authorizations to make suggestions and offer guidance. Usually (but not always) such suggestions and guidance are willingly accepted because they are taken to reflect the general consensus.

In general, Japan has been alert to the need to aid declining industries, not by propping them up beyond their time, but by helping capital and labor to move elsewhere and cushioning the economic shocks bound to result. It has been specially aggressive in spurring the development of new industries capable of capturing major shares of future export markets. Long-term projects for the acquisition of necessary technology and multiple arrangements for industrial cooperation are Japanese trademarks in these efforts. The Japanese have also distinguished themselves in regard to flexible use of the various financial tools available for these purposes. The result of all these measures taken together are the economic performance achievements detailed earlier in this section.

INSTITUTIONS AND POLICIES: GERMANY

There is no equivalent to MITI in Germany (or anywhere else in the world, for that matter). The nearest that the Germans come to a means for central guidance is an ongoing public-private consultative process organized through the larger banks. For a nation lacking a single central planning agency, however, Germany comes about as close as possible to duplicating such a function in this informal manner. The task is undoubtedly made easier by the fact that Germany is a leading member of the European Economic Community. The latter's data-gathering, consensus-generating, and cooperative mechanisms are at work in the external environment of German policymaking at all times. In any event, long-term overall planning is a hallmark of the German system.

Two key ministries carry primary responsibility for industrial policies. One is the Ministry of Economics, to which falls the task of restructuring capital investment away from prospectively declining industries. Much of this effort is actually accomplished through the German equivalents of state governments, which operate both as conduits for federal funds and as independent developers under a general plan. The German record of anticipating the decline of major industries is good, and so far Germany has not fallen into unproductive support for fading industries.

The other crucial ministry is a 1972 creation, the Ministry of Technology. It carries responsibility for developing new processes and products, and for creating new export markets. Germany has emerged as probably the most aggressive of the major countries in direct support for industries likely to establish new export markets in the high-technology fields. The Ministry of Technology can and does fund research and development for private businesses and averages about 20 percent of all such expenditures per year.

But perhaps the most distinctive aspect of German industrial policy is the effort expended in various forms of public assistance to workers. Germany is second only to Sweden in the proportion of its expenditures devoted to social welfare broadly conceived, and far ahead of other major countries in this respect. Germany focuses on its labor market, offering a wide variety of protections for workers against unexpected or uncompensated loss of employment. It requires severance pay after lengthy notice in the case of terminated employment and provides substantial aid to communities affected by plant closings. Extensive retraining is available to workers as a matter of right, together with job-finding and relocation assistance.

The German approach is thus one of relying on informal public-private consultation at the highest levels for overall strategy and basic implementing signals. Aggressive promotion of new industries and export opportunities are relied upon to draw capital and skilled labor in the right direction. Under these shifts, a real safety net of protection and assistance for workers helps provide the skills and motivation needed to spur the newer industries to world significance.

What the Japanese and German achievements have in common is a kind of foresightedness, an ability to take the offense and design industrial capabilities for future markets not yet visible. These governments provide assistance with the research and development stages, then financing needs, and finally trade help that enable fledgling industries to eventually dominate world markets.

France has a long-established central guidance system and competent bureaucratic support, yet in the case of its steel industry, was ultimately tempted to follow the British model of supporting declining industries whatever the real prospects for their futures. Great Britain actually has more national government ownership, and less actual control or effective national planning, than any of the other major countries. The British, and recently the French as well, seem distinguished by defensive policies intended to preserve whatever exists rather than reconstruct their economies for future needs. Both ended up sustaining their steel industries long after the latter achieved dinosaur status.

Critiques of Yankee Capitalism

It is really remarkable that Yankee capitalism, more or less the ruling ideas and practices of the twentieth century, can be met today with such hostility from both right and left—and even with rejection by thinkers from their own center ranks. Despite their entrenchment in the citadels of American culture, or perhaps because of it, their proposals have drawn a withering crossfire of denunciation. To the cowboys and their free market allies, the Yankees are defined by their advocacy of an active role for government, internationalism, and failure to "stand up for America" in the world. To economic democrats, they are defined by their often thinly disguised impatience with democracy and corporatist inclinations. To both right and left, they are indelibly identified with the Democratic party.

The critique from the right is most vigorous, perhaps in part because it is a replay of the great issue that has divided Americans for so long: the free market vs. government "intervention" in the economy. But there is also a contest going on for the allegiance of many business leaders in the middle here. Most of them by inclination prefer the old free market principles, but are vulnerable to the prestige and persuasiveness of Yankee capitalists and their army of eager propagandists.

To those for whom the market is real and compelling, there is simply no redeeming virtue anywhere in the partnership proposals. The free market can always send the appropriate signals, channel investment, and reward risk better and more efficiently than any politically managed system. Nobody has the knowledge to pick winners and losers, and if they try, they will only introduce massive new problems into an economy already struggling with too much government intervention. Bureaucrats and politicians will end up engaged in a great new pork-barrel operation, assisting their friends in a wasteful, disruptive, and potentially corrupt manner. The planning systems proposed seem either unnecessary appendages or tantamount to expropriation of private property. The phrase "fuzzy socialism" is one of the kinder terms used to describe these proposals.

Clearly, Yankee corporatists have already made one important contribution to the American political dialogue. Their frank support for a comprehensive government role in managing the economy has shifted the terms of debate significantly. Finally, 70 years after the Progressive era and 50 years after the New Deal, advocates of a government role are no longer apologetically asserting that just this one minor statutory improvement is needed in a basically sound laissez-faire system. As long as the "free market" was premised as the normal and desirable principle from which one or two exceptions nevertheless had to be made, the government's role would remain illegitimate and suspect—and politically much more difficult. Today's corporatists have almost been obliged to argue the reverse, that is, that government direction is the rule and the unaided market the exception.

In so doing, the corporatists have willingly taken on an additional political liability. The notion of the free market is deeply embedded in the minds of many Americans. Taking this position, however, has heightened the contrast with the Reagan administration and gained important visibility as an "alternative" policy direction for the country to take. Indeed, the media visibility quickly gained by the corporatists is a tribute to both the remaining strength of the eastern establishment in the national media and the supposed lack of other alternatives.

The critique from the left holds that the Yankee capitalist remedy will lead to closer and closer integration between the corporate-banking sector of the economy and the national government. Failure to include open, democratic decision-making institutions and accountability provisions will mean effective insulation of a corporate-government elite and opportunity for it to wield its power over the country in secret. Some advocates of the corporatist proposals are already defining the U.S. problem as one of too much democracy, and many democrats feel that this is their way of solving that problem. "Neofascism" is the label often heard from this side, and it does appear a bit unseemly for the Yankees to be quite so enthusiastic about the workings of two formerly fascist nations' economies.

How real are the risks that even the limited form of democracy that we now know will be restricted further in this manner? Corporatists, and the corporate-banking constituency whose interests they reflect, are committed to efforts to manage the world capitalist system as best they can for their own long-range needs. To a considerable extent, this means management of trade and investments implemented through the world financial system. It is essential to back that system up with ample military power because in its essence it is a system of exploitation that requires control over others to be effective. Tensions in the world, and the military buildup at home, will be only slightly lower under corporatist rule.

But it is in the domestic decision-making process that the antidemocratic effects of corporatist priorities will be most directly felt. The insulation of all major economic decisions from popular accountability, which is a hallmark of corporatist prescriptions, implies a new institutional system for managing the American political economy.

Why are corporatists so concerned to protect their "hard decisions" against popular preferences? Why are they unwilling to allow, let alone encourage, open discussion of economic issues and choices? Part of the reason may be that their goals are not just efficiency, which they see as unfortunately in conflict with equity in many cases, but rather a fuller version of corporate priorities and needs generally. In other words, what looks like a *technical* rationality when they set forth their program is really a *capitalist* rationality that will inevitably be at odds with equity and democracy.

It is in conflict with equity and democracy because it promotes inequality, redistributing scarce rewards upward instead of generally. This system *has* to be insulated from popular preferences, because those preferences would favor equity and democratic equality. What we are talking about is the conflict between capitalism and democracy in a not-so-new form. If future conditions preclude the enormous economic growth of the past, as seems likely under either cowboy or Yankee capitalism, there will be far more conflict over the proper distribution of rewards than we have previously known. But capitalism will have erected a new institutional line of defense against the claims of people to share more fully in what they have produced.

There are ample defenders of Yankee capitalism, of course. Many writers and politicians who support Yankee capitalist priorities and industrial policy proposals also consider themselves "neoliberals," by which they mean that they remain true to the social and civil libertarian concerns of 1940s liberalism in the new "era of (fiscal) limits." They are skeptical of the indulgent "excesses" of the Great Society years, ready to make hard choices, and anxious to adapt to what they see happening in the high-technology future. They argue that Yankee capitalism represents a welcome middle road between backward-looking free marketeers and people locked into the failed formulas of the days when it seemed possible to solve problems. Their focus is on finding a means of restoring notions of excellence and purpose in individual and public life.

Some Yankees are already arguing that people should put the needs of the nation ahead of their particular interests. The case of Felix Rohatyn is interesting in this regard. He is at once the leading corporatist opponent of Reagan's vast new military spending and the most determined to establish new insulation against excessive democracy. He is apparently moved, first, by a genuinely conservative concern for social stability, which leads to appeals to put the country ahead of personal interests. In this above-party appeal, however, he is speaking for many other corporatists:

> The country's problems are so deep-seated, domestically and internationally, economically and socially, that even temporary and partial solutions (and that is probably the best that can be achieved) will, in my view, be beyond any one man, one party, one ideology. They will require an enormous bipartisan national effort. . . .[10]

The problem with this recurring "above party" theme lies in what it conceals. It argues in effect that we all share a harmony of interests in which the needs of the whole should take precedence over the claims of any sector, class, or group. But denying or repressing conflicts almost always works to the benefit of those who "naturally" reap the rewards from the "neutral" workings of a system that is not to be challenged. It is an appeal that seeks to divert people from recognizing that the system does not work for them—or at least not as well for them as it does for others. In the worst of times, it was regularly used to prevent unionization, condemn Populists, and isolate all who spoke for the disadvantaged of the day. Denial of the existence of conflicting interests, or appeals to unity and necessity, often conceal covert (and perhaps unrecognized) service to the established order of things.

To compound the problem for Yankees in selling their industrial policy product, they were met in late 1983 by a critique from the center—indeed, almost out of their own ranks. Charles Schultze, President Carter's chair of the Council of Economic Advisers, argued in a celebrated article that industrial policy was an idea whose time would never come and that it might as well be put aside.[11] Calling it "a dangerous solution for an imaginary problem," Schultze maintained that neither American institutions nor American political practice could perform as the industrial policy advocates were urging. In other words, he seemed to take existing institutions and practices as fixed givens, and to conclude from these premises that industrial policy was unworkable.

But he also insisted that, while there were economic problems in the country, they were not of the order or the "deindustrialization" character that justified the proposed industrial policies. Specifically, he argued that the problems of the steel and automobile industries are not typical and that the changes ahead could be handled better through the free market than by relying on government to identify winners and losers among American industries. There were therefore both institutional practicality and economic necessity arguments raised against the almost-unanimous Yankee capitalist and Democratic party industrial policy bandwagon. More such arguments were sure to follow. The issue seemed unlikely to go away. Once again, the crucial determinant will be the conditions of the American economy over the long term.

7. Full Employment: Jobs Before Profits

The full-employment cause developed during the New Deal, in a battle for priority on Franklin Roosevelt's agenda. The Hamiltonian concerns of Yankee capitalism's predecessors were more powerful and ultimately decisive, but the notion of full employment as a national policy gained visibility as part of the social and economic side of the new liberalism. Full-employment programs today still show some of their old intellectual parallels with Yankee capitalism—a kind of "industrial policy *plus*"—and still struggle with Yankee capitalists for a policy role within the Democratic party. But their premises and goals are increasingly independent, and the breach between them and the Yankees now seems beyond temporary political patching.

Full-employment advocates see a much changed economic and political world since the end of World War II, not all of which should be accepted as a given. Giant corporations with vast aggregations of assets, privately owned and managed for private profit through a government-aided market system, are the defining characteristic of this world. Many more small businesses compete vigorously in a much more genuine free market underneath the corporate-banking sector. But the basic directions and health of the nation's economy are established by the larger units.

Like the Yankees, full-employment advocates have learned some economic lessons from the twentieth century. One lesson certainly is that it is possible for capitalist economies, perhaps even the whole world, to wallow indefinitely with high unemployment, low utilization of capacity, and general stagnation. Another is that most people will not long or willingly tolerate hardship and suffering from the workings of their economy. Some may be willing to wait for a supposedly self-regulating free market to rearrange the factors of production and direct capital and labor to new forms of activity. But however much they may profess support for the unaided free market, in practice most people want their government to *do* something. Social upheaval and chaos, real or threatened, force even reluctant governments into action.

Supporters of the full-employment cause are particularly impressed with the way that the mighty stimulus of massive government spending can send modern capitalism off on a new stage of growth, absorbing new generations of workers in productive labor. Historically, war has been the only justification for such decisive government action in free market economies. But an equivalent injection of public funds into civilian activities would produce even greater growth and income.

As growth gets under way, governments must play a constant guiding role, supporting here and shaping choices there, so that the entire aggregate serves its own best interests in ways that individual units might never see, let alone seek. The lesson of the 1970s is not that the U.S. government sought to do too much of this, but that it did too little and that badly. For an economy under competitive pressure and undergoing significant transformation, such guidance must be exerted even more systematically and purposefully.

Full-employment advocates put their highest priority on achieving full employment and equitable distribution of income for all, with particular concern for the poor and minorities and women. It would be difficult to overemphasize their contrast with Yankees in this respect. This is the first economic renewal program so far considered to have constantly in mind working people and their needs and problems.

Planning is central to this goal, and (for some) democratic planning has a high and independent priority. How well such planning can actually be designed and implemented remains to be seen. But the intent is clear: Government should be the senior partner and business the junior. Public needs should be decisively superior to private advantage in the management of the joint enterprise.

Some of the policy tools for accomplishing these goals are often similar to those employed by the Yankees, although the mix and the purposes are distinct. Despite the sharp and growing contrast in basic goals with Yankee capitalism, the political fortunes of these two programs still appear to remain linked. For these reasons, occasional contrasts are emphasized here, and their political prospects are considered together in the next chapter.

The Essentials of the Full-Employment Program

This economic renewal program is capitalist because it assumes the existing corporate structure, the legitimacy of private ownership and private profit, and a flawed but still useful market system. But advocates call for comprehensive and coordinated government direction of the economy in order to achieve and maintain full employment. They deny that there is any necessary conflict between equity in the distributions accomplished and the efficiency with which the economy operates. Instead, they argue that full employment is not a drag but an aid to the better working of the economy. The new balance between government and the market, and the public dominance of the partnership involved, are suggested in this quote from a major paper by the Full Employment Action Council, a coalition of some 80 religious, civil rights, trade union, and other organizations:

> While we must rely primarily on market forces, there can be little doubt about the need for a positive government partnership with the private sector in addressing important national problems. There is an important range of problems—particularly in fighting inflation and strengthening the international competitiveness of American industry—that will not yield to the uncoordinated actions of either the public or private sector alone. Public and private partnerships must be forged, establishing a new institution of governance. . . .
>
> While the market can be a marvel at promoting short-run efficiency, it cannot solve larger problems. Markets by themselves cannot protect the environment, secure the health and safety of workers, eliminate discrimination, promote equal opportunities and adequate income levels for households, foster long-run basic research and innovation, and ensure national security.[1]

In addition to full employment and greater equity, the concerns of this group focus on the need to rebuild the American industrial base without spurring inflation. All these goals are to be achieved through a system of decentralized democratic planning. For some advocates, the latter is an important goal in its own right. There is much more detailed consideration of the means of conducting such planning among such proposals, as if it were something to be taken seriously. This arrangement of priorities is indicated clearly in the preamble to the proposed Recovery and Full Employment Planning Act sponsored by Representative John Conyers (D-Mich.) and others: "A Bill to establish an enforceable right to earn a living based on democratic planning for sustainable recovery and a full employment society." Together they show clearly that there is a distinctive set of goals involved here that is simply indigestible to Yankee capitalism, whatever else they may have in common.

REBUILDING WITH DEMOCRATIC PLANNING

The commitment to full employment is to some degree based on a new "personal right." How will it be achieved? At this point, some of the policy tools begin to sound familiar, but their combination and purposefulness are not. First, interest rates will be held to a small margin ahead of inflation, not just by exhortation to the Federal Reserve Board but by opening up the membership of that board to union, consumer, and other public representatives.

Next, massive investments in public works are contemplated. Citing the various national studies that have assessed the sorry state of the American infrastructure and estimated the cost of repairing and upgrading highways, bridges, sewer and water systems, and the like at from $2.5 to $3 trillion, these proposals urge that this task begin immediately. Other major projects proposed include an interstate railway system to rival the interstate highway system and provide fast, energy-efficient transportation between cities, and a national renewable-source energy system to finally end dependence on foreign oil. These are seen as major sources of direct employment, but even greater effects are expected from the multiplier effects they have in creating new jobs and increased demand throughout the economy.

Financing for these investments and new private projects will be provided in part by a new national network of publicly run development banks. These banks will get their funding from major reductions in the military budget and from the use of pension funds, both private and public. Not all, but most of these proposals envision a frontal attack on the military buildup, with redirection of billions of dollars toward the public works program. Some use the combination of priority for full employment and military reductions as a basis for a new foreign policy posture that would call for a UN conference on full employment. The IMF in particular is urged to work for growth instead of the austerity it now imposes on Third World countries in order to improve their debt repayment prospects.

Finally, they see major new sources of national government income possible through changes in tax policy. Following the principle of equity would mean a truly progressive income tax. More than that, great sums of new revenue, more than $200 billion by some estimates, can and should be obtained by plugging tax loopholes and tax forgivenesses that benefit the rich almost exclusively. With this more equitable revenue system and sharp reductions in military spending, major new funding for stimulating the economy would be available without inflationary consequences.

This brings us to the goal of instituting democratic planning as part of the program for rebuilding the industrial base. It is no coincidence that these two goals are placed together in this manner; they are two sides of the same purpose for most advocates in this category, and one is incomplete without the other. The principle for economic renewal is to upgrade all important industries, not to try to pick winners and losers and thereby merely accelerate market tendencies.

Investment funds therefore will be channeled into needy modernization projects as well as new industry development. Democratic participation will in most of these proposals move the public into a share of the present private decision-making power in major corporations. There will be plant-closing legislation and controls on capital flight so that corporations cannot simply depart from their workers and communities. Instead, workers and the community will have a voice in corporate investments and other policies. Workplace democracy will be promoted so that the shop floor is also democratized.

An elaborate national network of democratic planning institutions will engage local and regional groups and citizens in the management of the economy. Overall strategies will be set by the planning body at the apex of this system, variously known as the National Planning Council or the National Economic Policy Board. Business, government, and labor are assured representation on industry and wider planning bodies in most proposals, although there are significant differences between designs on this point. But the main day-to-day decisions are apparently to be within the powers of relatively local units. Despite some internal differences in design and emphasis, it is impossible not to see a qualitatively much greater commitment to democratic practices in these proposals as opposed to Yankee capitalism.

INFLATION: ANALYSIS AND PRESCRIPTION

Full-employment advocates deny that their proposals will rekindle inflation. They point, first, to the slack nature of the present economy and its combined need for large new demand and ability to absorb such demand before overheating. They make good use of the generally accepted tradeoff between unemployment and the federal budget to argue that deficits will actually be lowered by making these huge investments.

For each percentage point of unemployment, to use the Congressional Budget Office estimate again, the federal budget is thrown out of balance by an additional $30 billion. Of this sum, $11 billion is added to federal outlays in the form of unemployment insurance, welfare, and other support programs; $19 billion represents revenue lost because people who are not working do not pay income taxes. Therefore a significant reduction in the unemployment rate through the creation of new jobs would move the federal budget toward balance, not greater deficits.

But inflation fighting remains a major policy focus, in part because it is a way of emphasizing the contrasts between full-employment proposals and the Reagan administration's preference for monetary measures. Advocates of the full-employment cause deny that the recession of 1981-82 was necessary. They put the blame for the hardships suffered by so many (and the damage to the economy) squarely on Reagan's "free market" monetarism. A better way to fight inflation would begin with the control of interest rates and democratization of the Federal Reserve Board described earlier. It would then proceed into deliberate allocation of credit, to ensure the availability of capital when needed and for the best uses.

Equally important, the key inflation-generating sectors—health care, food, energy, and shelter—would be addressed directly. A program for controlling health care, for example, would target the problem of a fee-for-service system in which most of the payments are made by third-party insurers, often run by companies controlled or strongly influenced by the providers of health care. Such insurers have little incentive to hold costs down because they can simply raise premiums. In fact, health care costs have risen at a rate well ahead of inflation for several years. The remedy is a national health insurance system with direct controls over doctors' fees.

Control of inflation might require an incomes policy in which there would be direct controls over, in this order, prices, corporate executive salaries, rents, and wages if necessary. Such policies can be implemented from different biases, of course, and several steps are suggested to keep enforcement equitable and effective. Open decisions based on the principle of equal sacrifice have never really been tried, despite the fact that confidence in the equity of the restraints is crucial to their success.

What is involved here is a different perspective on the inflation-unemployment tradeoff. Those who see inflation as the greater threat are almost always willing to impose relatively high levels of unemployment on workers through monetary or other policy means in order to control it. Not surprisingly, those who actually suffer the therapeutic unemployment may be less enthusiastic about the cure administered. The choice of remedy for inflation is a basic value choice but depends in part on the analysis one makes of the *causes* of inflation.

There are many candidates for blame as the cause of inflation. Serious possibilities often alleged in the 1980s may be grouped into three categories for brief comparison. One set of causes may be termed "cost push" because it puts the blame for rising prices on the increasing costs of factors of production, particularly raw materials and labor. This analysis points chiefly at sharply rising energy costs, particularly the oil price increases imposed by the Organization of Petroleum Exporting Countries (OPEC) and labor costs. While energy costs may have risen prohibitively for some industries, forcing them to raise their prices sharply, these increases were only a small proportion of the total inflation of the period.

It is also hard to see labor costs as the culprit, again excepting isolated industries, because real wages increased very little on the average during the mid-1970s and actually decreased in the late 1970s. But the notion that wages are to blame persists, perhaps in part because labor costs are a high proportion of total production costs, and businesses always aspire to do something to reduce wages. In the late 1970s and early 1980s, many businesses did more than aspire to cut wages—they succeeded to a degree that surprised most observers. Wage increases plummeted, and unions gave back as concessions both wage levels and working condition protections that had taken years to achieve.

The second set of causes for inflation is simple: The government did it. These allegations span the range of practically everything that modern governments do. Regulations add to business costs and must be reflected in prices. The national debt is too high, taxes and spending are too high, and the money supply has been allowed to increase too rapidly. There is too large a deficit between revenues raised and expenditures made. And government policies are too uncertain, following a stop-and-go pattern of first trying to slow inflation and then stimulating the economy to promote employment. Many of these charges are mutually inconsistent, but that has not affected their sound and fury.

A final set of reasons assigned for recent inflation is more congenial to full-employment advocates than either of the previous ones. It has to do with the acts and omissions of managers of the corporate-banking sector of the economy. Such businesses are seen as so dominating their markets that they can raise their prices almost at will, and can hold them up even in slack times. Their managers are so focused on producing short-term profits that they fail to plan or invest for long-term gain, in which productivity improvement could yield higher wages and profits without increased prices. Massive waste occurs in the production and sales of military and other unnecessary goods. Multiple speculators and profit takers make mostly paper profits all along the chain of production. The result is that consumers pay higher prices than they receive in value and are forced to seek higher wages to be able to continue to do so.

There is thus a considerable range of differences, in priorities and in proposed practices, between full employment and Yankee capitalism. If these were the only two groups of proposals on the agenda, their conflict might be bitter and definitive. Indeed, they go a long way toward reproducing the old Hamilton-Jefferson contrast. If Yankee capitalists have succeeded in linking Hamiltonian ends and means, full-employment advocates have finally found a way to really construct a Hamiltonian government for Jeffersonian ends. More interesting, perhaps, is the fact that they have also found room for a good number of Jeffersonian political means.

Specific Programs for Full Employment: Two Examples

The overview of the full-employment position just presented is a "center of gravity" position between two distinct versions of these proposals. One version is not very different from the Ottinger "High Production Strategy to Rebuild America" or the AFL-CIO industrial policy proposals noted under Yankee capitalism. It belongs in the full-employment category, however, for two important and distinguishing reasons. One is that it stresses full employment and stable prices first and the restoration of business profitability as a distinctly subordinate goal. The other is that it insists on equity in the distribution of income to workers generally and the poor and minorities particularly.

This set of proposals is well illustrated by the several publications of the Full Employment Action Council, particularly the earlier-cited paper "An Economic Strategy for the 1980s."[2] This is a major document endorsed not only by the many trade union, civil rights, and religious groups who make up the council but also by 34 prominent economists linked in various ways with the labor movement. It opens with a call to put full employment at the center of national macroeconomic policy and offers suggestions for coordinating monetary and fiscal policy so as to reduce deficits, maintain demand, plug tax loopholes, and provide job training. It proposes fighting inflation by means other than recession, such as a focus on key sectors, price-wage controls, and reduced military spending.

The next set of proposals urges that business-labor-government consultative mechanisms be created to guide the rebuilding of American industry. Citing the experience of the Reconstruction Finance Corporation, they endorse the idea of a National Economic Policy Board to coordinate industry-wide boards whose goal would be to maximize growth everywhere instead of "picking winners and losers." Targeting investment and expanding public investment in infrastructure are additional proposals. None of them sounds very distinctive from the industrial policy ideas of some of the Yankees, and it is really the continuing emphasis on the goal of full employment that holds these proposals in a different category.

But there is also a strong emphasis on the point that full employment—and only full employment—offers the opportunity to combine equity and efficiency. The Full Employment Action Council argues that there is no conflict between these two goals. The probusiness position is that efforts to improve equity by legislating higher minimum wages or requiring fair hiring practices impede the efficient operation of the economy and thus effectively punish everybody. The council's response is that full employment will provide satisfactions and better performance on the job, more income to purchase the increased goods and services available, and more than enough new tax revenues to pay for the human capital development programs that make the whole process possible. The council clearly has a strong commitment to the social and personal development of citizens and sees secure and satisfying employment as a crucial step in that direction. Such development is "the essence of the freedom we desire."

It goes on to stress that

> the national government cannot emphasize certain kinds of freedom and forget others. Free markets reward those who have market power, but they do not improve opportunities for those who have little wealth or income. . . . Freedom is indivisible. We cannot emphasize only those forms of freedom that benefit mainly the powerful.[3]

With these appropriate final words, the 50-plus-page document is concluded. But there is no mention of mechanisms for participation or accountability, no discussion of how any of these programs are to be planned or implemented, and no mention of the idea of democracy.

The other version of full-employment programs is built around expansion and practical applications of the concept of democracy in a variety of ways. Figure 7.1 on page 130 reproduces section 2, the statement of purposes, from Representative Conyers's "Recovery and Full Employment Planning Act." This draft legislation is the best example of a full-employment program, and probably the most specific and far-reaching proposal for democratic participatory planning to be put forward by any economic renewal advocate. Subsequent titles of the draft bill implement its various purposes in distinctive ways that also deserve further notice.

One of the most important provisions has to do with establishing an enforceable right to earn a living. Title 1 of the draft bill declares that every adult able and willing to work has a right to "useful, productive and fulfilling paid employment" and that those unable to work have a right to an adequate standard of living. To implement these possibly illusory new rights, a Commission on Rights and Goals is created and charged with proposing ways to shape federal policy toward these ends, setting specific five-year goals for employment, output, and prices, and drafting an Economic Bill of Rights for the President to submit to the Congress. Specific guidelines for target goals, and for ways of consulting broadly with the people, are written into the statute to assure achievement of full employment *and* democracy.

Policy for economic recovery includes significant planning roles for labor and the unemployed, an array of incentives and disincentives for business to conform to overall full-employment goals, and strict limits on plant closings. A permanent Works and Services Administration of high status within the government is created and charged with the tasks of rebuilding the nation's infrastructure, comprehensive training and retraining of workers, and expanding human services capabilities. An annual National Recovery and Full Employment Plan is mandated, by which the President and Congress are to be guided in all relevant budgetary and other policies.

FIGURE 7.1

DRAFT OF THE RECOVERY AND FULL EMPLOYMENT ACT

SEC. 2. The major purposes of this Act are to

1. develop a nation-wide commitment to democratic planning for the establishment of an enforceable right to earn a living at real earnings high enough to provide the purchasing power required for sustainable recovery and a full employment society,

2. through both market and non-market processes, expand useful employment toward the goal of sustainable recovery and full employment,

3. enlarge productive capacity by improving the infrastructure of the nation's public works, human services and private industries and developing natural resources in a manner consistent with the maintenance of environmental quality,

4. match enlarged productive capacity with the higher real wages and salaries needed by both middle and lower income people to buy goods and services and invest in the productive capacity of the country,

5. provide thereby larger markets and better opportunities for enterprises with smaller unit profit margins to earn larger, more stable and less subsidized total profits on invested capital,

6. prevent or counterbalance undue concentration of corporate and federal planning power by fostering recovery and full employment planning by

a. labor, the unemployed, racial and ethnic minorities, women, small and large profit-seeking enterprises, and cooperative, non-profit and voluntary organizations, and

b. town, city, county and state governments in urban, suburban, rural and agricultural areas,

7. establish a full employment context for the preparation of and action on the many local, state and federal laws and executive policies required for recovery and full employment,

8. reduce economic dependence on military outlays and promote conversion from military to civilian goods and services,

9. provide for greater accountability to the American people by elected and appointed government officials and by the directors and executives of corporations and other organizations operating under public charters,

10. create conditions for more self-empowerment by people victimized by discrimination in hiring, training, wages, salaries, fringe benefits or promotion on the basis of prejudice concerning race, ethnic background, religion, sex, age, political or sexual preferences or personal disability, and

11. in doing all these things, promote greater activism by all Americans in decision making affecting themselves, their families, workplaces, communities, states and nation and their country's place in the world community.

An annual "needs assessment" developed by local and state planning agencies is to be the basis for this plan. Specific guidelines for what is to be covered in all major areas of the society and economy, and for assuring democratic participation in the planning process, are written into the statute. In other areas, national and local development banks are created, the Federal Reserve Board is reconstructed and given new priorities for keeping interest rates down and assuring availability of credit, and a system for controlling inflation is mandated.

Finally, Title VII is devoted to means of promoting full employment on a transnational basis. The U.S. government is directed to cooperate more fully with the UN in developing a new international order with rising living standards for all. In part, this means greater government supervision over U.S. transnational corporations operating in other countries, and also U.S. initiative in getting the UN to hold a continuing series of conferences on world unemployment and living standards. Further U.S. financial support for the IMF is conditioned on that body's reversing its policy of imposing austerity on various countries in return for new loans so that efforts toward economic growth become a consistent policy throughout the world.

Taken together, this second set of proposals calls for a dramatic redirection of American public policy and sweeping changes in the way our economy is run. Moreover, the program is offered in such concrete terms that it cannot be dismissed as mere abstract theory or wishful and impractical thinking. That is not to say that efforts are not made to do so. In anticipation, full-employment advocates have mobilized certain precedents and models on their side.

Models for Full-Employment Programs

Ample precedents for full-employment capitalism exist in the American experience, but only in wartime. It may seem surprising that full employment is otherwise a profoundly radical notion in the United States, but its implications as the basis for an economic renewal program should be understood accordingly. Repeated efforts have been made to get the national government committed to the principle of full employment, but they have never succeeded. In the Employment Act of 1946, the original draft promised a job for all who were willing and able to work, but the final version spoke more of free competitive enterprise than of jobs. The Humphrey-Hawkins Act of 1978 as enacted limited its commitment to no more than an exhortation to the government to work toward a 4 percent unemployment rate and conditioned even that on also attaining low inflation rates.

From an initial 3 percent level, the notion of what constitutes "full" employment has worked its way upward. The definition reached 4 percent for most of the 1970s, then 5 percent, and the Reagan administration proposed in 1983 to abandon the idea of trying to define full employment in this way. Instead, the President's chairperson of the Council of Economic Advisers, Martin Feldstein, proposed an "inflation threshold" of 6 percent—the idea being that any government effort to get unemployment lower than that level would be inflationary (and undesirable). Because an official rate of 6 percent meant that anywhere from 18 to 25 million people might be unemployed at some part of any given year, that approach was simply unacceptable to many people, not just full-employment advocates.

The U.S. reluctance to be committed to the policy package involved in seeking to assure work for all who want it is consistent with widely shared values such as individualism and the work ethic. But it stands in sharp contrast to the practice of most advanced industrial nations and all our major competitors. If full-employment advocates have a model, it is usually Sweden that they cite. To be sure, there are some difficulties in making comparisons with a nation so much smaller than the United States. But allowances can be made for differences of scale and then some lessons can be drawn that have applications in the United States. Full-employment advocates are not using Swedish successes to design an American program, but to argue that full employment is neither impossible nor necessarily productive of all the bad side effects critics associate with it.

Sweden's economy is capitalist in the sense that it is privately owned. But government plays a very large role in directing the income produced toward serving public needs. Within that governmental apparatus, the trade unions play a leading part, not least because in Sweden more than 80 percent of the workforce is unionized. Since the 1930s, Sweden has followed consistent policy commitments to full employment, extensive government services (particularly health care), and equity in income distribution. The results have been dramatic. In GNP produced per capita, Sweden leads the United States by 30 percent, and Swedish workers average almost 50 percent more per hour than U.S. workers. In both cases, Sweden was well behind U.S. levels at the close of World War II. Faster productivity growth enabled them to overtake us even more rapidly than other countries did.

The fact that highly progressive taxes took more than half the Swedish GNP (compared to about a third in the United States) did not prevent the Swedish economy from performing in this way. But it did help enable Sweden to invest proportionally much more in education than we do, to maintain lower infant mortality and higher life expectancy rates, to have much less pollution, and to have the least income inequality of the advanced capitalist countries. Most of all, the broad scope of government responsibility enabled Sweden to maintain unemployment rates, computed in ways comparable to the United States, of 2 percent or less throughout the worst stagflation years of the 1970s. This was less than one-third of the U.S. average during the same period. Like all other countries in the new world economy, Sweden has struggled with inflation and low growth lately, but the overall record is much better than that of the United States.

How was all this brought about? The Swedish government has undertaken an elaborate system designed to enable workers to have jobs that they find satisfactory. It provides extensive job information and referral services, training and retraining programs, and relocation assistance. It provides incentives for some companies to maintain unprofitable plants in labor surplus areas, and for other companies to move into such areas. Public works expenditures are timed and allocated to maintain demand and employment levels and include direct government employment, particularly for regional and local economic development purposes. Major efforts are made to encourage worker participation in both quality improvement and overall management of the production process.

One point about the Swedish example that strikes home for Americans today is that full employment was achieved and maintained for a long period of time *without* either war or a military buildup—by greatly *increasing* public expenditures while *raising* taxes via a truly progressive income tax. Another important characteristic is the principle of "solidarity wages" in which workers are committed to a degree of sharing of the aggregate total income that they all derive from their work. The main form it takes is policies intended to raise the wages of low-wage workers more rapidly than those of high-wage workers, and secondarily to keep wages for the same work roughly comparable throughout the country. These policies have the effect of promoting income equality, increasing overall demand, and reducing conflict within the workforce (and thereby increasing workers' bargaining strength). Some studies have argued that the substantial reductions in the spread between highest- and lowest-paid workers accomplished in this way were primarily responsible for the rapid growth in productivity enjoyed in Sweden in the 1960s and 1970s.

Once again, there surely are important differences between the two countries, and export-oriented Sweden has had troubles with inflation and low growth in the late 1970s and early 1980s. A much lower proportion of American workers is unionized, for example, and the ratio is dropping every day. But the success of a national full-employment policy commitment is undeniably on the record in Sweden, certainly more clearly than is any general achievement on the part of cowboy capitalism's free market solution in the United States. And that success occurred in spite of, or perhaps *because* of, massive government taxation, expenditures, regulations, social improvements, and general commitment to a better quality of life for all.

Critiques of Full-Employment Democracy

For the most part, full-employment proposals have had their principal visibility as labor-sponsored appendages to some version of Yankee industrial policy proposals. They have not fully blossomed as independent programs in which the nature of the entire economic renewal program was adapted to fit the goal of full employment. The Conyers "Recovery and Full Employment Act" represents a major step toward combining the two goals of full employment and expansion of democratic qualities in the society. To be taken seriously, it will need support from an organized popular movement, a possibility that I will explore in later chapters. But if or when it reaches the threshold of real visibility, it will become the focus for critical reactions that the other full-employment proposals have never drawn. Analogizing from the reactions to other full employment proposals, it seems likely that the chief targets will be cost, dangers from "politicizing" control over the economy, and the impracticality and undesirability of planning.

Where the Yankees were seen as dangerously threatening and drew bitter attacks from both right and left, full-employment advocates are seen by both as pale shadows of the Yankees, unrealistic, and fuzzy-minded. Cowboys' and free marketeers' minds are literally boggled by the costs of the programs involved, and the Yankees are not left in much better shape. None can believe that such "extremes" have any relevance to the American reality they know.

While economic democrats share many of the goals of the full-employment capitalists, they charge that the latter have given away too much before the game really starts. By conceding the rights and powers of the giant corporations and their market system, they assert, the full-employment cause has been rendered toothless and vulnerable to cooptation. Most likely, the rhetoric of full employment will serve as a cover for corporatism, perhaps delaying it and conceivably softening it a bit.

Critiques of full-employment proposals do not flow only from exaggerations or basic disagreements. There are some real and even acute dilemmas inherent in any effort at political management of the economy. The case of "domestic content" legislation, which many full-employment advocates supported, may serve to illustrate this point.

The United Automobile Workers is at once a union deeply wounded by imports and the recession and one with a historically progressive record. It provoked much controversy in 1983 by sponsoring employment-defending legislation to require foreign companies with significant car sales in the United States to produce some share of their cars in America. The proposal would require any foreign manufacturer with more than 100,000 sales annually in the United States to demonstrate that a proportion of their cars commensurate with the total amount of their U.S. sales originated in this country. For sales of 200,000 cars, 20 percent of the content would be American-made; for sales of 600,000, 60 percent; and so on.

The proposal was attacked by some as protectionist, likely to trigger retaliation from other countries against American exports and to force higher prices on American consumers in behalf of a dying and uncompetitive industry. It was criticized by others as unworkable, in that components of all major products were now made all over the world, and nobody could ever be sure of the value or exact origin of various materials. Still others insisted that it was racist and shortsighted in that it would take jobs away from Third World workers and give them to Americans when the real target should be the high mobility of corporate capital. The UAW defended it as a practical, temporary measure that was characteristic of many countries and therefore not likely to trigger reprisals. Besides, it would save American jobs, and nobody else seemed to be doing much about that urgent need.

Critics from the right were quick to point out that this disruptive intervention into national import policy was just what could be expected from acceptance of political management of the economy. Corporatists smugly noted the need for greater insulation of decision making against such pressures. Full-employment supporters reminded both that current import policies were highly politicized, but in behalf of other beneficiaries than were now proposed. They argued strongly that the free market worked to the advantage of some, usually owners and managers, but to the disadvantage of others, usually workers. With no neutral way to shape outcomes that had to be shaped in some fashion, the best way might actually be an open and participatory process. What better institution to decide the issue than the U.S. Congress?

The notion of planning arouses great controversy in the United States. Perhaps because free market imagery is so pervasive in our culture, Americans tend to react to the idea of planning in exaggerated ways. A few treat planning as a magic incantation that, once invoked, can solve all problems. Many more view it as the death knell of free enterprise and the beginning of outright socialism. It is neither, of course. In an essay entitled "The Inevitability of Planning," the economist Robert Lekachman presents planning as no panacea but "merely a better response than uncoordinated, partly competitive markets to the problems of an ever more interdependent economy and ever more interdependent economy and ever more interdependent world."[4] It is inevitable, he says, because it is the only way to use resources rationally and distribute economic goods efficiently.

Nor is planning unprecedented in the United States. Indeed, a good argument can be made that we already have a comprehensive planning system in the form of the patterned decisions of the financial community about when and where to invest the capital that gives the economy its motive force. From that perspective, the only question raised by proposals for planning is whether planning should be conducted by different (public) bodies, under criteria other than those of private profit maximizing.

But we also have considerable experience with planning as national public policy. Comprehensive planning occurred in each of the world wars of the twentieth century, under the War Industries Board and the War Production Board. Sectoral and regional planning were common in the New Deal under the Natural Resources Planning Board, the Agricultural Adjustment Act, the TVA, the NRA, and so on. The commitments of the Employment Act of 1946, however reduced from their original versions, still amount to a form of planning. Price and wage controls, when instituted, are a far-reaching form of planning that allocates shares of national income in specific directions. Planning is going on all the time, by both private and public bodies, and the concept has many meanings. The issue is, what kind of planning, by whom, and for what purposes?

Two planning mechanisms are included within Yankee capitalist proposals. One calls for something like an economic advisory council linked directly to Congress. The other proposes a body analogous to the Council of Economic Advisers that would report first to the President, and through that office, to Congress. In both cases, the planning body is to include representatives of business, labor, and government (sometimes "the public," but government is what is meant). How labor is to be adequately represented when union membership is below 20 percent of the workforce is not addressed in any of the proposals for "tripartite" corporatist decision making. In neither case is the planning body connected in any way to lower levels of state or local planning, where more public participation might be anticipated.

Planning for the Yankees is a high-level, technocratic enterprise. Whatever linkage to public preferences must reluctantly be provided is accomplished entirely through Congress. But there has been little attention to the problems that Congress would encounter in analyzing and evaluating the planners' work or in developing implementing policies. Plans would have to be integrated with the annual Economic Report of the President and the President's budget proposals, a staggering task given the difficulty Congress has today with the budget alone. In the context of the American institutional system today, temptations will be very strong for the Yankees to seek a planning mechanism closely linked to the Presidency and the autonomous superagency that is to do the actual economy managing—and to bypass Congress as much as possible.

The tasks of any national planning body are vast, although not necessarily insurmountable. There are major needs for collection of new and different kinds of data, including some that have been previously categorized as "proprietary" or confidential by corporations and banks. Information about ownership, strategies, technological capabilities, and profitability will certainly be needed, and will as certainly provoke resistance. Forecasting from available data may be done using different assumptions, but at some point the goals to be accomplished must inform analysis and projections.

What is crucial is how early or late in the process of planning specification of goals is plugged in—and whose goals they are. Central planning will also be in constant tension with state and local action, particularly when the states take on new functions and enter fields of regulation that the national government is steadily abandoning. These examples are intended only to emphasize how much the planning process is a *political* process, one involving choices of values and goals amid basic conflicts of interest.

There is a sharp difference between the technocratic, top-down, depoliticizing Yankee version of planning and that of the full-employment democrats. The latter premise the political nature of planning and therefore seek to open it to wide public participation starting from the local and state levels and working up toward the national government. The national planning bodies they envision are frankly political arenas where contrasting views can be harmonized with the needs of the whole as they are perceived by national officials.

Two factors might help make the latter process more coherent than this cumbersome arrangement at first suggests. One is the shared commitment to full employment as the first priority at all times. The other is that there would presumably be many other forms of public participation and policy making available so that everything would not depend on what was finally decided by the national planning board or how it was eventually implemented. But the more democratic the intentions, the more tolerant of messiness and delays in the process one must be; such tradeoffs will not disappear, even if policy directions change.

Planning may thus be more of a symbolic obstacle than a real one. A genuinely participatory process ought not to be resisted, except by the business community. This resistance, and its resonance in many Americans' minds, should not be underestimated. But this may be only another way of saying that full-employment democracy depends heavily on a continuing popular movement, probably one organized in something like a political party.

8. Economic Democracy: The Transition to Full Democracy?

There is a qualitative difference between cowboy capitalism, Yankee capitalism, full-employment—our first three categories—and economic democracy. It is like stepping across a threshold and then seeing the world differently. Although there are sharp differences between them, all the other programs share certain premises. They all assume an economic system dominated by great corporations, a market that operates more or less well, competition, and the legitimacy of the private profit motive. These are givens, from which they begin to think about what to do and for whom. Even more important, they see the economy as a mechanical aggregate of working parts, a complicated machine with a few key levers that can be manipulated from above to determine its direction and speed. Their problem is to manage that machine so as to get as much out of it as possible. When they disagree, it is about how to make the machine work better or about how its benefits should be distributed.

Economic democrats differ in two important ways, one more fundamental than the other. The more modest difference lies in the ways that they use certain tools to analyze the machine that the others see. Without accepting the others' premises or givens, economic democrats can still talk their language and use similar analytic methods, although they usually arrive at quite distinctive conclusions. For example, economic democrats are much more likely than the others to find the causes of inflation in the power and practices of American corporations. But they do so using evidence and arguments that the others would recognize and respect, even if they would dispute the conclusions.

The economic democrats' fundamental difference, and their distinguishing feature, lies in their basic premises and ways of thinking about an economy. Not only do they deny that the market is a neutral or efficient way of allocating economic goods and all the other "givens" that the others accept; what they *see* when they look at an economy is different. They look at it from underneath, not from above. They do not see a machine with interacting mechanical parts that occasionally need repair, but social relationships between living people. They see some people trying to get others to work under their direction in order to produce the goods and services needed to sustain life for all.

The problem is that the owners and managers in the system claim the right to take the lion's share of these goods and services. They leave very little for the great bulk of the people, who do most of the work. This absolutely requires that owners and managers spend much of their time and energy maintaining control over the workers. This is essential both to keep them producing and to prevent them from finding ways to get a larger share of the total of goods and services they are producing. The task is accomplished initially by organizing the production process so as to maximize hierarchical control. Another important tactic is mystifying what is actually going on in a variety of ways so that workers do not see what is happening or are discouraged from doing something to change the situation.

But this introduces some very substantial inefficiencies and irrationalities into the process of making and distributing goods and services. The owners and managers have to do so much to ensure their control and keep on getting the lion's share that the whole process produces less than it could and wastes natural and human resources while doing it. Much of their effort goes into seeking military or economic domination over other countries, to assure raw materials and markets that they need. And their two dominant priorities, assuring control and maximizing profit, make life very difficult for the workers. The material conditions of people's lives are often far worse than they could be, and for many they are actually harsh and degrading. But the social and cultural side of human life is also warped under this system. So many subtle and deeply embedded means have been deployed over time to maintain the owners' and managers' control that people feel tensions with one another, they are frustrated in their lives, and they end up seeking a variety of compensating gratifications.

What people should have, and what economic democracy basically stands for, is a fully participative life. This means democratic control over all the forces that shape one's life—economic, social, political, and so forth. The citizen should be able to take part in workplace decisions, both about how work should be organized and who should do what in order to produce efficiently and humanely. The citizen should be involved in democratic planning of investment and the question of *what* should be produced. And the rewards of the economy should be distributed equitably, in accordance with criteria set by these same participants. The quality of people's lives—all people, and all dimensions of their lives—is what concerns the economic democrat. Economics is only one (vital) part of a fully integrated human existence that can and should be brought into being. It is a good place to start partly because in the compartmentalized capitalist world, people turn to economics for explanations of what is happening and prescriptions for what to do about it.

Martin Carnoy and Derek Shearer are perhaps more direct than other economic democrats when they state their basic perspective on the world. They say:

> We believe that economists and other governmental policymakers cannot improve the situation primarily because . . . they accept a set of ideological assumptions about the "naturalness" and "perfectibility" of capitalism as an economic order. . . . We think it is crucial to political-economic discussion to accept openly the fact that assumptions about ownership and power are part and parcel of the economic problem. Rather than discussing the best methods for "fine tuning" the economy, we want to shift the debate to strategies for changing the structure of the economy so that it better serves the interests and needs of all Americans. . . . Neoclassical economics represents a point of view, a political position, a set of assumptions about the way the world should be and about human behavior. We will present an alternative view based on an alternative set of assumptions.[1]

Let us imagine representatives of each of the four economic renewal perspectives arguing over how to get the U.S. economy going in the best possible manner. The first three can talk to one another—not with much agreement, perhaps, but with many of the same definitions. They argue animatedly about the relationship of growth to capital formation and productivity rates; the tradeoffs between inflation and unemployment and between imports and exports; the impact of tax incentives on the behavior of corporations and consumers; and the policy implications of various indices—exchange rates, net returns on investment, corporate profits, and so on. They talk of "laws" of various kinds, graphs of elasticity curves, and have a general air of certainty about the inevitable effects of changes in one rate or factor of production upon others.

Economic democrats can talk this language well enough, but at some point it begins to seem irrelevant to what really goes on in a working capitalist economy. One of them is sure to open the window and shout, "Economics is *politics!* If you want to fix things, change the power relationships—change the people who have control, and the private profit goals that dominate the whole thing. Everything else is a series of Band-aids to keep the rich secure and the rest of us struggling for crumbs."

The others react resignedly. The cowboy, secure with his pistol on his hip, wishes it were the old days when one shot could drop such a troublemaker on the spot. The Yankee smiles smugly, having learned all the flaws in such crude foreign ideas from trustworthy Ivy League teachers, and prepares to chart a course that, because it is in the interest of the banks, is surely in the best interest of all. The full-employment advocate tugs anxiously at the economic democrat's sleeve and says, "Yes, you've got something there, but be realistic—the only hope we have is to show the Yankees that they need us, and then they will give us a part of what we want."

And the fact is that economic democrats *do* have a real dilemma. If they talk the language of dominant beliefs, they end up playing somebody else's game and give up their unique perspective and the goals that go with it. But if they frame their appeals in their own perspective, most people just do not understand them. The problem involves both the intended audience and the manner in which the argument is made. Orthodox economists do not look at the world the way economic democrats do, and rational arguments using orthodox tools never convince them. Orthodox economists have their professional status and all the solid thinking of the "better people" to reinforce their convictions, although they are not above appropriating a good idea now and then.

But when economic democrats try to tell it like it is in their own terms, hardly anybody listens. Or if they do, they often quickly add that nothing can be done about it anyhow and move to a distant seat. More people listen when times are hard, and more of them breach the barriers that their culture has erected and come to understand what economic democrats are saying. More ideological and political walls remain, however, and the way to success is long and hard.

Faced with the prospect of failing to convince either opinion makers or the general public, economic democrats do what makes the most sense under the circumstances. They redouble their efforts in both directions. They are determined to win as much as they can in the conventional (capitalist) language of economics—to create as much doubt about the efficacy of capitalism as possible and to show that it works only for the few. And they offer detailed and plausible alternative policies for running an economy under their premises and goals in order to build confidence that there *are* practical, workable programs for fundamental reconstruction that can yield a better life for all. I look first at the analysis that they make of today's economy and then at the prescriptions they offer for its transition to economic democracy.

Economic Democracy's Analysis of the U.S. Economy

A common theme of economic democrats is that people generally will be made to pay the price for capitalism's efforts at recovery. They charge capitalist analysis with finding the causes of problems in the behavior of people—a kind of "blame the victim" approach that serves to mask capitalism's failures. For example, take the problems of low growth, low productivity growth, and inflation. "Mainstream" analysis finds the cause alternatively in low levels of saving and hence low investment, excessive consumption, and unions' pressures for higher wages and better working conditions. These findings lead to the widely shared view that the solution lies in greatly expanded capital investment. This new capital is drawn in most proposals from money that previously went to working people, whether in the form of wages, transfers or services from government, or comparatively lower taxes. In other words, the capitalist recovery and renewed profits will be provided by new capital investment obtained by reducing the standard of living of workers and other consumers.

Economic democrats charge that mainstream economists have never adequately explained inflation and are too ready to prescribe cures—such as balanced budgets during slack times or contractions of money and credit that cause unemployment—that punish workers most severely. They point to the larger role of government, and larger deficits, in other countries to refute the claim that the cause of inflation lies with government. They are much more likely to see inflation stemming from the power of corporations to keep prices high and rising because of their dominance over both supplying sources and the markets in which they sell. Acknowledging declining profits, they see inflation as partly the result of efforts to restore profit margins by raising prices.

But economic democrats are not comfortable with a narrow analysis of one characteristic in isolation. By looking at the capitalist system as a whole, its particular features come through most clearly. What should strike any open-minded observer is the sheer irrationality of the system. This irrationality extends beyond the contrast between opulence for a few and poverty and hardship for many to some features directly linked to the search for private profit and the need for social control. Three are currently urged most often, and may serve as an illustration of the economic democrats' indictment of contemporary capitalism.

First is the point that the search for immediate, short-term profit has created a situation where it is the *misuse* and not the shortage of capital that has created problems. Moreover, this misuse has been destructive for the economy in general and workers and their communities in particular. The term "capital flight" was coined to describe the mobility of capital out of declining or low-profit industries and areas and toward regions or countries where labor costs were lower and unions nonexistent. Mergers, speculation, and other nonproductive uses of capital offered other sources of profits, and capitalism had no incentive to reproduce itself in ways that could sustain its workforce.

Second, economic democrats argue that the economy suffers from a number of "costs of corporate power." That is, corporations use their power in self-seeking ways that send a surge of unnecessary costs running through the economy. They impose such heavy controls on their workers, for example, that workers are led to resist in various ways. One argument along these lines holds that more than half of the drop in productivity can be attributed to sheer worker resistance to speedup and other work rules that were unnecessary to production and did not cut costs. A more fully shared position is that corporations used their power to break the implicit postwar "social contract" with labor as soon as their profit margins were squeezed. This social contract was to the effect that corporations would share some part of their rapidly growing profits with workers via wage increases and taxes that translated into government services and transfers to those in need. Instead, corporations sharply reversed themselves, fought their unions, and at the same time campaigned to have their taxes cut and funds slashed for social services.

Third, this imperious use of power leads to a defining characteristic of capitalism that requires independent analysis: economic waste. There are many potential kinds of waste, from unnecessary production (military goods or goods intended to become obsolete very quickly) to unused labor or plant capacity to excessive advertising and overpriced goods (particularly health care) and crime control made necessary by unemployment or uses of corporate power. One recent study, appropriately titled *Beyond the Waste Land,*[2] has tried to give an estimate of the total amount of waste in the economy per year, using 1980 as the base year.

The various components of waste identified include all the items listed above and some others as well. The two largest items, wasted labor effort ($455 billion) and unutilized labor hours ($234 billion), reflect the economic democrat's bottom-up, social approach to understanding economics. In this case, the way to increase productivity and make use of human resources would be to end forced overtime, employ everybody, and institute workplace democracy as a way to permit workers themselves to define the best ways of doing their job. Only the authors' "work intensity" or wasted labor effort figure (the level of worker resistance to unnecessary work requirements) would be disputed by more than a handful of economic democrats, and all would agree that some entry was appropriate here. Many would argue that their estimate of $50 billion wasted in military spending is much too low. In any event, the total estimate comes to nearly half the total GNP of the American economy. Even if some exaggeration is involved, the sums represented by simple waste are huge.

The conclusions that economic democrats reach is that the U.S. economy, by almost any standard, is working very poorly. By contrast with what it could produce, or the needs of many people, it does not deliver. This is bad enough, but the remedies urged for its ills by mainstream economists and other probusiness spokespersons are even worse. The latter see no alternative but a recession, and many even recommend it, with all its hardships for working people. They *want* a recession to stop inflation, to discipline labor and force down wages, and to create conditions for a new round of growth and profits. Moreover, in the context of recession and declining real wages, corporations have stepped up their attacks on unions through decertification campaigns, demands for wage and working-condition concessions in collective bargaining, and the use of bankruptcy proceedings to break existing contracts.

Nor is there any prospective benefit for ordinary people in the remedies proposed by the Yankees, which would create a secret, authoritarian mechanism for economic decision making in the interest of the big corporations and banks. An irrational economy, whose mandarins propose to help it by worsening the plight of working people in any number of creative ways, simply must be exposed for the perverse, power-based system that it is before it does more damage to itself and to people generally.

Economic Democracy Prescriptions: Principles

The economic democracy movement gained broad public recognition in the early 1980s with the publication of several comprehensive and detailed programs for the reconstruction of the U.S. economy. By now, the movement has produced an alternative program with highly specific components. In part, economic democrats have felt this necessary in order to show skeptics that concrete and practical policies that would add up to reconstruction really were available, and to give supporters something to rally around.

Some have presented the principles of reform and illustrated them with specific proposals; others have offered comprehensive inventories. An example of the first category is drawn from Bluestone and Harrison's *The Deindustrialization of America:*

> First, there must be a rising standard of living for working people, more equally shared, and an adequate supply of useful goods and services, whether or not they can always be made at a profit . . . more hospitable, more interesting, less authoritarian, and safer work environments . . . it will be necessary to radically transform the nature of active popular participation in the day-to-day running of the basic institutions of the economy and the society.[3]

The authors proceed from these principles—"economic growth, production for use, a humane work environment, and economic democracy"—to specify a number of policy changes that would accomplish "reindustrialization with a human face."

Another version of a set of principles followed by specific proposals is found in Martin Carnoy and Derek Shearer's call for a "New Social Contract," which

> must reaffirm and energize the fundamental dynamic of our history: democracy—a democracy where individuals working together politically make government ex-

> tend their economic and social rights. In the new contract, government does not restrict liberty, it expands it and makes it a reality.[4]

The authors argue that the goals of economic democracy can be obtained only through greater, not less, democratic participation. They cite the economic bill of rights developed by Franklin Delano Roosevelt in his 1944 State of the Union message and, expanding on that, develop a ten-point set of rights of their own.[5]

An even more comprehensive approach is found in the "Economic Bill of Rights" offered in Bowles, Gordon, and Weisskopf, *Beyond the Waste Land,* shown here as figure 8.1 on page 146.[6] The authors describe in 130 pages and an appendix how each of these 24 points could be accomplished through specific national policies. An economic bill of rights of a more specialized sort, focusing on the prospects of future high-technology developments, was developed by the International Association of Machinists. It is shown here as figure 8.2 on pages 147-48. Together, the two sets of listings give an idea of the scope and purpose of the economic democracy movement in about as concrete a fashion as can be articulated; if there are problems with these proposals, it is not their lack of specificity.

Economic democracy prescriptions all share two premises that should by now be familiar. The present economy is a slack economy, with great unused capacity and much waste, so there is ample room for growth right now. There is no need to impose austerity on people to direct new capital into investment. We do *not* face a "zero-sum" situation where anything gained by one group or sector of the population must come at the expense of others, and there is *no* conflict between equity and efficiency. We can all gain, and can have both better distribution and more production, by massive government stimulation of the economy toward full employment. Second, the place to start is from below. Reconstruction begins where the economy and society begin—with individual people and their communities—and not with reindustrialization from above.

Economic Democracy Prescriptions: Implementation

In this section I review the basic shared components in the economic democracy program synthesized roughly in the consecutive order that they would be implemented, because I want to be able to return to assess *political* practicality in the next chapter. I do not mean to suggest that completion of one stage must precede the start of the next or any sharply prioritized distinctions. Efforts would undoubtedly proceed on almost all fronts at once. But some components of the program clearly must be in place before others are practical, and it is this sequence that I want to indicate.

FIRST STAGE: DEFENSE

The first task is to stop the current process of erosion of productive capacity and begin the democratization of everyday life. A general program of workplace democratization should start immediately, and communities should become more conscious of "their" major companies as components of a viable

FIGURE 8.1

AN ECONOMIC BILL OF RIGHTS

I. *Right to Economic Security and Equity*
   1. Right to a Decent Job
   2. Solidarity Wages, Comparable Pay, and Equal Employment Opportunity
   3. Public Childcare and Community Service Centers
   4. A Shorter Standard Work Week and Flexible Work Hours
   5. Flexible Price Controls

II. *Right to a Democratic Workplace*
   6. Public Commitment to Democratic Trade Unions
   7. Workers Right to Know and to Decide
   8. Democratic Production Incentives
   9. Promoting Community Enterprises

III. *Right to Chart Our Economic Futures*
   10. Planning to Meet Human Needs
   11. Democratizing Investment
   12. Democratic Control of Money
   13. Promoting Community Life
   14. Environmental Democracy
   15. Democratizing Foreign Trade

IV. *Right to a Better Way of LIfe*
   16. Reduced Military Spending
   17. Conservation and Safe Energy
   18. Good Food
   19. A National Health Policy
   20. Lifetime Learning and Cultural Opportunities
   21. Payment for Home Child Care in Single-Parent Households
   22. Community Corrections and Reduced Crime Control Spending
   23. Community Needs Information and Reduced Advertising Expenditures
   24. Equitable Taxation and Public Allocation of Resources

SOURCE: Samuel Bowles, David Gordon, and Thomas Weisskopf, *Beyond the Waste Land* (New York: Doubleday Anchor, 1983), 294.

FIGURE 8.2
THE NEW TECHNOLOGY BILL OF RIGHTS OF
THE INTERNATIONAL ASSOCIATION OF MACHINISTS

I

New technology shall be used in a way that creates jobs and promotes community-wide and national full employment.

II

Unit labor cost savings and labor productivity gains resulting from the use of new technology shall be shared with workers at the local enterprise level and shall not be permitted to accrue excessively or exclusively for the gain of capital, management, and shareholders.

Reduced work hours and increased leisure time made possible by new technology shall result in no loss of real income or decline in living standards for workers affected at the local enterprise level.

III

Local communities, the states, and the nation have a right to require employers to pay a replacement tax on all machinery, equipment, robots, and production systems that displace workers, cause unemployment and thereby decrease local, state, and federal revenues.

IV

New technology shall improve the conditions of work and shall enhance and expand the opportunities for knowledge, skills and compensation of workers. Displaced workers shall be entitled to training, retraining, and subsequent job placement or reemployment.

V

New technology shall be used to develop and strengthen the U.S. industrial base, consistent with the Full Employment goal and national security requirements, before it is licensed or otherwise exported abroad.

VI

New technology shall be evaluated in terms of worker safety and health and shall not be destructive of the workplace environment, nor shall it be used at the expense of the community's natural environment.

VII

Workers, through their trade unions and bargaining units, shall have an absolute right to participate in all phases of management deliberations and decisions that lead or could lead to the introduction of new technology or the changing of the workplace system design, work processes, and procedures for doing work, including the shutdown or transfer or work, capital, plant, and equipment.

VIII

Workers shall have the right to monitor control room centers and control stations and the new technology shall not be used to monitor, measure or otherwise control the work practices and work standards of individual workers, at the point of work.

FIGURE 8.2
(Continued)

IX

Storage of an individual worker's personal data and information file by the employer shall be tightly controlled and the collection and/or release and dissemination of information with respect to race, religious, or political activities and beliefs, records of physical and mental health disorders and treatments, records of arrests and felony charges or convictions, information concerning sexual preferences and conduct, information concerning internal and private family matters, and information regarding an individual's financial condition or credit worthiness shall not be permitted, except in rare circumstances related to health, and then only after consultation with a family- or union-appointed physician, psychiatrist, or member of the clergy. The right of an individual worker to inspect his or her personal data file shall at all times be absolute and open.

X

When the new technology is employed in the production of military goods and services, workers, through their trade union and bargaining agent, have a right to bargain with management over the establishment of Alternative Production Committees, which shall design ways to adopt that technology to socially useful production and products in the civilian sector of the economy.

social-economic entity and not as some investors' projects. Long-term goals include development of local democratic planning bodies that will have the capacity (first human self-confidence and intent, then legal and practical) to shape the community's future as its citizens prefer, and democratic control of investment. The latter is the key to shaping the future in terms that people generally, as opposed to corporate profit seekers, actually want and need.

Central to this first stage is plant-closing legislation, to be enacted at the national level as soon as possible but perhaps preceded by some state models. Statutes would require advance notice by corporations of their intent to close or reduce operations at any given location, financial assistance to workers and communities, and opportunities for the latter to purchase and operate the facilities. Corporations intending to close or move would have to offer workers retraining, relocation, and/or opportunities to acquire the company or plant at fair prices. Government or other financial assistance would be made available to enable workers or the community as a whole to acquire the facilities. Planning boards of workers and community members would have the legal authority to make these decisions.

This legislation would clearly be a major step toward social control of investment, workplace democracy, and community self-development. A national statute is much to be preferred because it would apply everywhere and would eliminate competition between states. Models are available from other countries' experience, and the issue offers a sharp enough focus that a national campaign might achieve such a statute more readily than might at first seem likely. But probably state action is more immediately feasible, and efforts to experiment with such models are already under way.

Another component in this defensive first stage is the restoration and improvement of the "social wage" or "safety net" of national government protection for workers and their families in times of need. The assurance of job security, health care, and adequate retirement income are the major needs. Bluestone and Harrison make this point very strongly:

> Productivity is a *social* relation. To promote it requires *more,* not less, social security. Only as the fear of poverty, disease, and joblessness recedes can human energies be totally released for creative, truly productive effort. Thus, before Americans can embark on any major planned structural transformation of the economy, they must reject the claims of those who would promote insecurity as a matter of policy, find ways to re-establish the social safety net, and *extend* the range of the regulatory system to make that net even more secure for more groups in the population. These are the preconditions for any fundamental restructuring of the American economy.[7]

Most economic democracy programs place a heavy reliance for early success on the trade unions and their historic support for basic government social security provisions. Union support for plant-closing legislation is assumed, and to some extent is in fact mobilizing. The unions also play a major role in the expansion of workplace democracy, worker ownership schemes, and the development of community control of investment. Although it is only obliquely suggested in a few places by economic democrats, let us assume that the general democratization process proposed also applies to the unions. In other words, as democratic participation and control extend to the workplace and investment, they also extend to the trade unions and render them newly democratic organizations as well.

THE SECOND STAGE: REVIVING THE SLACK ECONOMY

The task of reviving the economy must begin by shifting government priorities into a truly massive full-employment program, in which there is high concern for equity in distribution. Instruments for accomplishing the latter include the actual employment of all who are able and willing to work, which economic democrats assume will mean a merely "frictional" (people changing jobs or merely taking time off) unemployment rate of about 2 percent. They also include an effective and really progressive income tax with no loopholes for the wealthy, and programs to raise the lowest levels of wages in ways that would ultimately benefit all wage earners.

The major components of the full-employment program would be the rebuilding of the nation's crumbling infrastructure with particular attention to new transportation systems, development of new and decentralized energy-producing capabilities, and a variety of other public projects under community development auspices. A coordinating national agency modeled after the New Deal's Works Progress Administration (WPA) is envisioned, variously titled but uniformly included. There is little doubt of the urgent need for infrastructure reconstruction or for expanded rail and mass transit systems. Energy remains an important component of any comprehensive program for growth with stable prices, and local needs have been postponed during the stagflation and recession years. It is worth stressing these points again, however, to emphasize the point that a new WPA does not imply "make work" public jobs—as all economic democrats know will be charged.

But public efforts are only the beginning of the full-employment program. A major new expansion in the private sector is to be expected from the new demand generated by the first wave of public-sector and public-investment generated jobs and income. But there will also be funds available for private-sector modernization, new industrial development, and research and development purposes. Both national and regional (and, presumably, state and local) development banks are contemplated. They could employ as capital direct appropriations from the federal government, pension funds from public employees' retirement systems, and private pension or institutional investors' funds.

Along with the full-employment efforts, economic democrats intend a vast health insurance program that would once and for all remove the threat of ruinous medical or hospital bills from Americans. But it would go beyond paying the bills to help create healthier lives and living environments. Shifting the American health care system from a focus on high-cost (and often high-technology) cures to a wide-ranging preventive system is long overdue. Preventive efforts would embrace environmental health measures including nuclear safety, toxic waste, and other hazards, and occupational safety standards. Medical costs would be reduced in this way, and ceilings placed on them as well, with important side benefits for inflationary pressures.

How will all this new activity be financed? One source will be reductions in the military budget. One reason for what may appear to be a relatively low priority for curtailment of the military buildup is that economic democrats think it vital to have the full-employment program in place and job security assured before tackling the controversy involved. The unions are of a mixed mind about the job-producing necessity of military spending. Immediate confrontation with the military issue might fragment needed popular support for the basic reconstruction program. But economic democrats have no doubt that the military buildup is very costly, dangerous, and wasteful in the extreme, and they mean to drastically cut back this category of expenditures.

Other sources of the necessary financing will be the radically improved progressive income tax system in which the elimination of loopholes favoring the wealthy is estimated by conservative specialists to produce about $200 billion in new revenues. A corporate income tax, with tighter controls for foreign profits and deductions, will also be implemented. But the largest new source of funds will be derived from full-employment itself. Tax revenues generated by the income earned by 10 million people who do not now have jobs is a giant new resource to be shared by the federal government among all the various projects under way. Other taxes and excises will increase as economic activity picks up and reaches new levels.

The most detailed estimates of the costs involved are provided by Bowles, Gordon, and Weisskopf in connection with their Economic Bill of Rights. In a carefully worked out series of projections covering the first two years of such a program, detailed in an appendix to their work, they estimate that an increase in useful output of some $600 billion would be produced.[8] This sum greatly exceeds the government investment involved, so much so that about $400 billion would in their eyes be available for a combination of increased personal consumption and government social programs.

Finally, all economic democrats deny that these programs would lead to inflation. Because the economy is so slack now, and useful output is to be increased drastically under high-productivity conditions (worker-controlled processes), the pressures that lead to inflation are unlikely. But just in case and to provide double assurance that past experience does not lead to "inflation psychology," standby controls over prices in key sectors are always available.

THIRD STAGE: MAKING PLANNING REAL

Achieving social control over investment and money is the final stage of transition, after which the economic democracy program would be fully in place. It assumes that the processes of democratization and decentralization have gotten well under way throughout the economy and society—in workplaces, in communities, in organizations, and in local, state, and national governments and the institutions and processes connected with them. It assumes that real achievements in job security, full employment, and general economic activity are evident. Next on the agenda are matters that consolidate economic democracy and establish it in ways that are not likely to be undone except by decisive popular action. These are democratic control over investment and money, and the inclusion of such powers in an effective bottom-up planning system. What makes this such a crucial stage is that it probably involves a head-on confrontation with corporate power that will make any previous conflicts seem tame by contrast.

The first and most attainable move in this direction is an effort to democratize the Federal Reserve Board. Control over the availability of money and credit is essential to a planned expansion of the economy. Elements of the public, not just bankers, must be able to exercise this control. Economic democracy proposals envision elected members on the Fed, representing important constituencies such as unions and consumers in sufficient numbers to make up a controlling majority.

The opening wedge in achieving *social,* instead of private profit-seeking, control over investment occurred with the advent of plant-closing legislation. But the problem of the mobility of private capital was barely touched by that essentially defensive measure. If capital remains free to move wherever it wants to, into whatever uses happen in capitalist irrationality to bring today's maximum profits, the economy cannot produce for people's needs, be truly efficient, or provide the largest possible number of jobs. There must be a way to direct private as well as public capital into socially desirable investments. These need not be unprofitable. Owners can make ample profits. But new investments must fit into a socially projected pattern of needs so that they are neither wasteful nor redundant. So stated, this may sound reasonable enough. The capitalist version of "freedom" is at stake, however, and corporations, banks, and the wealthy are likely to resist bitterly.

Some early beginnings of a national claim to direct private investment in a general manner can be accomplished in the ways that public capital is used to help particular private firms. Financial aid from the network of public development banks can be conditioned upon either some degree of control over such corporate beneficiaries or an equity position within the corporate ownership structure. And government subsidies or other forms of assistance such as special regulatory concessions or trade protections would be extended only under specific contractual arrangements. These would provide that the recipients agree to act in certain ways with respect to their workers or communities—or even grant public bodies power to take part in major investment decisions.

Another way in which the public could acquire a major role in directing the private economy is through extending the role of public enterprises. Public ownership is a direct route to social control over investment, and multiplying public enterprises extends those effects widely into a variety of manufacturing industries and service providers. Such enterprises give people a chance to do things together, develop confidence, and provide quality products or service. People become much less dependent on the jobs kindly provided by private employers, and more able to resist the terms offered for such employment.

But the extensive use of public enterprises can also affect how private enterprises operate. Public enterprises provide a way of demonstrating that there are markets where private investors are skeptical or timid, serve as "yardsticks" to force competitive pricing, and enable the public to acquire intimate knowledge of important areas such as the energy field. Overall, they put pressure on private industries to perform as well and in equally socially beneficial ways. Public enterprises must be thoroughly democratized in their operations, of course, lest they become as bureaucratized and unaccountable as any other large organization.

In the end, however, there will have to be planning mechanisms, national and local, with authority to approve major investment decisions. Local planning bodies will have to certify that intended investments within their jurisdictions meet their standards for the nature and quality of new developments. These terms would include environmental impact, tradeoffs between services demanded and quality of jobs provided, and so forth. They would have to be met before new public *or* private projects could be undertaken. Regional or national planning bodies will have to certify that such investments are consistent with overall plans for orderly and desirable development and, most of all, impose restraints on capital flight overseas.

One way that economic democrats have suggested for guiding the entire planning process is through an annual or biannual "needs inventory." Public wants and needs would be assessed in various ways and made known to the planning bodies. Each level beginning with the most local would then generate requests and plans to meet those needs, and would send their views on up through the planning network. The national planning body at the apex of the system would make a report to the President and Congress in the same way that the annual Economic Report is now made, and there would then be concerted national action in accordance with the priorities indicated.

Critiques of Economic Democracy—and Prospective Opposition

Very few critiques of economic democracy arguments are available. Opponents usually dismiss economic democrats as visionary or un-American without engaging any substantive issues raised or proposals offered. This is partly because mainstream opponents do not want to legitimate such arguments even by denying them, and partly because the arguments are distinctive enough to impose serious obligations on any who would try to respond specifically and in their own terms. If mainstream economists or policy makers were to accept the premises of economic democrats, even for purposes of argument, they would be likely to have lost the ballgame before they began. By and large, they solve that difficulty by ignoring economic democrats as much as they can. But that does not mean that they would sit idly by if economic democracy had a real chance for power.

What most economic democrats anticipate would be threatened, and certainly follow institution of any major part of their program, is a "capital strike" — a refusal by corporations and the wealthy to invest under these terms. There is bound to be a point of basic confrontation with corporate power and prerogatives, and determined resistance should be anticipated. At what stage would such a confrontation occur? Economic democrats are scrupulous about following the rules of electoral politics and hope that business would be the same. The confrontation might then be postponed until after economic democrats acquire power by democratic means. What form would it take? There are various ways in which a refusal to invest could be penalized financially without confiscating assets entirely, and of course the legal authority of the planning bodies could be disputed in court and in the electoral arena. Economic democrats are willing to take their chances in any open debate in which the final decision would be made by popular majorities. They would not deserve to be called democrats if they were not.

But what if corporations and the wealthy would not accept such a basis for the decision and sought instead to impose their preferences through military or other coercive means? The historical record suggests that property rights take precedence over due process, civil liberties, *and* majority rule whenever owners feel sufficiently threatened—and the threat need not be real but only fancied to trigger such a reaction. This is obviously a critical moment for economic democracy, but one that has not yet been addressed. There are so many vital thresholds to be crossed before that moment arrives that there will be ample time in the future to think about such needs.

Let us assume that the economic democrats have succeeded, at least this far. What would they have produced? It is certainly not centralized classical socialism, a concept with little application to the United States at any time. It is even more clearly not one of the so-called socialisms of the contemporary socialist world, or even the democratic socialisms of European imagination. It looks much more like a genuine American hybrid, responsive to American democratic and other traditions and circumstances, that includes real space for individual innovation and advancement—but balanced with a sense of interdependent obligation and collective purpose. It is a powerful argument, with potentially broad appeal.

PART THREE

Political Prospects—And Implications for Democracy

9. Political Implications of Economic Renewal

The current economic decline and transformation in the United States, combined with the political stalemate, have contributed to building up pressures on our social order for more than two decades. They are creating conditions much like those of the great transformation of 1877-1920. The four economic renewal programs analyzed represent the range of choice open to the United States a century later. They are in one way restoring, in other ways changing and renewing, the options of those times. No matter which economic renewal direction is chosen or imposed, major changes are in store; a transformed political-economic system will emerge.

Once again, the question is whether capitalism or democracy will have priority. It is our enduring Hamilton vs. Jefferson conflict in only modestly new form. Cowboy and Yankee capitalists compete for primacy with each other, in part by seeking the electoral support needed to empower them to implement new forms of capitalism. Full-employment and economic democrats seek to mobilize an electoral coalition from below that could achieve national power without submerging itself in the capitalist framework asserted by the first two programs. Once again, the issue focuses on whether capitalism can clear a path for itself by preserving the current partial version of "democracy" against the challenge of people who (consciously or unconsciously) seek the fuller social-economic-political "democracy" that their predecessors once took for granted.

The present era owes its initial form to the extent by which Hamilton had bested Jefferson (and capitalism had submerged democracy) by the close of the transformation ending in 1920. For most of the nineteenth century, Jefferson's laissez-faire philosophy prevailed. But the practical consequences were to encourage capitalist development—an end that progressively terminated the social and economic equality Jefferson thought essential. By the close of the nineteenth century, Hamilton's preferred institution, the Supreme Court, had turned back Jefferson's successors' search for greater equality and democracy. And the Court used Jefferson's own principle of laissez faire to accomplish Hamilton's ends; indeed, Jeffersonian means served without exception to accomplish Hamiltonian ends throughout this period.

Hamilton's greatest triumph occurred in the Progressive era, when the new corporate-government partnership was established. Later, purposeful government in the interest of business first and public welfare second was confirmed in the New Deal. At this point, Hamiltonian means had been recoupled with Hamiltonian ends. Industrial inequality was a stark fact, although continued pressure from ordinary people led to occasional government efforts to promote greater equality.

Jefferson was represented neither by means nor ends but merely by rhetoric. Despite the solemn assurances of one of Theodore Roosevelt's close advisers that the United States had built "a Hamiltonian government for Jeffersonian ends"[1] the basic Jeffersonian goals of equality, independent citizenship, and political power for ordinary people were clearly in eclipse. It only added insult to injury in 1981 that, when Jeffersonian laissez faire became a serious principle of government again for the first time since the 1890s, it was in the cause of the most open service to the wealthy that the twentieth century had seen.

Let us return for a moment to the question posed earlier by the fable of sibling rivalry between democracy and capitalism. Can capitalism restore itself through new accomplishments under cowboy capitalism? Or can it hold the throne by means of the new forms proposed by Yankee capitalism? Or is this the transformation in which the dispossessed return to establish a humane new democratic political-economic system? The outcome depends in important ways on what people *want,* and how clearly they see their options. Such clarity depends, first, on locating the four programs in the evolving historical context of American political-economic ideas. Then it requires exploring their positions with respect to the question of partial versus full definitions of democracy and how the latter is to be implemented.

Crisis and transformation induce polarization as new demands are made and each one produces new reactions from the opposition. The political spectrum is spreading more widely every day, it seems, with the center dissolving toward the poles. But this may be only the dropping of some illusions about harmony that is characteristic of a period of crisis and change. It may be necessary to a process in which economic change and changes in ideas, institutions, and policies are occurring at the same time.

In any event, our four economic renewal alternatives arrange themselves across the entire American political continuum and link up clearly with the dominant groupings of beliefs and practices that have shaped American history. Cowboy capitalism marks the right-hand pole as the modern successor to 1890s laissez-faire and free market principles, with perhaps more of the jingoism of 1898 than many would have thought consistent with such principles. Yankee capitalism is a centrally managed system that seeks to maximize the profits of a somewhat different set of interests in a more complicated world. Both endorse Hamiltonian goals, even though they differ significantly with regard to the most appropriate means. In particular, they are both concerned about the prospect of popular intrusion into their handling of the economy.

Next in sequence is full-employment democracy, which seeks more egalitarian goals in the context of an initially unchanged corporate structure and its market system. Closest to the democratic pole of the continuum is the economic democracy program for new policy directions. Both sets of proposals are Jeffersonian in their concern for the economic and social conditions necessary to making democracy real. Both follow Jefferson in urging more opportunities for decentralized planning and control by participating citizens. Economic democrats would extend these powers for ordinary people in a variety of ways, into the workplace and over crucial investment decisions. Full-employment democracy may be in some respects more realistic, but economic democracy—farther from the prospect of power—is at least rhetorically more democratic.

Once we have located the alternatives in their historical context, it is time to ask how they bear upon the "democracy problem." By this I mean the double issue of first understanding "democracy" in either full or partial versions and then linking the imperatives of *preserving* and *expanding* democracy in the United States. The second part of the problem is more readily dispatched. I do not believe democracy can be preserved without being expanded under the economic and political conditions of our times. Either we will institute one form of economic renewal program, and yield democratic rights and powers in order to do so, or we will institute another economic renewal program that simultaneously expands democratic rights and powers. But that leaves the crucial first part: How do the four alternatives affect our understanding of "democracy" in *full* or *partial* terms?

Cowboy capitalism and Yankee capitalism do not even preserve what we now have in the partial sphere of political democracy. They consistently foreclose consideration of additional dimensions to the notion of democracy and emerge as efforts to constrict American democracy more fully than it already has been. The full-employment alternative involves no similar limits with respect to political democracy, and at least one major version certainly endorses the extension of democracy to economic and social circumstances. Economic democracy, like a true heir to the early democratic tradition, insists from the beginning and with a single voice upon the full definition of democracy. Economic democracy argues that political democracy can never be realized until it includes economic and social democracy.

Our political context is one in which only the cowboy capitalists and Yankee capitalists have significant grounding in the institutions and elites of the first power system. But they do not have the sustained electoral support, available only from a second power system coalition, that is necessary to implement their economic renewal programs and the institutional changes implied in them. The American electorate may be too balkanized, withdrawn, and volatile to line up affirmatively behind either of these alternatives at this time. What that means, along with some dangerous possibilities, is that there is an opportunity for either full employment or economic democracy (or both together) to fuse with a developing second power system coalition. Probably it is only as a joint program that they could rise to state and national offices from which to implement *their* programs. The route would be difficult, requiring reconstructing or transcending first power system elites, but it is *possible.* That is the point of this book, and the remaining chapters explore the political prospects of each of the economic renewal programs with this special focus in mind.

Political Support: The Capitalists' Problem

Analysis must start with the goals and strategies of cowboy capitalists and Yankee capitalists because they each have solid grounding in first power system elites and can play a shaping role over events. I have argued that both propose economic renewal programs that are profoundly damaging to the physical and social well-being of great numbers of Americans, and necessarily if not deliberately destructive of democracy as well. Each can rather readily acquire office in the national government. They are firmly rooted in the two major parties, which serve as vehicles for evicting each other in response to repeated failures to cope with the events and problems that threaten to overwhelm us.

But they cannot implement their renewal programs—fortunately—because they do not have the electoral coalition from the second power system that is needed to make basic policy and institutional changes. The sustained, affirmative mass support that is crucial to carrying out such a fundamental shift in direction has not yet been found. Moreover, under today's conditions it probably cannot be found. And that is both good and bad. It is vital to see the ways this is true.

The cowboy capitalists' threat to the health, safety, and welfare of Americans is clear and present. They will accomplish a massive redistribution of wealth from poor and working people to the wealthy and impose social costs for generations to come. In addition, their program *requires* military adventurism, aided by war or the threat of war and possibly by internal security purges of the opposition as well. Those dynamics are built in to the drastic expansion of the military that is such a fundamental commitment of cowboy capitalism. Morever, invoking threats to national security—or racial conflict—is the only way that the cowboys can hold their unsteady voting support together long enough to implement their otherwise contradictory program. What they will create if they succeed is fortress America, a right-wing plebiscitary regime that is bellicose abroad and viciously intolerant at home.

The Reagan administration's version of a "free market" approach makes sense in terms of the current cowboy world view and its constituency, and so does the military buildup and hard line with respect to the Soviet Union. The nonmilitary cuts are aimed at the very groups that gained in the previous two decades, and whose gains effectively generated the populist conservative reaction that elected Reagan. By undoing the Great Society, Reagan fulfills his constituency's wishes. Moreover, nonmilitary cutbacks are aimed at Reagan's least likely supporters, many of whom—the poor and the minorities at least—have been politically inert groups whose voter turnout has been historically low.

The danger that Reagan or any successor faces, however, is that economic hard times or perceived failure to move fast enough and far enough can fragment the populist conservative coalition behind him. Many of these people once supported the New Deal policies of Franklin Roosevelt and the Democratic party, and sustained hardships could well send a substantial share of them back to pocketbook voting again. Many also believe that Reagan can and should do more to serve their goals in regard to social issues and the restoration of American power in the world. As I noted earlier, the New Right has been continuously dissatisfied with President Reagan's "moderate" course, in foreign policy particularly but also in staff appointments and level of enthusiasm for social issues. There have been threats of forming a new political party, and an advance commitment to making the 1984 election into a referendum on stopping the Soviet Union in Central America.

To hold that constituency together even in moderately bad times may require special appeals. One obvious appeal already invoked is that of the "social issues" of abortion, prayer in schools, and other "family preserving" causes. Another is to patriotism, cold-war memories, and resentment over the Vietnam war. This could take the form of even more aggressive counterinsurgency in Central America, or more direct confrontation with the Soviet Union, or new attacks on the loyalty or intelligence of such internal opponents as nuclear freeze supporters—or all of these things.

Such a strategy involves some real difficulties as major portions of the electorate are likely to react against the prospect of being dragged into—or provoking—a war. The image of Reagan as likely to involve the country in war is already damaging his reelection prospects or those of any Republican successor. The goal would be to make the provocation appear that of the Soviet Union and assume the stance of one who resolutely "stood up" in the ensuing crisis.

The dangers to the country from the latter appeals are profound. Even the military buildup contains the germs of a garrison state mentality and a challenge to the patriotism of all who question it in any way. Once the arguments are marshaled in support of a vast new national spending commitment, they embody a dynamic of their own—a self-confirming effect that will make both the Soviet Union more powerful and domestic opponents possible communist sympathizers. *I doubt very much that the contemplated buildup can be sustained in the face of continuing large deficits without unleashing a classic anticommunist purge within the United States.* Such a campaign would be a necessary adjunct also to any major commitment of American forces in Central America. The free market flag is not simply a cover for the installation of raw cowboy capitalism. It is also, potentially, the American flag employed in an explosive reactionary scapegoating surge that could rival any Red Scare in our history.

Yankee capitalists are an improvement only in style, not in substance. The difference between cowboy and Yankee capitalists is that between a "tough cop" whose methods are brutal but open and a "soft cop" who achieves the same ends by manipulating incentives, except when it is necessary to silently savage the opposition. Yankee capitalists are concerned primarily for the long-term profitability of key American units of the world economy—a different sector of the U.S. economy, but one whose needs are as demanding as any supported by the cowboys. Yankees *began* the military buildup, and need it to accomplish their world-defining ends. They must implement a comprehensive program of industrial development that will require austerity for most Americans, and they will have to devise new means of social control to prevent effective resistance. Their program already includes a variety of ways in which new decision-making institutions will be dominated by technocrats and insulated against political accountability.

The Yankees' program is comprehensive and far-reaching. It will lack a mass base, however, unless one of two possible routes is followed. The first is an alliance I explore in the next section, in which the full-employment advocates offer the vital electoral support that their cause can generate for a figurative pat on the head from the Yankees—and little or nothing else. The second is a link with sunbelt corporatists, amounting to accepting a somewhat more right-wing version of the Yankee design in trade for the support of part of the sunbelt electoral coalition. Kevin Phillips characterizes a sunbelt version of corporatism this way:

> Sun Belt corporatist policies would demand that the government manage the economy more closely than is done today, mobilizing a USA, Inc. to cope with France,

> Inc. or Japan, Inc. Meanwhile, the morality of the majority would be upheld and enforced, though with politically convenient lapses; the star-spangled banner would wave with greater frequency and over more parades; increased surveillance would crack down on urban outbreaks and political dissidents perceived as extremists.[2]

Given the present electoral trends—dealignment, nonvoting, volatility—the prospects are for continued flipflopping between Republican and Democratic administrations. Each will gain office principally because of the other's failures, and neither cowboy Republicans nor Yankee Democrats will be able to develop the sustained support needed to implement a basic change of direction. Meanwhile, economic conditions and their social consequences will continue to worsen. Then cowboys may accelerate their efforts, or Yankees may make one of their two possible alliances; and either could seek to implement their programs with a minimum of support and a maximum of urgency. Or some other drastic and authoritarian solution might offer itself as the answer to the country's problems.

These grim prospects are what make a ground-up movement for one of the democratic alternatives seem so desirable, however difficult to bring about. And that is why I seek to show that such alternatives are *possible*—electorally and institutionally—in this context. They are possible in *many* ways, and the precise routes to be followed can be determined only by participants under conditions yet unknown to any of us. My point is established by showing only that there is an opening for democracy—that permissive conditions exist for at least one of probably many democratic possibilities. Everything depends, as it should, on what ordinary American citizens think and do in politics.

Political Support: The Democrats' Problem

Many full-employment advocates are thoroughgoing democrats, but almost all are firm Democrats, accounting for a good part of the party's left wing. They are a vital complement to the Yankee capitalists, who essentially own the party. The two programs are tied to each other not only by common origins in the New Deal and their common opponents but also by their enduring loyalties to the Democratic party. Between the Yankees with their many resources, and the full-employment advocates with little but a principle long deflected, there lies the great middle of programmatically inert Democrats and the party apparatus. Their allegiances fixed, they wait for a candidate or an idea that looks capable of mobilizing a winning electoral majority in ways that do not threaten the status quo too much.

The strength of the full-employment cause, with its strong support from the labor bureaucracy of the AFL-CIO, should be seen for what it is and not discounted prematurely. The Yankee capitalist program fundamentally lacks a mass appeal. It is too complicated, too elaborately rational and technical to ever become the focus of a mass following in the American electorate. *What the corporatists absolutely require in order to gain power is some support from the full-employment cause.* Only the full-employment program and the power of its appeal to the rank and file of the blue- and white-collar working population, the poor, and minorities can give corporatists a working majority in a future American government.

What we have seen as the differences between Yankees and full-employment supporters is also a preview of the coming struggle for control of the Democratic party. It is an unequal struggle that the Yankees are likely to win. But this result will be owed partly to the fact that some full-employment advocates *want* such goals only on Yankee terms of business priority. And another part of this prospect is that full-employment advocates historically underestimate their strength and yield too easily—perhaps out of deference to their social superiors. It is a mini-replay of Hamilton vs. Jefferson in which the conventional wisdom suggests another in Hamilton's seemingly endless series of victories achieved under cover of Jeffersonian rhetoric.

Consider the advantages that Yankee corporatists have on their side. The underlying dynamic in American economic circumstances seems to be clearly establishing that *some* kind of comprehensive government direction of the economy will have to be established. The historical precedents are all Hamiltonian. The Progressive era set the model, and World War I provided the arena for Woodrow Wilson's Democratic party to show how business and government together could mobilize resources and manage the economy. The New Deal was a second stage of that model for Franklin Roosevelt's Democratic party, and World War II finally convinced much of the larger corporate community that the business-government partnership could generate new levels of growth and profit.

The present offers an apparent third stage of greater integration, with business retaining its decisive role as the senior partner. Corporate priorities have dominated in recent versions of the Democratic coalition, although they have been obliged to yield more to the welfare cause than they might have wished. In compensation, they received a degree of mass support—and the unchallenged political power that made their governing role far easier than it might have been. Jimmy Carter tried to move the nation in this direction, but he was so timid and ineffective that nothing happened. But his "moral equivalent of war" (MEOW) campaign might be only a forecast of what later followers might accomplish in something like an "Economic Emergency Equivalent of War" mobilization (and I leave that acronym for others).

As in history, the Yankees have the edge within the party today. All the "serious" candidates and officeholders resonate with their policy premises. None stands with the full-employment advocates except in the context of the larger industrial policy proposals. The eastern establishment, always strong at the upper levels of the Democratic party, has been rudely evicted from its prior role within the Republican party. If the New Right stays within the Republican party, Yankees may have no better place to go than to a unified role in control of the Democratic party. Organized labor is divided and weakened, but its traditional leadership clearly seems ready to stand with business and the corporatists. All that the full-employment democrats—the supporters of the Conyers version of full employment—have within the Democratic party hierarchy are some left-leaning congresspersons, some labor, and minorities.

But outside the hierarchy, they have the potential for mass support among working people, the poor, and minorities—in other words, in the traditional and essential Democratic electoral constituency. If past precedents apply again, the full-employment cause will support the corporatist leadership and once again will see their policy goals absorbed into and coopted by the basic corporate priorities of the Democratic party. When that party is in power, it delivers to the "progressive" corporations and banks first, and to the poor and minorities second, when they make a big enough fuss about it.

In some ways, the full-employment cause faces the reverse of the Reagan political problem. Full employment as a rallying policy goal has the capacity to generate a national electoral majority, particularly in hard times. It could break the "populist conservative" loyalty to Reagan. But as a potential majority it is vulnerable to the appeal of the "social issues," and even more to patriotic cold-war bluster, military priorities, and Red Scares.

To protect themselves against these appeals, all Democrats will be tempted to prove their loyalties to these symbols. Yankee capitalists will find these appeals at least partially functional. They not only help control the demands of full-employment advocates but fulfill corporate needs for a lower level of direct popular pressure for government services at the same time. The advocates of full employment could find themselves devoting their energies to individual defenses of civil liberties, more general defenses of labor's earlier gains and government social programs, and/or trying to justify their participation in the Democatic party to their friends among the economic democrats on their left. At that rate, full-employment advocates could be exhausted before they even began to mount an effective campaign for their own cause.

But what if full-employment advocates, led by full-employment democrats, were to suspend the conventional wisdom of past politics (or, perhaps, relearn its lessons) and try a bolder strategy? A comprehensive new full-employment program could be the basis for a popular movement that aimed squarely at taking control of the Democratic party, or failing that, establishing its own national Full Employment party. To take such a step, and make it effective, full-employment advocates would have to break with their enduring faith as Democrats. That is, give up their belief that only the Democatic party—regardless of how full its leadership is committed to Yankee capitalist goals—stands between the country and the Republican recessions, depressions, and military adventurism that would follow if it does not hold the Presidency.

Decades of supporting the "lesser evil" have produced some concessions from the Yankees and some improvements in people's lives, but the price has been some seriously self-limiting habits. These decades have also led to many failures and disappointments, and perhaps have merely postponed the day when bolder, more independent action has to be taken. At the least, there are two new sets of arguments why a bolder strategy might be successful today.

First, there are several compelling reasons why a full-employment program should be the centerpiece of a reconstructed Democratic party. They apply almost equally to justify an independent Full Employment party if that alternative is necessary.

1. The vast reservoir of nonvoters has been growing steadily for decades and now amounts to almost half of all eligible voters. These people are disproportionately drawn from the less-educated and lower-paid ranks of society, groups with much to gain from a major full-employment program. Many of them are politically cynical and alienated, possibly because they see little difference between the parties and rightly believe the system is not intended to work for their benefit. They might very well turn out to vote in substantial numbers if the full-employment cause was the focusing issue of an election. Historically, the advent of just such new blocs of former nonvoters has reshaped the directions of American politics.
2. The Reagan administration cutbacks in social programs have hit hard at minorities, the poor, and lower-paid working people generally. At the same time, they have greatly advantaged already wealthy people. It is not just being singled out for reductions in assistance that mean real family hardships—unemployment, illness, lack of food and shelter—but the *unfairness* of it that is likely to lead to an outpouring of votes for a program that promises real change. Moral outrage combined with financial hardship can move people in ways that neither cause could alone, and only a full-employment program promises a real remedy for both.

3. The full-employment cause, moreover, has had long support among the traditional New Deal voting coalition. Surveys have shown over and over again that a majority of voters believes that, particularly in hard times, government should see to it that everybody has a job. But this support has been specially strong among blue-collar, urban, and ethnic constituencies that gave the New Deal repeated support. These are the very groups whose defection elected Reagan in 1980. They could be brought back to the Democratic party if full employment was its basic commitment.
4. Full employment is the issue to which blacks and other minorities are likely to be most responsive. The Democratic party cannot win without overwhelming minority support, and *no* party deserves to—although the Republicans have proven that they can. The full-employment cause could hold blacks within the Democratic party or provide the rallying focus for them to move to an independent party.

Second, there are several equally compelling reasons why the Democratic party is less valuable as a vehicle for gaining office than it once was. Most important is the fact that it is dominated by Yankee capitalists, whose money and status and political expertise make it very difficult to dislodge them. Yankee capitalists will always work to limit the scope of any full-employment program, particularly between elections when their relative power is greatest. They have done so in the past, and both their recent practices and their corporate interests suggest that they have little wish to be of serious help to working people, organized or unorganized. Yankee capitalists support the military buildup at almost the intended Reagan administration levels. Indeed, the buildup began under their guidance during the Carter administration. They have been enthusiastic supporters of the campaign to reduce real wages, break unions, and reduce taxes and regulations on business.

Voters' loyalties to political parties as such have been declining steadily along with turnout on election day. Parties simply do not mean as much as they used to, and do not provide the voting cues for people that they formerly did. Why tie a potential popular movement to an empty shell if there is a program capable of attracting massive support in its own right, particularly if that empty shell is miraculously discovered shortly after election day to be firmly in the grip of Yankee capitalists?

There is a real dilemma, not just a problem of maturity or self-confidence, involved here for full-employment democrats. Full-employment democrats, to be effective, will have to be ready to give up the Democratic party if necessary. Not that they ever had it, but it provided an umbrella and allies when needed.

To go it alone means to risk isolation. Full-employment democrats will have to appeal for support to former nonvoters, minorities, the unemployed, and others who would benefit particularly from a full-employment program. To do so effectively, they will have to develop and campaign on a view of the United States that emphasizes something like class conflict.

Such talk is frightening to some, anathema to others. It provokes reactions from the "better people" everywhere, and misgivings even from supporters steeped in American ideology. It represents another risk.

Full-employment democrats *must* address the issue of the military buildup, and they must vigorously favor reduction in such spending and arms limitations. This is a moral imperative as well as a practical one for advocates of social justice and democracy. Here they risk losing some of their constituency, particularly some key unions; and their opponents (including Yankee capitalists) will use their position to make them seem unpatriotic, unrealistic, or even subversive.

By taking such risks, full-employment democrats will add to the already existing danger of seeing their potential majority fragment into several pieces. There seems to be no way to avoid taking those risks, and the best approach might be to try to meet the issues involved straightforwardly. There is something to be gained, surely, by putting an end to temporizing "lesser evilism" and meeting hard problems head-on. It might even be the best way to mobilize the necessary new coalition of voters and former nonvoters. Treating voters as mature people who appreciate honesty might be exactly the dramatic new approach that would draw "apathetic" nonvoters into action. If the full-employment cause is to lose again, it might as well be by telling the truth independently and forthrightly. At least it would be a different way to lose.

Economic democrats' plans for developing the political support necessary to be able to implement their programs have not advanced very far. Indeed, they contrast rather sharply with the comprehensive specifics of their policy programs. But it may well be asked why they should be expected to have everything orchestrated in exquisite detail. They are feeling their way along in thoroughly uncharted waters, with little precedent to guide them. Each of the other economic renewal programs has deep grounding in one or both major political parties and does not seem to feel the need to face such questions at all. Only the weakest tendency among them, the full-employment democrats, have given much thought to the political problem of attaining power—and then with more or less resignation to staying within the Democratic party.

The most compelling question seems to be whether the economic democrats can find a constituency on the American electoral scene to embrace and support their program. That constituency, at least eventually, must be a large number of ordinary people who genuinely adopt these ideas as their own and are prepared to act on them, or the whole idea of democracy will be a fraud. I think the program offered is responsive to—or perhaps creative of—such a constituency. That constituency currently exists only in potential. It is not only not yet organized, but some elements are not yet even politically active. The most organized elements are some of the important single-issue movements of the times, but the least organized are the real potential mass base of the constituency—rank-and-file workers, poor people, minorities, and the like, who are disproportionately nonvoters. And there are real obstacles in the way of pulling these elements together.

The economic democracy program contains strong potential bridges to the nuclear freeze, antiwar, and environmental movements, more fundamental ones than any other economic renewal direction. But the nature of single-issue politics in the United States makes these linkages far from automatic. The United States powerfully encourages single-issue movements because they do not imply fundamental confrontation with the structure of power or the nature of the economic system. Single-issue movements are functional safety valves in several ways. People can vigorously, even violently, challenge one set of policies without having to go through the intellectually demanding, anxiety-producing task of understanding why such undesirable policies exist in the first place. They do not have to confront the unhappy fact that such policies are often fundamental to the nature of capitalist American society and that they cannot be significantly modified without seeking changes in the essence of that system. But many intelligent and well-meaning people are deeply engaged in these movements. When and if they begin to see the interconnections of the policies they oppose with characteristics of the underlying capitalist economy, they may well move toward economic democracy.

The potential constituency is highly dependent on separate fragments that have historically been unable to overcome their differences to join in a single coherent movement for basic changes in the American system. Divisions between races, ethnic groups, occupations, sexes, and classes have broken progressive movements at every moment when they seemed on the verge of unified action. If there is a way to overcome the individualism and self-interestedness of these fragments, it surely lies in the direction charted by economic democracy—job security, equity in distribution, and democracy. The crucial step, and one that economic democrats understand very clearly, is to make the principle of interdependence as real for the people as it is for the owners and managers of the capitalist economy.

The next question is whether this constituency can organize and move itself effectively in American politics. This is where the sequence of economic democracy program implementation becomes important. It is integral to electoral success and expansion of the constituency to the point where it will be ready for the final stage of consolidation.

I think it unlikely that economic democracy can become a shared perspective among many people without (1) having an electoral focus, and (2) proceeding in stages. Merely intellectual or ideological views of the world do not easily make their way into people's minds under any circumstances. Moreover, the people to whom economic democracy must appeal are not people with the time, money, or education to do a lot of careful reading. They have the visceral insight that something is very wrong with the way things work, but they do not have all the reasons or alternatives neatly laid out.

A major mutual education effort is implied, along the lines of the old Alliance lecturer system of the Populist days in the Midwest and South, in which organizers and people talk through the things they want and need and how to get them.[3] In a nation whose media are dominated by mainstream national networks and wire services, only candidates for election can give a new interpretation and program the living substance that it needs to gain strength. Moreover, some early victories, and some continuing bases of strength and achievement in cities and states, would be highly desirable.

This brings economic democrats to the key question of whether to form an organization like an independent national political party (a different *kind* of political party, as befits the democratic commitment) or support the Democratic party in some critical and distant manner. There is a need for some sort of national focus, to go along with the various local and state electoral coalitions in existence.

Most economic democrats have few illusions about the progressive potential of the Democratic party. But full-employment advocates are correct when they say that third parties have been a losing proposition on the American scene. This is a vital dilemma, one that splits economic democrats and finds some full-employment democrats on the side of a third-party movement. I consider this debate in detail in chapter 12.

Much depends on what other groupings do in the way of political strategy. If the Democratic party were to split between Yankees and full-employment democrats, there would be every reason to join the latter. Economic democrats tend to be long on officers and organizers and short on troops on election day. But that would make them a good partner for the full-employment democrats, perhaps even foreshadowing a consolidation of the two movements. The central images for the economic democrats to retain in the midst of uncertainty are full employment and democracy. The former is the key to a future constituency. The latter is the essential shield with which to fend off the red-baiting whose advent will mark the moment when economic democracy arrives as a real threat on the American political scene.

If the analogy with the Great Transformation of 1877-1920 holds, there may be a decisive election on the order of 1896 in our future, perhaps in 1988 or 1992. The election of 1896 marked the point where a Republican majority solidified and enabled the party to govern effectively for 36 years, with the exception only of the Wilson years. During this period, and because of the electoral realignment, progressive Republicans and their allies were able to change the structure of national government institutions to adapt them to new economic realities. Simultaneously, like-minded elements at the local level were able to change the rules of political participation to help them stay in power both locally and nationally. These possibilities link the political implications of economic renewal progams directly with the politics of institutional change.

10. The Politics of Institutional Reconstruction

The prospect of institutional change is the other half of the analogy to the transformation of 1877-1920. The current stalemate must soon give way under the implacable pressures of decline, transformation, and popular dissatisfaction. Whether one of the capitalist economic renewal programs is chosen or imposed, or some version of the democratic programs is successful, substantial institutional change will *necessarily* follow. Each program is at once a proposal for redistributing wealth and power by means of basic changes in institutions, overall policy directions, and the nature of the government's role in the economy and society. In other words, no economic renewal program can be implemented without reconstructing the American national government in basic ways.

For a nation that prides itself on "Yankee ingenuity" and technological innovation, we are certainly incrementalists when it comes to politics. Really structural changes at the national government level have been few, and then seemingly accidental. Neither scholars nor citizens invest much energy in serious consideration of ways to fit governmental forms to the functions we ask of them. The question of when or how the structure or practices of our national government institutions *change* under pressure is seldom explored.

One important study has addressed exactly these questions with respect to the key period of the earlier comparable transformation, 1877-1920. This is Stephen Skowronek's *Building A New American State: The Expansion of National Administrative Capacities, 1877-1920.*[1] Skowronek sees the essential nature of institutional change as a political process in which the existing state structure serves as a focus or an arena where the basic conflicts of the nation are played out. He says it this way:

> State building is prompted by environmental changes, but it remains at all times a political contingency, a historical-structural question. Whether a given state changes or fails to change, the form and timing of the change, and the governing potential in the change—all of these turn on a struggle for political power and institutional position, a struggle defined and mediated by the organization of the pre-established state.[2]

According to Skowronek, at the outset of the transformation in 1877, the United States was a nation with a weak state apparatus, compensated for by strong political parties and an active court system. Most of the important decisions needed were brokered and made through the two latter sets of institutional arrangements. Parties were specially sensitive to local needs and provided democratic input and consent, insofar as they were required at the national level. Courts provided a standardizing and arbitrating service, and helped economic development go forward unimpeded by law or national policy. What was required to serve the needs of a centralizing national industrial economy, however, was a national government with regulatory and administrative capacity. The economy needed to be rationalized, seen as a single unit, and protected from both self-damage and parochial intrusions.

Skowronek characterizes the first decades of the transformation as a patchwork process in which needed reforms were not successfully accomplished primarily because the system of parties and courts remained strong enough politically to defeat them. This period was followed (after the realignments of 1896 and their aftermath) by the Progressive era, in which the political forces finally gathered themselves and were able to reconstitute the national government in accordance with their needs. These political forces, of course, were the major corporations and banks and professionals, allied as I earlier described with reform-oriented middle-class voters.

There then ensued a series of expansions of national administrative scope and power, to the point where an essentially new bureaucratic apparatus arose to take the place of the former system. The ingredients that made this process possible were for Skowronek, "the promise of a new democracy, the embrace of corporate conservatism, the lure of professionalism, and the quest for administrative rationality, all . . . caught up in an intense and extended struggle for power."[3]

The result of creating this new system was to permanently undermine the older one of parties and courts, but not to replace either the democratic or the limiting roles once performed by those institutions. What took their place was then undemocratic, unlimited bureaucracy, with its vast regulatory and financial capabilities. This bureaucracy reached new heights in the 1930s, when:

> . . . the New Deal turned bureaucracy itself into the extraconstitutional machine so necessary for the continuous operation of the constitutional system. Like party patronage to the old order, bureaucratic goods and services came to provide the fuel and the cement of the new institutional politics. They became something valuable for Presidents to offer and for congressmen to support. They articulated a new set of concrete institutional ties between the state and the citizenry. This bureaucratic solution to the problems of governing under the Constitution prom-

> ised to work in benign confusion as long as administrative services and supports could expand.[4]

When administrators' overreaching provoked reactions and fiscal constraints made further expansion impossible, this system lay dead in the water, a friendless target for the frustration and resentment of all. What we have today is what Skowronek calls "a hapless administrative giant."[5]

The model of institutional change that Skowronek suggests is thus a two-stage one involving first the *patchwork* process and then, as political forces mobilize more coherently, a period of *reconstitution*. Skowronek argues that the United States today has passed through the period of trying unsuccessfully to mount patchwork solutions. Minor reforms in the organization of the executive branch and the upper civil service, the Congress, and the political parties have had few consequences. In his eyes, we may now be ready for "the opening of a new reconstruction sequence,"[6] which is made more likely by the Reagan administration's frontal attack on bureaucracy itself. By campaigning against the government in Washington, and by seeking to dismantle or redirect major parts of the bureaucracy, President Reagan may have opened the way toward much greater reconstruction—for purposes and in directions yet undetermined.

There seems little doubt that the patchwork efforts so far have failed to adapt institutions to new realities, nor could they have done so without a break in the political stalemate. The question is, what kinds of institutional reconstruction would follow from the implementation of either capitalist or democratic economic renewal programs? Can we speculate about what the process would look like, and what some of the consequences might be? Skowronek's model seems to depend also on an extraconstitutional vehicle of some kind that makes the old institutions workable under new conditions. If direct change in the Constitution's prescribed institutions is not possible or even sought, then presumably we should be alert for some other means of performing the missing functions.

The place to begin is where I believe the process must start, with the needs of the corporations, banks, and their surrogates in the first power system. Initiative lies with them, insofar as they can exert influence in their own context of multiple pressures. These elites are motivated and constrained not only by their own interests and those of opposing groups in this first system but also by other powerful forces. Some of these emanate from the economy (inflation, unemployment, recessions, etc.), others from foreign affairs (debt payments, trade, war and the threat of war, etc.), and still others from the power of coalitions working through the second power system.

Institutional changes sought by elements of the first power system will reflect power relations at that level. But they also involve reactions to what is coming up from below: the goals and forcefulness of electoral coalitions. The terrain or arena in which these two power systems meet—and merge, clash, or adjust to one another—is the structure and function of the state. They play out their conflicts and seek accommodations by creating and implementing institutional changes. In the pages that follow, I look first at the institutional changes as they have been proposed or are needed by cowboy capitalism and Yankee capitalism. But I *focus* on what potential there is for such changes to be converted to the joint purposes of full employment or economic democracy. And then I take up some of the latter's institutional proposals.

The Capitalist Agenda

I suggested earlier that both of the capitalist economic renewal programs might, in the event they were able to implement their designs, have need of new arrangements for maintaining social control in a context of austerity before the transformation was over. The Republican platform of 1980 promised new internal security committees of Congress, and a comprehensive new system of information management has been proposed by the Reagan administration. A new system for managing immigrant workers, and indirectly other workers as well, was pending in Congress in 1984. The most concrete proposals for institutional change now projected, however, are President Reagan's "new federalism" efforts and the pending call for a constitutional convention to frame a balanced-budget amendment to the Constitution. The New Right has added to these a call for introducing the initiative and referendum at the national level.

Yankees are already on record with several proposals along parliamentary government lines, and would undoubtedly produce more if they seemed about to acquire office again. There is considerable respect among Yankees, as there was for Hamilton, for the British model of managing empires. The efficiency of the parliamentary system is much admired, along with the use of financial leverage to attain ends that would otherwise require excessive uses of visible power. Yankees particularly need institutions for coordination of American policy and integration of that policy with the international economy. At the same time, they need to assure insulation of the actual decision-making bodies from political pressures.

These considerations suggest that the planning bodies actually included in the various industrial policy proposals made so far are only the beginning. If internationalization is indeed the wave of the future, as Yankees assume, such planning bodies might actually fulfill the nightmares of some cowboy capitalists and eventually lead to some form of superagency for coherent management of the entire economy. Clearly, the target for analysis in regard to Yankee institutional changes is the planning mechanism that they envision.

FEDERALISM: A NEW ROLE FOR THE STATES?

The Reagan administration began with a commitment to reinvigorating the states. It accomplished some consolidation of programs into block grants that were made available to the states with greater discretionary control over their use than had previously been the case. But much of the early fanfare about New Federalism evaporated when it became clear that the administration intended to devolve functions without the accompanying financial resources. The recession had squeezed many states' revenues to the point where they were raising taxes, cutting services, or both, and further cuts in a wide range of federal programs put additional pressure on state capacities. Federal cutbacks led to state cutbacks in most cases, instead of to state assumption of new governmental responsibilities.

The states' economic circumstances, rather than any conscious Reagan administration policy, led to a new state role in the development field. In addition to the usual tax giveaways and other concessions that the states employ to compete with one another in attracting footloose businesses ("the new war between the states," as some have called it), the states began to assume direct promotional roles. Several states experimented with forms of financial assistance that would encourage formation of new businesses, particularly high-technology companies and community-based businesses in areas of high unemployment.

Some states made available both technical and financial assistance for the formation and operation of producer cooperatives, or undertook development of infrastructure or other facilities through public enterprises. Many moved to make some portion of public employee pension funds newly available for housing or other developmental purposes within their jurisdictions, partly because their own borrowing capacity or debt limitations were exhausted. Most of these new directions were born of necessity and the imaginations of higher-level technocrats and legislators. With one or two exceptions, they were not products of popular efforts from below. But they suggest a welcome stirring of innovation and challenge at the state level.

THE BALANCED-BUDGET CONSTITUTIONAL AMENDMENT

A more characteristic movement emanating from the states, and one that had the Reagan administration's somewhat hypocritical but nevertheless enthusiastic endorsement, was that for a balanced-budget amendment to the Constitution. There are no precedents regarding a constitutional convention called at the initiative of the states, and no procedures yet established for electing delegates, convening the convention, or conducting its business. Nevertheless, because only two more states' endorsements were needed in 1983 to create the constitutional obligation on the Congress to call such a convention, proposed enabling statutes started to make their appearance in both houses.

The idea of balanced-budget advocates joined together in a convention with the power to propose amendments to the Constitution calls up a broad range of fears for many people. It probably should. The last time a group was called together to amend the governing document of the country, they produced a whole new constitution and successfully accomplished its ratification. No matter how constraining to a single subject the enabling legislation might be, there will always and properly be fears that such a convention might go too far and endanger established liberties, power relationships, and the general stability of the political system.

But not all the prospects from such a convention are necessarily bad. It would certainly bring the vital notion of "balanced budgets" up for public attention and thoughtful consideration in a way that never could be accomplished otherwise. How important is it for the national budget to be "balanced"? What is the experience and practice of other countries in this regard? "Balanced" in what terms, and as of what point in how long a budget cycle?

If the budget were balanced in terms of the revenues and expenditures that would be realized under a reasonable definition of full employment, for example, it would be a very different budget from one balanced in terms of a fixed revenue pot. What sorts of expenditure commitments would be assumed as obligatory? What kind of flexibility and progressivity would be assumed in the revenue-raising system? Budgets might be set up for longer than one-year periods in order to provide greater opportunity for planning and more time for Congress to attend to other matters. "Balancing" could be required at repeated intervals as estimates of revenue and expenditure changed, or at the close of the budget period in the form of retroactive taxation or transfers.

Clearly, the issues are ones on which a genuine national debate could be immensely valuable as an educational and mobilizing experience. If the elections of convention delegates were made the focus of a full-employment organizing campaign, who knows what interesting debates or results might ensue from such a convention? In any event, there would be a series of state-level debates and electoral campaigns around the issue of ratifying any proposed amendment that did emerge from such a convention.

On balance, the calling of such a convention might be a vitally constructive development, one that contributed significantly to breaking the combination of hopelessness, complacency, and the fear of the unknown that have bred much of our current political stalemate. What a marvelous media event with which to celebrate the bicentennial of the ratification of the present Constitution!

THE INITIATIVE AND REFERENDUM AT THE NATIONAL LEVEL

One additional institutional change that draws on state sources and has been proposed by the New Right for adoption at the national level is that of the initiative and referendum. These provisions are variously designed and in use in a number of states, primarily the newer states whose constitutions were influenced by the Populist period in our history. They are being used today with growing frequency and effect in those states.

The initiative, as the name suggests, is a method by which a certain number of voters can by petition place a proposed statute on the next ballot for adoption or rejection by the people as a whole. The legislature and executive are thereby circumvented, and "direct democracy" is substituted in their place. In another version, the form of the ballot can call for the legislature to take up the proposed statute at its next session, and if it does not pass, the issue will go before the entire electorate in the same manner as before. The referendum is a method whereby a certain number of voters can by petition require that a statute enacted in the previous legislative session be submitted to the people at the next election for their acceptance or rejection.

In all these cases, vigorous and expensive campaigns are waged around the relatively narrow issues raised, and unpredictable results are injected into the public policy process in many states. Whether one views these consequences as desirable or undesirable depends both on what policy preferences one holds and on how one thinks a political system ought to operate. It probably is too soon, and may never be possible, to reach a generally applicable judgment about what these provisions accomplish. While I would like to think of them as extensions of democratic opportunities and contributions to voter efficacy, in the present context they have more of the appearance than the reality of either.

What they really have done so far is to sharply increase the workload and policy-making roles of state supreme courts (and even national courts) and lawyers generally, hardly a democratic development. Every successful initiative is likely to be challenged in court by the losing side. This is partly because a lack of technical expertise and the need to simplify for electoral purposes lead to drafting the new legislation in vulnerable ways, and partly to use the delay obtained thereby to appeal to legislatures for modification of the new laws.

PLANNING: THE FEDERAL RESERVE AND DEVELOPMENT BANKS

The Federal Reserve and development banks must be considered together because they jointly determine the availability, cost, and allocation of capital for investment. Interest rates are at the center of economic policy concerns, almost without regard to the political perspective one holds. But those who wish to exercise more direction over the ways that capital is used and by whom need to go much further toward managing incentives and disincentives for investment and actually making capital available directly when necessary. Let us look first at the Fed as it stands and then at what the various economic renewal programs would do in this area.

For an independent agency with long standing in the national government, the Fed is a remarkably political body. The system consists, first, of a seven-member Board of Governors appointed by the President for 14-year terms. The Chair is designated from among the governors by the President also, but for a four-year term. The system includes all the national banks of the country, organized in 12 districts, each of which has a Federal Reserve Bank at its center. These 12 Reserve Banks are effectively controlled by the member banks in that district. But the important powers of the Fed are to set interest rates and control the amount of money in circulation, both of which policies are set from the center under the special influence of the Chair of the Board of Governors.

Historically, the Chair has (usually) been willing to help incumbent Presidents win reelection by loosening the money supply and lowering interest rates as an election approached, thereby boosting the economy. But not always, and the Fed lives under constant pressure from both Congress and the President to do more and different things at different times. The current Chair, Paul Volcker, was initially a Carter appointee, but declined to play the usual game in 1980 and helped to keep unemployment up and interest rates relatively high during the presidential campaign. A committed monetarist, he nevertheless relented enough in 1982 to keep interest rates headed down and the stock market booming as the election drew near.

Part of the reason was that the continued high interest rates he had imposed for the previous two years had built up a major effort in Congress to trim the independence of the Fed and mandate certain targets for interest rates and money supply. The chief constituency of the Fed is the banking industry and its needs for flexibility, credibility, and profit. But the Fed must also maintain its status with the President and Congress in order to be able to deliver to its primary constituency, and much of its behavior can be understood only in these terms.

From the perspective of those who would like interest rates to be lower, credit easier, and employment higher, the Fed seems far too independent as it is. Certainly such far-reaching powers could be made more accountable to public preferences in a variety of ways. But that is just the point: Bankers and their allies among creditors and hard-money advocates would be very unhappy with such arrangements. So the Fed lives amid politics, conflict, and controversy.

Yankee capitalists would like to be able to exert more control over the Fed's functions, but to have them isolated from the capacity of *other* interests to do the same. If interest rates are kept reasonably low, more money and credit will be available from private sources at affordable rates so that businesses can expand. But these effects are general, not targeted toward the industries that *should* expand and away from those that should not. There are several possible ways to accomplish the vital targeting. One is through tax incentives that encourage certain uses of capital, and disincentives that penalize other uses of capital. Another is through a development bank, whether an adjunct of the Fed or a separate institution.

A development bank can make public funds available, either as part of a package including private capital or as the sole financing, for projects that the government considers desirable. Conditions can be attached to the use of government funds that require corporations to act in ways considered likely to further the competitive position of the economy as a whole. Such indications of government confidence and purpose should provide cues for investors and entrepreneurs to move in similar directions, and thus multiply their effects.

This kind of articulated direction over both public and private capital is an essential component of Yankee capitalist economic renewal policy. But it is not the only major goal. Another vital aspiration is that of devising an international mechanism for allocating reserves and credit so as to foster a coordinated growth within the integrated world economy. The United Nations is not an appropriate body for such functions because it is controlled by the Third World. Yankees need to manage the Third World and see that debts are repaid and opportunities for further investment are promoted. Thus, whatever financial control mechanisms are developed in the United States will be designed in part for their capacity to serve as participants in the international management of the availability, cost, and allocation of capital and credit.

In addition, Yankee capitalism envisions control over investment as part of a more comprehensive program to shape the direction of the economy. This means that the revised Fed, the new development bank, tax policies, and any direct investment of public funds such as infrastructure projects must be harmonized with import and export policies and perhaps other areas. And all of this array of policy-making capabilities must be insulated from parochial popular pressures. This is why I suggest that nothing less than an autonomous superagency for management of the economy will really serve Yankee needs. And I have little doubt that this would amount to reconstitution—perhaps even reconstitution run riot, to adapt Justice Cardozo's famous characterization.

Much of the planning to be accomplished by Yankees would be through the decisions of the new or refurbished national financial institutions, supplemented by consistent patterns of decision making by lesser banks all the way down the line to small local banks. But there would also be the need for industry-wide and coordinated national planning by the tripartite boards so much discussed in industrial policy proposals. The essence of such planning, as I have suggested, is technocratic and managerial. Rather than seek to learn what smaller local units or people generally think they need, centralized bureaucracies will decide what is needed by the whole and then where it can be produced most efficiently. The technical and rational needs of the major units of the economy will take precedence over all but the loudest demands from people and lesser units. Undoubtedly there will be a necessity from time to time to forcefully conform the behavior of the latter to the perceived needs of the larger corporations and banks.

The Democratic Agenda

Full-employment and economic democrats have three goals in the area of institutional change. One is widespread democratization of existing institutions, including some of the same ones proposed by the capitalists. Another is the creation of a whole new democratic planning system, one that connects with existing state and local governments but also draws on new versions of participatory institutions at the local level. The last is to greatly expand and democratize the use of public enterprises. All require sustained popular support, and that raises a further issue for consideration in a final section.

DEMOCRATIZATION

The issues posed in democratizing the Yankee capitalist institutions are challenging, and go to the heart of the question of practicality in large-scale democracy. For example, is it possible to decentralize and conduct planning democratically at state and local levels at a time when the principal dynamic of the world economy is toward international integration? How can labor really ever hope to balance the international mobility of capital that is already a fact? Workers would first have to agree throughout the United States, and would then reach agreements with workers from other countries, before they could present a united position against the relentless search of capital for lowest-cost labor markets.

To take another example, what does it mean to "democratize" the Federal Reserve Board? Surely not to have the President appoint one or two representatives of labor or consumers to sit as tokens among the bankers. But would it be more democratic to elect them, or even to elect a majority of the board?

Whose expertise would be dominant under almost any circumstances, and whose priorities therefore controlling? The point is not at all that it cannot be accomplished, but that the task of democratizing expert-dominated agencies is very difficult.

Armed with different priorities and intentions, would the financial systems of the full-employment or economic democrats end up differently? I think so. If employment and not private profit is the paramount goal, the system changes. There would be no need to design and implement policies at odds with what people generally wanted, or to thereafter find ways to present them in terms that people might nevertheless find acceptable. Democratizing and accountability remain problems, but they are procedural questions and not threats to the basic purpose of the whole enterprise. Much more direct control could be exercised by Congress, or by the President and Congress together in some fashion, without the same kind of threat to the substance of the intended actions.

But before we explore this planning system and its practical implications, we need to take seriously the prospect that all this effort toward democratization is likely to be politically explosive. One simply cannot imagine the banking industry submitting to serious democratization of this crucial function without having first attempted and lost every possible avenue of appeal—including questioning the basic power and legitimacy of the forces favoring democratization. Determined resistance must be assumed, and the forms of new institutions will depend on what forms that resistance takes and how it is overcome.

This is one more way in which the task of institutional reconstruction is intimately linked to the strength and organizational continuity of an electoral coalition. A variety of setbacks must be anticipated as the two capitalist groupings join forces to impugn the motives and perhaps the character of those in the forefront of implementing democratization. Supporting electoral and other popular groupings will be under heavy fragmenting pressure of various kinds. The willingness of capitalist elements to play the game of politics by democratic rules even if it means losing some of their major holdings and other advantages has never been established historically. Their behavior when such losses have seemed merely possible, on the other hand, suggests that democrats should be prepared for the worst.

PLANNING

Most of our understanding of planning comes from the effort of advocates to devise or implement a system for making certain decisions more "rational" in some way. This "rationality" usually embodies some policy-maker's or expert's or other technocratic manager's view of how efficiency should be promoted—and greater profits generated with the same or lower costs. The relationship is purely instrumental: Given the intent of the owners and managers, how can the means of employing resources be improved so as to more efficiently fulfill those intentions?

But as projected by the full-employment and economic democrats, planning is a political process integrated with the "coming to power" of a new popular movement. It is the way that people gain more knowledge, leverage, and self-confidence. Where once planning was a way to mask value choices behind the technocratic jargon of experts, it is intended to become an open arena for popular empowerment. One of the leading full-employment theoreticians, the political scientist Bertram Gross, explains that this much-expanded concept of planning would include:

> (1) a growing commitment to human rights and needs as guiding values for democratic planning, (2) the effort to build a popular political party able to unite people behind plans that express this commitment, (3) active participation by all private sectors, not just big business alone, (4) public planning that is locally rooted, has national scope and can take part in transnational decision making, (5) and the nurturing of management and budgeting approaches that break with established traditions of hierarchy and bureaucracy. Last but not least are (6) new styles of educating hierarchs and bureaucrats, (7) horizontal communication among society's lower and middle strata and (8) working toward more responsible and accountable leadership.[7]

What the full-employment planners have in mind is thus a vast interactive process in which no social entity or person need be left out—in other words, a newly active society constantly engaged in reshaping the conditions of its life.

PUBLIC ENTERPRISES

The development of public enterprises is a central commitment of both full-employment and economic democracy. This is the best way to gain the information, experience, and leverage to ultimately exercise control over the corporate economy. And it is the only way to really have social control over investment. An important side benefit is that it enables workers to set standards of participation and accomplishment in cooperative efforts. But public enterprises are not easy to start, and even more difficult to continue, in the images of their original democratic goals.

There are at least three major kinds of public enterprises. One is the "yardstick" enterprise, often a public corporation in a major industry that undertakes operations in competition with private corporations in order to improve services, force more competitive pricing, or achieve some other public goal such as learning about an industry. Another is the infrastructure-providing public enterprise, such as a port authority or municipal electric utility, that provides services to all users at a lower cost than might otherwise be possible. The third is the explicitly developmental public enterprise, in which the goal is primarily to provide jobs not otherwise available or develop resources or provide services that private investors would not undertake.

Each of these kinds of public enterprise can easily lose sight of the "public" nature of its origins or ownership and begin to act exactly like private businesses. If they do, they serve no democratic purposes, although they may be successful in other terms. These consequences are possible whether the controlling body is appointed or elected, and regardless of the extent of worker participation at the ground level. Both workers and elected managers grew up and live in a capitalist environment, and it is natural for them to act accordingly if they somehow acquire responsibilities for managing a publicly owned enterprise.

At least the first two kinds of public enterprises above, for example, are often evaluated in terms of whether they "made a profit" or not, and whether they should have made more. Scale is a problem in both public and private enterprises; the larger the size, the more likely it is to have bureaucratic tendencies. Accountability is an endemic problem, not one dependent on the intentions of the founders of an organization.

For all these reasons, it is easy to be skeptical of the long-term viability of public enterprises as vehicles of democratic education and accomplishment. In fact, any number of examples provide grounds for skepticism about lasting and effective democratization of *all* of the institutions discussed in this section, from planning boards to banks to local governments. But this does not say only that the notion of democratization is a romantic ideal unfit for practical souls. It also says that those who seek democratization can do so realistically only when their efforts are continuously and firmly grounded in a sustained popular movement.

Without such a popular movement, everything ultimately becomes a top-down operation, run by experts, despite their best intentions of acting in the name of "the people." With such a movement, there is at least a chance that actions are taken in keeping with popular preferences and do not—because they are not allowed to—end up in efforts to manage them. Such a movement must sustain itself for a considerable time, and that is not easy either. In this case, however, the prospect of continuing opposition should serve more than adequately to keep a popular movement alive and alert to dangers from within and without. If full-employment or economic democracy ever linked with an electoral coalition capable of raising it toward national power, it would never lack for the opposition to keep it vibrant and creative. What we need to know now is whether it will ever have a chance to do so.

PRACTICAL PROSPECTS FOR THE DEMOCRATIC AGENDA

The question seems to be whether the proposed changes offered by the democrats can command popular support and serve as continuing foci of mobilization. Popular movements have become experienced in the last decades in making public institutions more responsive to their demands. Many issues or problems once the exclusive preserve of bureaucrats have become "public property" in this way. Examples include the management of welfare, or public education, or other services that people have come to think of as at least partly their "rights." It does not seem a very long step for a new electoral coalition to seek institutional changes that would serve immediate goals and as longer-range visions of a desirable future system.

The place to start, given American traditions, probably *is* with an Economic Bill of Rights that amounts to a modern parallel to the political bill of rights contained in the first ten amendments to the Constitution. As a premise, the individual is surely entitled to certain levels of economic security, including the right to a relevant education, a job, health, and a dignified life as a senior citizen. This Economic Bill of Rights should be national, and enforceable against both national and state governments. But enforcement need not be exclusively the function of lawyers and courts, in this or other areas of newly created rights. Wherever political decision making can be substituted, such as by hearing boards of ordinary citizens, the opportunity should be welcomed. It will speed up the process, simplify it, and engage people in important decisions to which they can make real contributions.

Next in importance is the maximum use of increased powers and responsibilities at state and local levels. These are reachable, useful bodies of decision-making power capable of providing many early electoral victories and policy achievements. The days when states were districted against majorities of their own people are past, and many previously quiescent sectors of their populations have been thoroughly politicized in the last decades. State and local governments can be the laboratories where ideas and people are refined and developed for national leadership.

The question is always raised about the danger that states will discriminate against local minorities. The possibility is real, but the best remedy is a responsible (and therefore a more public-interested) electorate. Some outer limits contained in the Economic Bill of Rights can be enforced when necessary by a system of citizen juries (without judges, court procedures, or lawyers) where swift decisions embodying essential justice can be rendered.

Here as elsewhere in any developing democratic system, we shall have to come to terms with the notion of trusting and accepting the decisions that people make in their capacities as governing officials. If democracy proves not to work very well, we should try to improve on it. But in the meantime, we should be ready to give it the genuine trial that it has never had. None can know now with certainty how people or institutions act under conditions that have never existed. If we design institutions or otherwise act as if people were not to be trusted, we shall soon find that to be a self-fulfilling expectation.

National budget making should be an open, highly participative process. Presidential candidates should be obliged to run on platforms that include a national plan for the two-year and five-year future—a statement of needs, priorities, and ways of accomplishing goals that the President and his or her party are prepared to implement if installed in office. The national budget should also be for a two-year period, linked to the plan. People generally would thus have one occasion for choice about a combination of candidate and plan, and another with respect to the budget that implemented the plan.

The local and state planning bodies created to take reponsibility for planning development at those levels could also serve to focus state and local preferences with respect to the national plan and budget. The process would occur every two years, leaving time for other things and allowing longer-range planning and administration within governments. Presidents would be required to submit two-year plans in the so-called off-year congressional elections as well, thus keeping the general public focus on plans, budgets, and national political party responsibility for carrying them out. The National Planning Council should be dominated by politically accountable members, including some from Congress and some from state and local planning bodies. It should monitor and periodically report on both economic and social consequences of implementing present programs. Its reports should also serve to alert policy makers and the public to potential future problems, needs, and opportunities.

Additional streamlining of national government institutions to enhance political accountability would also be desirable. Some adaptations of parliamentary forms would make sense, particularly the open politicizing of functions and powers now rendered invisible or unaccountable by their "independent" status. For example, the three key departments of State, Defense, and Treasury could be much more closely integrated with the relevant congressional committees. The Treasury could be reconstructed into a Department of the Economy, with the Federal Reserve Board and new powers over corporate activities and import-export policies lodged there. Headed by the vice president, this could become a politically responsible arm of the President and his or her political party.

One of the crucial needs of any new democratic government is for technical expertise—more than equal to that of private business and the banks—for managing the complicated political-economic enterprise. There needs to be a new version of the civil service and a new pool for higher appointments that are not merely projections of corporate experience. New international political-economic capabilities of an unprecedented nature need to be developed.

The scope and importance of these needs suggest that an Academy of Democratic Management, incorporating the rigor and sense of service of the military academies and the idealism of the proposed "peace academy," should be part of the new program. One of the functions of such an academy could be the "mid-career" educational development of large numbers of citizen participants of various kinds, including those who serve on appellate-level juries in the ongoing replacement of judges, lawyers, and courts.

All these changes could be accomplished by statute alone. For tactical purposes, this is certainly important. The program should be something that is within proximate reach of a large majority, not dependent on years of effort in a variety of states. But for similar political reasons, some of the more far-reaching changes, such as that for an entirely new budget process, should be enacted for a limited time only. Provision should be made to submit them to a constitutional amendment process within a fixed period of years, partly to reduce initial reactions and partly to keep the movement alive and focused on ongoing political tasks.

Perhaps the most controversial change will be the reduction of the role of courts, judges, and lawyers. It will raise due process constitutional objections as well as igniting fears about the loss of political liberties. Congress does have the power to create new court systems, however, as well as to manage the ones it has created previously—which includes the federal courts below the Supreme Court. It will simply have to proceed slowly and experimentally, backing up citizen juries with new administrative courts until the problems become clear enough for a focusing constitutional amendment. One way to do this is to attach the new citizen hearing boards initially only to newly created rights and procedures, thereby avoiding the more direct constitutional confrontation until considerable experience has been developed and broad support is available.

More changes would be appropriate as experience was gathered and support increased. There would undoubtedly be ways to further reinvigorate the (democratically reconstructed) political parties. The new national plan and open budget process would give rise to many such opportunities. Congressional terms could be extended to four years and integrated in a variety of ways with such plans and budgets. The list literally is endless.

What is important here is the apparent fact that institutional changes can be made to fit with a new democratic movement's aspirations, fulfill its policy promises, and contribute to its further development. And they can do the job of governing at the same time. The real question is whether a democratic popular movement capable of these sorts of changes is possible in the near future in the United States. Stated only slightly differently, can full employment and economic democracy find the electoral coalition necessary to gain power and implement the policy and institutional changes they propose?

11. The Changing Shape of American Politics

The shape of the future depends on whether the electoral system can organize and deliver sustained support for *any* coherent policy direction. In the balkanized state of American politics, with its emphasis on special interests and single issues, this is a very serious question. To institute changes successfully, support must be drawn from electoral components that are themselves changing and pursuing their own ends. Political parties may or may not be able to mobilize a sufficient body of voters for a long enough time to see the changes through to completion. Other forms of organization or mobilization may be necessary. And it is always possible that no adequate coalition will be available. If that is the case, then I join the authorities cited earlier in the conviction that the regime itself is in danger.

In this chapter I explore some current developments among the basic building blocks of American politics in an effort to assess the chances that the four economic renewal programs have for finding a supportive electoral coalition. I look first at changing patterns in employment opportunities and underlying demography, and then at some leading value conflicts as they are represented by contending political movements. Then I focus on the threshold question: Who doesn't vote now, and why, and what would it take to bring them to the polls in large enough numbers to make a difference? Although I assess the prospects of each economic renewal program, my primary concern continues to be with the potential for realization of the democratic alternatives.

Employment: Patterns and Prospects

The dominant fact in the American economy in 1984, as in 1981, 1982, and 1983, was the extent of unemployment. Unemployment, the fear of unemployment, and the related drop in standards of living are by far the most significant economic factors in our politics. Despite "recovery," poverty levels increased, wage rates continued to decline, and unemployment levels seemed likely to remain high in some older industrial areas for the next few years. Many more people had been out of work for longer periods than in any other postwar recession, and this situation seemed likely to continue. Workers were still being asked or forced to accept wage concessions despite the recovery, and general wage levels seemed likely to remain depressed for some time. In the summer of 1983, the number of people living below the official poverty line rose to 34.4 million, 15 percent of all Americans and the largest total since 1965. Continuing concern about the possible return of inflation suggested that there would be only modest government efforts to combat unemployment *or* poverty.

Who are the unemployed? Keep in mind that both totals and percentages of people unemployed are only snapshots. In any 12-month period, it is estimated that probably three times that number are actually out of work at some time. Many more, of course, are anxious about the prospect of unemployment on a daily basis. These estimates were borne out in a 1982 national survey that found one-third of all households reporting that an adult member had been unemployed at some time during 1982, and by the extent of discouragement felt by respondents in several surveys.

In November 1982, at the peak of the 1981-82 recession, about 12 million people were out of work, or about 10.8 percent of the labor force. Another nearly 2 million persons were not counted in this total because they were "discouraged workers" who were not currently seeking employment. Uncounted others remained in school or at home because they did not believe that they would be able to find work, and some others worked only part time when they needed and sought full-time work. Among those actually counted in the statistics, there were some sharp and predictable differences. White adult women had the lowest rate of unemployment, 8.0 percent, while white adult men were only slightly higher at 9.2 percent. The rate was 16.7 percent for black adult women and 19.0 percent for black adult men. For teenagers, the figures soared: 21.3 percent for whites and 50.1 percent for blacks. For a significant and growing sector of the population, in other words, there is the prospect of a continuing lack of job skills, job experience, and the capacity for a self-supporting life.

The industries with the highest unemployment were the smokestack and other vulnerable industries. Metal manufacturing, which includes steel and other basic metals, stood at 26 percent, while automobiles trailed closely at 24 percent. Construction was at 22 percent, and lumber and wood products at 20.4 percent. Industries with relatively low unemployment tended to be in the service sector, such as communication (2.9 percent), finance, insurance, and real estate (4.7 percent), and government (5.0 percent). These patterns carried over geographically, and so states with the highest unemployment were those in the Midwest most dependent on metals and automobiles and those in the South and Northwest most dependent on lumber and construction. States where high-technology industries, energy production, and/or farming played a large role tended to be low in unemployment. Many older blue-collar workers seemed to face permanent unemployment, and some states—the Midwest "rust bowl," for example—might become permanent depressed areas.

As suggested earlier, a brisk debate rages over the proportion of workers whose jobs have been more or less permanently displaced by the ongoing transformation. Their jobs were in effect moved to Third World countries or absorbed by new technologies or automated processes. One figure from a Congressional Budget Office study set the number of displaced workers at 1.6 million, which would suggest a major task for government support systems and public-private retraining efforts. Other estimates, usually from the business press, set the figure much lower and argued that most of the unemployed were merely victims of the recession.[1] All estimates acknowledged, however, that new jobs for displaced workers are not likely to be found in the vicinity of their former employment (and homes and families), but in distant areas of the country where the mix of jobs is different.

Economic recovery may prove elusive, aborted by inflation or rising interest rates or some unexpected factor. Or it may be comparatively sustained and still not result in much reduction of unemployment—if a good share of the latter is linked to race and poverty or to long-term decline and transformation. For the democratic economic renewal programs, unemployment is the major reason for a new government role in the economy; for the Yankees, it is one good reason among many. Cowboys maintain that the revived ("unleashed" is their other term) free market will eventually pick up all willing workers, perhaps with the aid of some government-rewarded private training programs. On occasion, they point with hope to the coming population patterns in the United States. In a few years, fewer people will be seeking employment for the first time, and most women who want to work will have found jobs.

It is true that the actual total of jobs in the United States has been increasing, not declining, for the past several years. There are more jobs and more people at work today than ever before. About 350,000 new jobs are created every month. But so many people are seeking work that these increases have only little effect on the unemployment rate. New technological developments will lead to automated production processes, moreover, and repeated waves of older blue-collar workers will be displaced from their jobs. And the United States is experiencing a surge in immigration that seems likely to keep pressure building for more employment opportunities.

A major shift in the occupational patterns of the American economy is under way. Many applications of high technology may actually reduce the skill levels needed, and rapid changes in the nature of production processes may make any but the most flexible worker education programs obsolete. Older workers will need both retraining *and* relocation as population shifts to the West and South continue. One reason to retain some older industries is that they can still provide large numbers of jobs, even if they are not growing as rapidly as some of the newer fields. Industries that grow spectacularly from a tiny base are still not going to provide anywhere near the number of jobs that declining mass production industries can for a period of years remaining.

TABLE 11.1
THE CHANGING AMERICAN WORKFORCE,
1950-80

	1950	1980
Workforce (millions)	62.2	106.9
Men	43.8	61.4
Women	18.4	45.5
Participation rate[a]	59.2%	63.8%
Men	86.4	77.4
Women	33.9	51.5
Occupations (share of total)[b]		
White collar	35.9%	52.2%
Professional, technical	8.4	16.1
Managers, administrators	8.6	11.2
Clerical	12.0	18.6
Sales workers	6.8	6.3
Blue collar	40.1%	31.6%
Craftsmen, foremen	13.9	12.8
Operatives	19.8	14.2
Service workers	10.2%	13.3%
Farm workers	11.6%	2.8%

SOURCE: *Statistical Abstract of the United States, 1983.*

a. Proportion of noninstitutional population 16 and over in labor force.
b. Excludes the unemployed in 1950.

Tables 11.1 through 11.3 help illustrate the problems involved. First, note the large increase in the actual numbers of people in the workforce between 1950 and 1980. As population increases taper off, the pressure for the economy to produce new jobs may slacken. But before too much hope is drawn from the passing of the postwar baby boom, analysts should take into account the rapid rise in immigration (legal and illegal) that has characterized the last few years. The skill levels of these immigrants are much the same as the American workforce, and they are not all coming in at the bottom to take menial jobs.

TABLE 11.2
THE TWENTY LARGEST JOB CATEGORIES, 1980

	1980 Employment	Projected Growth 1980-90	Percent Growth
Secretaries	2,469,000	700,000	28.3
Nurses' aides, orderlies	1,175,000	508,000	43.2
Janitors and sextons	2,751,000	501,000	18.2
Salesclerks	2,880,000	479,000	16.7
Cashiers	1,597,000	452,000	28.4
Professional nurses	1,104,000	437,000	39.6
Truck drivers	1,696,000	415,000	24.5
Fast-food workers	806,000	400,000	49.6
General office clerks	2,395,000	377,000	15.8
Waiters, waitresses	1,711,000	360,000	21.1
Elementary teachers	1,286,000	251,000	19.5
Kitchen helpers	839,000	231,000	27.6
Accountants, auditors	833,000	221,000	26.5
Construction helpers	955,000	212,000	22.2
Automotive mechanics	846,000	206,000	24.4
Blue-collar supervisors	1,297,000	206,000	15.9
Typists	1,067,000	187,000	17.5
Licensed practical nurses	522,000	185,000	35.5
Carpenters	970,000	173,000	17.9
Bookkeepers, hand	975,000	167,000	17.2

SOURCE: Bureau of Labor Statistics.

A second factor making for continued pressure for more jobs is the rising proportion of women who are seeking jobs. A vigorous dispute exists between specialists as to whether this is a dispensable luxury that is part of the women's movement or a necessity forced on women because men's real wages are inadequate to support families. In any event, a major task in this economy is simply finding jobs for people who want and need to work.

The shift in occupations shown in table 11.1 is also very substantial. Blue-collar and agricultural jobs are declining; technical, managerial, and clerical positions are growing rapidly. The growth areas of the future are expected to force a reconstruction of these categories. The Census Bureau is dropping its "blue collar" category as no longer meaningful and instituting new subclassifications in the service field. The latter will no longer be oriented only to personal services such as domestic workers and waitresses, but also to business services like data processing and hospital services of a semiskilled nature.

TABLE 11.3
THE TWENTY FASTEST-GROWING JOB CATEGORIES, 1980

	1980 Employment	Projected Growth 1980-90	Percent Growth
Paralegal personnel	32,000	35,000	108.9
Data processing mechanics	83,000	77,000	92.3
Computer operators	185,000	133,000	71.6
Computer analysts	205,000	139,000	67.8
Office machine servicers	55,000	33,000	59.8
Physical therapists	34,000	17,000	50.9
Fast-food workers	806,000	400,000	49.6
Computer programmers	228,000	112,000	48.9
Tax preparers	31,000	15,000	48.6
Employment interviewers	58,000	27,000	47.0
Speech, hearing clinicians	35,000	16,000	46.6
Correction officials	103,000	45,000	46.5
EDP equipment operators	49,000	21,000	44.0
Aero-astronautical engineers	68,000	29,000	43.4
Travel agents	52,000	22,000	43.4
Nurses aides, orderlies	1,175,000	508,000	43.2
Insurance claims examiners	40,000	17,000	43.0
Economists	29,000	12,000	42.0
Brickmasons	146,000	58,000	40.2
Psychiatric aides	82,000	33,000	39.9

SOURCE: Bureau of Labor Statistics.

Table 11.2 and 11.3 show the fields where the largest number of jobs and the fastest-growing employment can be found. Only two kinds of jobs appear in both tables: fast-food workers, and nurses' aides and orderlies. The largest job producers are the older, lower-status jobs. The fastest-growing areas are somewhat more "interesting" and high-technology work, but only relatively small numbers of jobs are involved.

What is implied here is a major task of adapting education and skills to the needs of the changing economy, and perhaps of finding or making an adequate number of jobs. Some would argue that only very substantial economic growth, sustained over years, will make it possible to have enough jobs *and* an opportunity for people to choose the careers they want to have. Satisfaction in work has much to do with being able to develop skills and choose among several possible kinds and locations of jobs. Not much progress has been made in thinking through ways to do this, or how such growth might be achieved. Employment—or unemployment—problems seem to be the principal fact of political life in the next decade.

The Underlying Demography

Closely related to employment is the distribution and makeup of the population. As Kevin Phillips emphasizes, demography is destiny. Population characteristics can be projected into the future with greater accuracy than most social statistics because so much is known about such large aggregates—and it takes time for new patterns of births and deaths to arise and change these projections very much. The basic facts shaping American politics today all have to do with the rise and character of the sunbelt, and its future. Population moves there, jobs follow, and movement accelerates. Soon enough, the House of Representatives and the Electoral College reflect such changes. Because the sunbelt includes so many religious fundamentalists, wealthy free-enterprise worshipers, and retirees, it is thoroughly conservative in outlook. The sunbelt mandates a conservative perspective—a move to the right—in national politics for the next period. This is so much our current conventional wisdom that I hesitate to explore it in detail. But I do so because I want to enter some important reservations to this thesis about the American future.

TABLE 11.4

POPULATION AND JOB SHIFTS, SNOWBELT TO SUNBELT TO YEAR 2000

	Northeast	North Central	South	West
% of U.S. population, 1980	22.7	26.6	32.5	18.3
Net change in % of U.S. population, 1980-2000	-1.6	-1.3	+1.5	+1.3
Net change in % black, 1980-2000	+2.3	+1.6	-0.9	+0.9
% of U.S. jobs, 1973	23.5	27.5	30.6	17.6
Net change in % of U.S jobs, 1973-2000	-4.4	-2.1	+3.2	+3.6
% of U.S. manufacturing jobs, 1973-2000	-7.0	-3.2	+5.8	+6.2

SOURCE: U.S. Census Bureau.

A gross statement of the conventional wisdom would say that the sunbelt is becoming so dominant that its needs and interests will control American politics for two decades or longer. There is an important sense in which this is true. Table 11.4 summarizes many of these changes, and will repay close consideration.

First, we should be clear about definitions. The idea of a "sunbelt" permits several possible definitions. As originally labeled by Kevin Phillips, the sunbelt began at North Carolina's northern border and ran across the bottom tier of states to California. Fifteen states were in this group, including nearly all of the fastest-growing states of the country. I have used the broader (and easier) Census Bureau categories of South and West in the table, partly because the Mountain and other Pacific states have many of the high-growth, energy-boom, and other characteristics of sunbelt states. Along with the notion of a sunbelt, there has developed the idea of a "snowbelt," by which is usually meant the 15 New England, Mid-Atlantic, and Great Lakes states. These form the core of the Northeast and North Central categories of table 11.4. The latter permits some broad comparisons in which the entire country is involved, and we can narrow to electoral contrasts between the two key groups of 15 states later.

The first facts confirmed in table 11.4's projections from the present to the end of the century are those of population movement. It is hardly news that population has shifted, but of some importance that it will continue to do so. Perhaps more important is the implication that the white population is moving. The black proportion of the total regional population will rise most in areas that are losing population.

But the last four rows of table 11.4 may be the most instructive. The proportions of all jobs in the country, and particularly manufacturing jobs, will fall and rise in different regions in an exaggerated manner consistent with population change. That is, areas gaining in population shares will gain much more in shares of jobs. Those losing population will lose proportionally many more jobs.

The job pattern used to be tilted toward the snowbelt states; it is shifting even more dramatically than population toward the sunbelt states. The West will end up with a distinctly larger share of all jobs than it has population, while the Northeast and North Central states will be short on jobs. What this means, and probably will continue to mean, is that skilled and educated whites will be migrating South and West to take the new technical and professional jobs, while blacks remain in the Northeast and North Central states in the old smokestack industries and unemployment lines.

These changes have already started to be felt in the House of Representatives and the Electoral College, and will develop greater impact after the census of 1990. They will mean changes in the balance between parties and in the nature of the interests represented within each party. A quick characterization would be that congressional seats and Electoral College ballots are moving from center cities in the Northeast and North Central states to new suburbs in the South and West. Seventeen seats shifted from the first pair of regions to the second as a result of the 1980 census. Because of Democratic successes in districting at the state level, the party shift in the House was negligible. But there will be 17 more Electoral College ballots in normally Republican states in 1984. If the population projections hold for 1990, between 15 and 19 more seats and ballots will shift in this manner for the elections of 1992 and afterward.

But now it is time to enter some reservations about the conventional wisdom regarding the sunbelt and its implications. The first set has to do with the impact of sunbelt ideology, particularly within the Democratic party but perhaps also within the Republican party. Just as we saw in analyzing the cowboy capitalist economic renewal program, the free market emphasis of the sunbelt coalition is neither unanimous nor unequivocal. There is both experience with and need for government planning and guidance for economic activity, which leads some to support essentially corporatist programs for economic renewal.

Next, inspection of the contrasts between representatives elected in 1982 from older, "smokestack" congressional districts and newer "high-tech" districts leads to some provocative (if speculative) contrasts. The party breakdown in the high-tech districts favors the Republicans, but by only a slight margin. All but one of the smokestack districts were Democratic. The population change contrasts are dramatic: high increase in high-tech areas (greater in Republican districts), and actual decrease in smokestack areas.

There are also sharp contrasts between Republicans and Democrats in new high-tech areas: Republicans score much more conservatively on the standard measures of liberalism-conservatism published by various lobbying groups. A more limited difference is visible between Democrats: high-tech Democrats score lower in liberalism than do smokestack Democrats. In microcosm, these relationships say a great deal about the relationships developing between the basic sectors of American industry and the political parties that seek to represent them.

The pattern of support for Representative Ottinger's "High Production Strategy to Rebuild America" discussed in chapter 6 may serve to foreshadow emerging differences within the sunbelt and in its representation in Congress. Certainly the most politically attractive version of Yankee capitalism, it was developed by a group of 75 House Democrats organized in 16 task forces. A total of 148 Democrats eventually signed on as "members or endorsers." Snowbelt initiative is visible in the fact that ten of the task force heads are from those states, and only one is from a sunbelt state (five are from what I shall now call "middle" states, which will turn out to be primarily Maryland, Missouri, Iowa, Colorado, Oregon, and Washington). Among the others associated with the final program, however, there are 80 snowbelt representatives, 17 from middle states, and 35 from the sunbelt. Of the latter 35, 24 are from California (out of 29 Democrats in the California delegation).

Clearly, Yankee capitalism can expect to draw some support from a not-so-solid sunbelt. And other economic renewal programs might similarly find bases of support within those states. Social security, health insurance, and a variety of other income transfer and social service programs can certainly count on support from the growing elderly populations in the key sunbelt states as well. As a group, such voters may not be consistently progressive, but they are likely to be solid on questions of economic welfare.

There is also a time bomb ticking in the sunbelt, as table 11.5 demonstrates. Among the 15 core states of the sunbelt, six are distinctively high in black proportions of the eligible electorate. Two others, Texas and California, have very high proportions of blacks and Hispanics. These minorities have historically been supporters of economic welfare programs and the strongest opponents of cowboy capitalism and free market policies. In hard times, or with a viable full-employment or economic democracy movement, these groups might well form the basis for a new electoral coalition that would have a strong grounding in the sunbelt. At the least, this part of the underlying demography spells trouble for simplistic sunbelt thinking.

But the minority-focused analysis can be taken a step further, with even more far-reaching implications. Table 11.5 also shows the proportions of the populations of several of the most populous states with the highest number of Electoral College ballots that is made up of the two largest minorities, blacks and Hispanics. It demonstrates that these minorities are located for maximum impact in the Electoral College and that they are factors of large and growing importance to the outcomes of presidential elections.

Some caveats are in order. Many Hispanics in the West and Southwest will not become citizens (and thus eligible voters) for years; some may never do so. Puerto Ricans, however, the basic Hispanic population in the Northeast and Mid-Atlantic states, are U.S. citizens and eligible voters at all times. Hispanics are by no means as solid a block of voters as blacks. Their turnout rate is even lower than blacks, and many Hispanics have historically been associated with the Republican party. The Latin population of Florida, for example, is likely to be particularly subject to cold-war or military adventurist appeals.

On the other hand, California has come to notice recently as being our first prospectively "Third World" state. At some point in the 1990s, according to demographic projections, California's minorities will together make up more than half the state's population. One reason for this is the substantial and growing number of Asians in California; another is the influx and rapid increase in the number of Hispanics. As the latter group rises to the status of the nation's largest minority and acquires greater political awareness, it will become

TABLE 11.5

POPULATION SHIFTS, MINORITIES, AND THE NEW ELECTORAL COLLEGE

	The Elections of 1992-2000[a]				The Election of 1980			
Ten Most Populous States	Electoral College Ballots	Percent Black	Percent Hispanic	Total Percent Minorities[b]	Electoral College Ballots 1984	Electoral College Ballots 1980	Percent Black	Total Percent Minorities[b]
California	50	10	30	50	47	45	8	33
Texas	33	13	32	46	29	26	12	34
New York	31	19	12	32	36	41	14	25
Florida	25	13	13	26	21	17	14	24
Illinois	22	17	10	28	24	26	15	22
Pennsylvania	22	12	2	15	25	27	9	11
Ohio	21	12	2	14	23	25	10	11
Michigan	18	13	2	16	20	21	13	16
New Jersey	15	16	10	27	16	17	13	21
North Carolina	13	24	2	27	13	13	22	24

Note on the sunbelt: In additon to California, Texas, Florida, and North Carolina (shown above), Alabama, Arizona, Arkansas, Georgia, Louisiana, Mississippi, New Mexico, Oklahoma, South Carolina, and Tennessee had in 1980 an average minority proportion of 28 percent of their populations.

SOURCES: 1980 data from Michael Barone and Grant Ujifusa, *The Almanac of American Politics, 1982* (Washington, D.C.: National Journal, 1982), lx and lxi. 1990 population and Electoral College data compiled from Cary Davis, Carl Haub, and JoAnne Willette, *U.S. Hispanics: Changing the Face of America* (Washington, D.C.: Population Reference Bureau, 1983), 12 and 39; *American Demographics,* August 1983; and U.S. Census Bureau estimates.

a. Electoral College ballots as estimated after census of 1990; minority populations estimated for the year 2000.
b. Includes black, Hispanic, American Indian, and Asian, as appropriate.

a major political force. If blacks and Hispanics were ever able to cooperate consistently, they could change the direction and character of American politics significantly.

The sunbelt, therefore, may appear to be dominated by the new free enterprisers and religious fundamentalists, but it has some very important underlying differences within it. These contending blocs of political power may find even greater expression in the Congress than in the presidential elections because the cowboy elements may be sufficient to carry pluralities in the most populous of the sunbelt states. But even then, there are ways in which presidential elections can become more competitive than they have been in recent years. Republicans have dominated of late in part because party attachments are weakest and media influence strongest for that most visible of offices, the Presidency of the United States.

If economic welfare issues become the focusing aspect of campaigns, however, snowbelt states and sunbelt states are likely to reach a rough standoff in which the middle states will determine outcomes. The 15 sunbelt states will have about 200 Electoral College ballots after the 1990 census reallocations, and the 15 snowbelt states about 200. About 135 electoral ballots rest with the "middle" states, the major ones being old "border" states, Central Plains states, and Rocky Mountain and Pacific Northwest states.

This is not an unpromising constituency from which to define the American future. Even conceding the border states to the sunbelt, Populist, cooperative, and public enterprise traditions run through all the other states as they do in no other combination of states in the United States. Many of these states were represented in the 1983 formation of a radical-progressive 14-member "Populist Caucus" among Democrats in the House: Tennessee, West Virginia, Iowa, North and South Dakota, Minnesota. Other states represented included sunbelt strongholds: Texas, Arizona, New Mexico. The new caucus's founding principles echoed many of the old Populist positions in modern forms, taking care to excise many of the racist dimensions included in some uses of the term populism.

What underlying demographic trends suggest, therefore, is change and uncertainty, not any decisive advantage for cowboy capitalism. What happens within the minorities, particularly Hispanic minority groups—Mexican, Puerto Rican, and Latin in origin—will be very important. Once past the relatively predictable employment and population change factors, we enter a much more volatile and less predictable field. This is the realm of changes in values and attitudes, and different levels of mobilization around particular issues—all of which depend on the unpredictable ways that people react to what is going on around them.

Value Changes and Group Mobilization

Changes in basic values are occurring for some people more rapidly than for others, and the feeling of unjust deprivation is widely but unevenly distributed. Much of this ferment is expressed in organized efforts to obtain or prevent specific changes in American life. The three leading movements of this sort in the 1980s are mounted by women, minorities, and the New Right. These groups have the capacity to bring new millions to the polls and to shift their votes between parties and candidates in decisive ways. Some other groups, both ethnic and ideological, are also important but do not reach this level of significance. I consider them briefly at the end of this chapter.

The changes that are under way in our fundamental values and beliefs, as elsewhere in our social world, are both recognized and subterranean. They have occurred gradually, sometimes behind our backs, throughout the twentieth century—perhaps ever since the Hamiltonian-capitalist structure was actually put in place. They are by-products of recurring and irresistible democratic pressures, however awkwardly imposed through the maze of our deflecting political processes, to which even the Hamiltonian model had to give ground. People simply saw or viscerally knew that the system was producing for its favored few. They demanded a larger share of the economic returns for themselves, and a larger part in public decision making at the same time. What they got was literally half a loaf: a somewhat larger share of the economic and bureaucratic goods available, and little or nothing in the way of a greater voice in government. (These characterizations apply equally to all three groups cited—women, minorities, *and* the New Right.)

Some significant change in values and beliefs occurred, and some very tangible policy accomplishments were realized, in the developing crisis 50 years ago that was terminated by World War II. But the current crisis involves greater potential. Barring nuclear war, no longer to be dismissed as unthinkable, we have already embarked on a process of change that will far surpass the 1930s. Not only are the ways that many people understand fundamental American values changing, as I described in chapter 2, but many other forces built up during the 1960s and 1970s are still at work among us. For example, an entire generation has deep experience with fundamental change in values and beliefs, always in the direction of expanding their meanings and widening their democratic implications. One component of that generation tasted success in basically altering national policy, with respect to the Vietnam war, in civil rights, and in the treatment of minorities and women generally. Another and perhaps larger number of people reacted against those changes and succeeded in slowing or stopping the trend—at least temporarily.

What the antiwar, civil rights, minority, and women's movements had in common, knowingly or not and despite some painful differences, was the fact that they took the Declaration of Independence seriously. They believed that people had the right of self-determination; that they were inherently equal, and that they were entitled to the tools with which to pursue life, liberty, and happiness. And in many cases, they too pledged themselves, their honor, and their lives to these ends. Whatever the economic crisis and transformation brings, it will come on top of this profound experience, at once very current in our social memory and fundamental in politicizing significance.

The New Right took the Declaration no less seriously, and sought in similar mass participatory fashion to reverse the gains that had been made. Although the New Right was mobilized first by reaction against the changes accomplished in the 1960s and 1970s, there are important similarities between its members and major elements of the women's and minority movements. Nor are they merely mirror images of each other, in the sense that white voters move to the Republican side as black voters enter electoral politics, usually on the Democratic side. Economic issues particularly might find the two sides lining up together, and they certainly share commitments to mass involvement in efforts to generate electoral impact in opposition to traditional elites. The New Right has been as disappointed as the others ever were at the failure of candidates they supported to deliver what they had expected after the election, and as full of resolve to see matters to a better conclusion in the future.

Each of these three major groupings has already had profound effects on the structure and policies of the American political system. Each has the capacity to further reconstruct both institutions and policies. It is not much of an exaggeration to say that these movements hold the key to the future direction of the American system in their hands. Whichever group(s) succeed in mobilizing supporters and bringing out the current nonvoter in large numbers can effectively break our continuing political-economic stalemate. No other political identities hold the primary loyalties of numbers of people in the same way.

The Crucial Threshold: The Decision to Vote or Abstain

The present stalemate is unlikely to be broken without a major influx of current nonvoters. Realignments of lasting character have always required the entrance of a major bloc of new voters, as well as the shift of a substantial fragment of regular voters, to develop momentum. What can be expected of our current near-majority of nonvoters? The steady decline in voting turnout and the potential it appears to carry for "disruptive" impact on our politics have led to several recent studies of who such nonvoters are and what might lead to their participation in the future. The results of one of these studies were analyzed at length by the experienced electoral observer Arthur Hadley in *The Empty Polling Booth.*[2]

Hadley shares the concerns of most commentators for the implications of nonvoting, but uses the term "refrainers" to avoid pejorative implications. I cited his characterization earlier of nonvoters as a "bomb" waiting to explode and change the course of history. Hadley's goal is to promote a steady, stabilizing increase in voting, just to avoid such an explosion. But he is one of the few analysts to take seriously the possibility that nonvoters are such because of flaws in the political system and not for reasons having to do with their moral character or mental capabilities. He states this as follows:

> But here a word of warning. Voters become refrainers for a variety of reasons. An important one is voting, winning, and then not getting what you want. . . . More and more citizens see examples of the elites making decisions that are against the will of the majority. And the majority need no poll to tell them this. Or the decisions are made in places the voters can't reach or influence, such as the courts or the bureaucracy. All this leads to growing feelings of impotence.[3]

Table 11.6 summarizes the categories into which Hadley sorts his "refrainers" and shows the proportions of nonvoters involved in each. While in general nonvoters are drawn disproportionately from those sectors of the population that normally vote Democratic, Hadley emphasizes that there are all kinds of people and many different reasons among refrainers. The largest group is what he calls "positive apathetics." These are happy, well-off people with characteristics much like voters. They feel effective politically, but seem to have too much to do in life to bother with voting.

TABLE 11.6

NONVOTERS CLASSIFIED BY REASONS FOR NONVOTING

Category	% of All Nonvoters
1. Positive apathetics	35
2. Bypassed	13
3. Politically impotent	22
4. Physically disenfranchised	18
5. Naysayers	6
6. Cross-pressured	5

SOURCE: Based on national sample surveys, as reported in Arthur T. Hadley, *The Empty Polling Booth* (Englewood Cliffs, N.J.: Prentice-Hall, 1978).

One reason for not registering to vote is to save time and trouble by avoiding jury duty, which is based on voting rolls. Politics is unimportant, in part because they feel that they have the capacity to take care of themselves. But if ever politics should *seem to be* important, they have all the psychic qualities to simply walk in and vote. In a much-cited paper at a forum on the problem of nonvoting in 1983, political scientist Austin Ranney argued for acceptance of nonvoting on the grounds of a "right" to abstain. This and the "naysayer" category (see below) can be the only group of nonvoters to which such a characterization would apply.

In the "bypassed" category are the people who are most inert politically. They have low incomes, low education, and very little political awareness. Two-thirds are women, people whom American life seems genuinely to have left behind. This group as a whole was not particularly cynical or bitter about politics, but simply lacking in political awareness.

In sharp contrast were the "politically impotent." These people were found to be much better off financially than the "bypassed" group, but to have deep feelings of political powerlessness and cynicism. Hadley characterizes them as having done their duty, lived up to the rules, with nothing to show for it—not happiness, not real affluence, and no feelings of satisfaction. (Not only is this a profoundly alienated group but a sizable number of voters show similar attitudes. Hadley terms this 21 percent of current voters the "vergers"—people who are likely to drop out of the voting electorate at any moment and for the same reasons of frustration with the way the system works. My guess is that Hadley is talking about the same people from which are drawn the group that Phillips calls "populist conservatives.")

Hadley's next category is the "physically disenfranchised," people who have moved recently, are out of town on election day, or have other physically preventing reasons, and people who are ill or disabled. The health-disenfranchised refrainers are about a third of this category. But the other two-thirds are the most likely voters of all refrainers—reasonably happy, affluent, interested in and confident about their capacity to affect politics. They just were not able to vote because of something that intervened in their lives.

The "naysayer" category is one of the useful findings of this study because it too represents a group that is otherwise psychically ready to vote if voting seemed important enough. Relatively few in number, these are people who are particularly well educated and deliberately refuse to vote for reasons that are important to them. Some of these reasons are religious, but others have to do with the lack of choice or the corruption of politics.

The final group is one of people who are "cross-pressured" by contending loyalties who solve their problem by not voting. Neither of these groups is very much different from voters in income or efficacy, and most have voted in other elections.

The point of Hadley's book is to find ways of bringing refrainers back to politics. To his apparent surprise, he found that most refrainers were such for reasons that are *political.* He notes that about 70 percent of refrainers do not vote because "they feel the act is meaningless or they lacked a reason to go to the polls. The vast majority of the refrainers will return to the polls for political reasons. . . . To be blunt: it is their disgust with politicians, not needed 'reforms,' that are keeping the refrainers from the polls."[4]

There is no doubt of the moral imperative associated with voting. Most people believe it is their civic and social duty to vote. Most nonvoters feel guilty about not voting and wish life had made it possible for them to do so. The task for a democratically oriented electoral coalition is, first, to make voting meaningful and then to help make it physically easier. Only the democratic economic renewal programs *really* want to make voting meaningful, and that is the secret ingredient for increasing turnout. Most of the rest of the reforms are likely to produce substantial results only if the precondition of meaningful elections has already been met.

Hadley's reforms include postcard registration with 30-day residence requirements, making Election Day a national holiday, and having easy absentee-voting arrangements. They are certainly worth supporting and implementing. But a decisive commitment to a meaningful program would be an absolutely necessary means of generating the new voter turnout that would carry any new coalition to power.

There would be some merit to an across-the-board effort to increase registration and turnout because the majority of votes added would probably be Democratic and perhaps supportive of democratic goals. The qualitative merits of the *program,* however, and the determination to carry it out as promised, would be the decisive attraction to current nonvoters. They have the capacity to make a new agenda possible in the coming years, but only for those who play the game openly and honestly for goals involving economic well-being and democracy. The idea of "keeping faith with the nonvoters" sounds bizarre, but not inappropriate to the world we live in. Consider the alternatives.

Some Political Implications

Given present conditions, what will it take for one or another economic renewal program to find the necessary electoral support? Much depends on the way that elections are understood, which is in turn at least partly a product of international conditions that American elites cannot control. As a general principle,

I think it can be said that the only way that either full employment or economic democracy can develop a viable new electoral coalition is if a series of elections are seen as involving primarily economic justice and well-being. Even then, the Yankees are more likely to win out unless hardship is widespread and these alternatives gain wide mass acceptance. But if conditions lead to understanding of elections as involving primarily national security, race relations, or the social issues, the advantage will lie with the cowboys. Yankees might win at such times, but their chances are less likely under most imaginable circumstances.

Other significant organizations and groups within the electorate should receive consideration in any comprehensive analysis of what is happening in American politics. Indeed, it is just this proliferation of ideological, ethnic, and other special-interest groups that has led some to talk despairingly about the "balkanization" of American politics. No analysis can go far at all without taking into account the truly significant role that religion plays in the United States. And the opposition to Central American policy, plus the nuclear freeze and environmental movements, should be recognized as significant progressive factors. They are, of course, relevant chiefly to middle-class professionals and are likely to produce a backlash from others that might be even more significant.

Most of these movements will go their own way without much regard for economic welfare issues. This is one of the problems of coalition building on the American electoral scene. Single-issue movements tend to make demands and exert their efforts in narrow terms, each insisting on its own first priorities and denying their connections with anything else. The only more destructive tendency in these characteristically American movements is their habit of evaporating as soon as some achievements have been recorded.

Part of the task for any economic renewal program is to show at least some of the single-issue movements of the day that their goals are bound together with the problem of economic renewal. Failing that, the only other route to sustained power—long enough to effect the institutional changes needed—for one of the economic renewal programs is to maintain the threat of war or social turmoil as a kind of cover while the program and changes are being instituted. Of course, that route is possible only for cowboy capitalism or Yankee capitalism. The other programs must come to power in an open and straightforward—and much more difficult—manner.

The cowboys have the organizational structure of the Republican party, for what it is worth, but must gain the support of either the New Right or the free market and middle-class moderates who are not congenial with the New Right. The only way to secure such support is to reach for the strengths of the party, national security or race relations, a strategy not unwelcome to cowboys. Military adventures or the orchestration of the threat of war are dangerous games, however, though probably effective for at least some time. The brute fact is that in economic hard times, cowboys are vulnerable. If prosperity cannot be achieved, something else will have to be done to gain or stay in office. If not the national security trump card, then the race conflict card. Cowboys have no alternatives.

The Yankees have the Democratic party, but lack a mass base for their program. This is why I have argued that they must come to terms with the full-employment advocates. They could delude themselves for some time, as perhaps they have already, with the notion that the leadership of the traditional unions effectively represented "labor." But Yankees are so uncomfortable mixing it up with people, and their program is so rational-technical, that they will keep on trying to find some arm's-length cause or organization that can bring them the masses. They will pay handsomely, and have no end of suitors for that reason. Whether they can find any grounds other than a full-employment program on which some substantial bloc of voters will support them for any length of time, however, is doubtful.

These reflections bring us to the possibility of third-party alternatives. In the 1980 election, the candidacy of John Anderson looked promising at first but faded by Election Day to about 7 percent of the total vote. Anderson was a centrist candidate who appealed to middle-class professionals, university communities, and others now known as "Yuppies" (young, upwardly mobile professionals). He took an essentially Yankee position without the resources that make the Yankees formidable. And he may well have cost Carter the election. But this sort of third-party candidacy has little long-term viability unless some drastic changes occur in the major parties.

The next possibility in the third-party sweepstakes is a new party started by the New Right. This is likely only if the Republicans seem bent on governing in a manner consistent with the twentieth-century consensus, and if their leadership slides back toward their free market and moderate middle. Such a party could come about also if economic conditions worsened substantially. It is a real possibility for the later 1980s, and because of its strength could trigger a realignment among the other "major" parties.

Another, somewhat less likely, possibility is for Yankee capitalists and sunbelt corporatists to come to terms somehow and strike out together in a centrist party. This would require that the Democratic party move to the left or that major elements leave the party to the Yankees so that their accommodation with the sunbelt could be struck under the umbrella of the Democratic party. As we have seen, there are grounds on which Yankees and some sunbelt elements could cooperate. Only the Yankees' determined internationalism really stands in the way, and sunbelt industries will soon enough need import-export assistance. Both have a real need to impose order on the rest of the society, and their orientations would be complementary in this respect.

The last in this list of decreasingly likely possibilities for political party development is a party of the left. Perhaps organized around the full-employment program, such a party would seek to build support over time from a coalition of minorities, former nonvoters, and the disadvantaged generally. It would start on much the same basis as the Republican conservatives did in 1964, and undoubtedly would lose at the presidential level. If it did not have the staying power to entrench itself in local and state offices and grind its way to visibility and then national office, it would deserve to follow other such efforts into the status of a footnote to history. The best hope for full employment-economic democracy is probably a gradual but genuine takeover of the Democratic party. This would require a staying power, and a level of organizational skill, not previously characteristic of the left. But it would result in possession of the still potent appeal of the Democratic party, one of the two historic major parties in American politics.

What does all this say about the prospect for a democratic future? Neither cowboy capitalism nor Yankee capitalism offers much promise. The best that can be said for them is that they will have difficulty establishing themselves and implementing their programs, and may very well fail. That is the good news. The bad news is that their failure may well lead to a drastic authoritarian remedy, when the nation appears so threatened that neither elites nor people can see another way out. This is what makes understanding the chances for a democratic alternative all the more urgent.

12. Toward a Class-Based Realignment of American Politics?

What conditions would make either the full-employment or economic democracy solutions possible? I have made a major point of the need for replacement of partial understandings of democracy with full versions, and a general integration of economic and political understanding. Three more strictly political conditions follow this initial one. First, such a democratic future requires that national elections be understood almost exclusively as posing questions of economic welfare. At the least, the focus on economic welfare must be so strong for many people that it can withstand efforts by others to interpret the elections as primarily involving national security or race issues. If economic welfare is *not* the basic focus for a potential majority of voters, there is no future for a democratic movement. Strong words, but defensible in the context of the historical record of voting behavior.

Next, such a democratic coalition must be built from (not necessarily around) minorities, former nonvoters, disadvantaged strata generally, and a new version of working-people-organized-politically. The older unions, with a few honorable exceptions, will be an obstacle—except in some wounded smokestack areas. New forms of organization of working people, such as associations of public employees, will have to take on the responsibility of organizing their fellows for the purpose of being able to do their job better, not just to make more money. An emphasis on the quality of work product, as well as the quality of work life, can bind people collectively and lead to a necessary confrontation with mere private profit as the basic motivator. Belated recognition of the full citizenship of minorities along the lines that were laid down by Martin Luther King, Jr., in the 1960s offers a chance for the cause of minorities to be everyone's cause.

The next condition is that nonvoters become genuinely politicized and engage on Election Day in large numbers and on the right side. This implies that something happens, either in the mix of events that surround former nonvoters or in the appeals made to them by new democratic candidates, that genuinely changes people's attitudes. It has to change them enough to convert them into supporters of the full-employment or economic democracy cause, and has to hold them there long enough for results to start coming in and others to join in support.

I doubt that any of these conditions can be met without the development of some shared and felt rather than articulated identity among Americans in relatively deprived levels. I have been alluding to this notion as the American equivalent of class consciousness. The empirical form would be a coherent mobilization around the basic goal of economic welfare, and a sense of the right and power of working people to attain such ends.

This sort of group commitment to achieving a collective purpose is unusual in American politics, but it is crucial to a sustained effort to accomplish the democratic ends involved. Just as there must be a continuing popular movement to give reality to the attempted democratization of institutions, so must there be the equivalent of class consciousness to sustain and give identity and purpose to that popular movement. Behind all this, let us hope, is a growing recognition that democracy could and should become a pervasive and active reality in the everyday social relationhips of all Americans. How far any of these hopes for such a new popular movement have support in evidence about how people think and feel today is the subject of this chapter. I start by posing what is surely the most powerful and best-known scenario for the way in which this sort of movement might rise to power.

The Class-Based Realignment Thesis

Perhaps the most insightful academic analysis of twentieth-century American social movements has been done over the past decade and a half by Frances Fox Piven and Richard Cloward. They began with *Regulating the Poor*[1] in 1971, which argued that the liberal state essentially "bought off" the protests of poor and unemployed people by expanding the financial support provided to such people as welfare payments or other social services and transfers. Once the protests subsided, benefits were cut back so as to keep the pressure on people to accept work even at low wages. They argued that poor people should apply for all the benefits to which they were possibly entitled as a general strategy to put maximum pressure on the state and the capitalist economy it served.

In *Poor People's Movements*[2] in 1977, the authors turned to comparative analysis of various American movements from the 1930s forward. Here they argued that progress for the underprivileged in the United States historically came through mass protest movements rather than the regular channels of electoral politics. By 1981, however, they had begun to see changes occurring in the way that people understood their relationship to the liberal state as a result of the cumulated experience of decades of protest. In their eyes, many people had come to feel entitled to certain minimum standards of living and other entitlements from the state, which served as a recognizable substitute for the capitalist economy. In other words, decades of struggle for economic justice had made the state an accepted battleground.

Thus, when corporate forces mobilized and, acting through the Reagan administration, sought to cut back on transfers and services to the poor, Piven and Cloward anticipated vigorous resistance from various groups of poor people. In *The New Class War*[3] they characterized the cutbacks as a class war of the rich against the poor, intended to reduce workers' bargaining power, improve business's profit margins, and thus restore general prosperity. The label they applied was simple: "capitalism against democracy."

This new class war against the poor, they argue, was made necessary by two developments. One was that the state had been injected more and more into the economy on behalf of capital in the late nineteenth and early twentieth centuries. The other was that, over time, people had begun to see that role, and to get the idea that their democratic rights should extend to the state's role in the economy also—meaning that they had a right to a decent standard of living and the state should guarantee it to them, just as it assured capitalist profits. Summing up, they say: "A century and a half after achievement of formal democratic rights, the state has finally become the arena of class conflict."[4]

Accordingly, they conclude by predicting the rise of a class-based resistance to Reagan's policies in which leading elements would be organized labor, the elderly, women, and environmentalists, as well as the basic groups of the poor, minorities, and the unemployed. In addition, social service workers and state and local agencies were thought likely to join. This alliance of groups and interests is what they mean by a "class" that would be called into active political efforts by Reagan's policies, and ultimately would triumph in the name of democracy.

One of the most interesting aspects of this analysis is that, by a different route, it arrives at the same fulcrum or condition precedent for change as has this book. In short, once people transcend the "wall of separation" that marks politics off from social and economic life and come to see their worlds (and entitlements) as one integrated whole, new forms of democracy are possible. The achievements of the past 50 years, Piven and Cloward maintain, cannot now be withdrawn without awakening the class-based resistance that will mean the final triumph of democracy over capitalism.

By 1983, Piven and Cloward argued that this resistance could be furthered by massive campaigns to register currently unregistered voters.[5] Their strategy was to bring a protest-oriented body of new voters into the Democratic party and force a party realignment along class lines. Because there are now few institutional limits to voter participation, and considerable voter experience with seeing the state as the source of economic benefits, they believe that nonvoters can be motivated to register and vote if they are caught up in a protest movement.

Piven and Cloward believe three special conditions make nonvoters more readily available today than ever before. First is the impact of the cutbacks, which they see as widespread and powerful. Next are the opportunities to organize and register voters provided by the way that the welfare state aggregates its clients—in welfare offices, food stamp lines, unemployment offices, and so forth. Finally, instead of depending on volunteers to find potential voters in the manner just described, human services workers could do the job themselves, perhaps in company with ministers and civil rights groups, as an expression of solidarity with their clients.

Piven and Cloward anticipate immense conflict as a result of these registration tactics and believe that it will be functional to maintaining interest and helping inspire nonvoters to actually get out and vote. Indeed, they depend on this conflict to generate a real protest movement capable of "disrupting and transforming" the Democratic party. They say:

> The great power of protest movements is the communicative force of the conflicts they generate. It is through conflict that movements project alternative visions in the face of the ruling-class monopoly on ideas, raise popular aspirations and hopes, and reach and mobilize millions of people.[6]

Piven and Cloward count on the reactions of elites to reveal their economic stakes in excluding the poor from the electoral process, and perhaps add to the conflict by making it appear that the rich are attacking democracy itself. Once a class-oriented party politics has been established, an as yet indefinite program could be shaped in its image. They recognize the need for a substantive program and anticipate great opposition from the business community, but see the development of a protest movement of nonvoters as the first major step in the direction of a transformation of American politics.

In addition to the high likelihood of controversy from these projects, some important strategic and tactical issues have to be considered. Some questions address Piven and Cloward's beginning assumptions. Are mere shared characteristics enough to constitute a "class" for purposes of continuing political impact? Can a protest movement be sustained on conflict alone, without a specific program and an organizational vehicle to keep it alive and focused on particular goals? Is the Democratic party a viable means to effective political power that can serve the needs and goals of the protesters?

More empirical issues include how much and what kind of impact the Reagan cutbacks have had on people; what changes in attitudes, beliefs, and behavior have been generated thereby; and what various components of this potential coalition are actually doing in their recent voting. I take up the latter group of questions insofar as available evidence permits and then move on to the first set of questions. In effect, I am trying to test and perhaps refine this leading scenario for the rise of a democratic economic renewal alternative with the scraps of evidence and historical precedents that happen to be available at this time.

The Polarizing Impact of Reagan Administration Policies

Some major components of the Piven and Cloward prediction clearly seemed to be taking shape in 1984. In one respect—that of the development of shared attitudes that I have been calling the American equivalent of class consciousness—some people even appeared to be moving farther than Piven and Cloward dared to hope. To begin with, the impact of the Reagan administration cutbacks and redistribution from poor to rich was evidentially irrefutable, as well as deeply felt by the people affected. Table 5.3 (p. 97) summarized the combined effects of the cutbacks in cash transfers, in-kind transfers, and taxes on the different "income fifths" of American families. It showed that the lowest fifth, who were far more dependent on federal assistance, suffered substantial losses, while the upper fifth gained even more new income.

The same point can be made with a variety of different comparisons. In one such comparison, the Congressional Budget Office compared cuts in the "means-tested" programs with those programs that are not means-tested.[7] The first category consists of programs for which people are not eligible unless they can prove that they lack the means of subsistence; the other programs go to people at all income levels. The means-tested programs were found to have been cut by a total of 8 percent in real terms, twice the proportion by which the other programs were cut. The CBO also found that the average household with income of less than $10,000 would lose $1340 during 1982-85. Although this group represented only 23 percent of all households, it was absorbing 40 percent of the cuts. By contrast, the average household with income that was over $40,000 would lose only $390 from the cuts, and reap benefits of $7500 or more from tax cuts.

Even more interesting was the pattern of reactions to such felt injustice. Not only people directly affected but many others seemed to be feeling a shared sense that President Reagan was biased against the poor. Women and minorities felt this unfairness particularly strongly, and for some people it seemed to be developing into a shared sense of the need to do something about it. With time and an opportunity for expression, this resentment might become the basis for an electoral movement that would be even more purposeful than Piven and Cloward predicted.

I argued earlier that a democratic alternative depended on the formation of an unprecedented coalition fused together in an active popular movement, in part by some sense of shared identity and purpose that elsewhere would be associated with the notion of "class consciousness." In this analysis, I start with the issue of how the latter "glue" might develop so as to hold together blocs of voters normally tending in distinctive directions. The first question naturally concerns the extent to which people may be breaking free of the powerful grip of the orthodox ideology that holds everything and everybody in their current places. If they are not, there is little reason to hope for development of *any* new way of thinking or acting that could provide a basis for a permanent new electoral coalition.

On this first point, there is striking supportive evidence. I stressed the decline of confidence in the American political system and the various leadership groups within the American social order in the first chapter. Confidence levels have never been lower. To be sure, they are very gross ways of understanding how people feel about their society and government. In direct questions about attitudes toward the political system, some sharp differences regularly show up. Well-educated, high-income people feel confidence in and support major institutions and the political system. As status levels drop, so does confidence in the political system. People at lower-status levels regularly show a greater sense of the need for government, but a lower rating of how well it is working, than do people in higher social strata. In all cases, support for the existing system is declining. In such a context, people are at least free to consider alternatives to what they no longer find deserving of their confidence.

THE RISE OF A CLASS IDENTITY

With such clear evidence that the ideological grip of existing institutions is slipping, we may start the search for new ways in which people are beginning to identify themselves in politics. Some important new dimensions evident in voting patterns of the 1982 election and other recent data suggest a new attitudinal structure taking shape around economic welfare issues. First, there was a modest increase in turnout for the 1982 election over previous midterm elections; 1982 actually saw the highest voting proportion since 1970. Sustained recession and unemployment may be capable of reversing the turnout decline that has gone on so long. More important were the totals of some key groups whose participation would be essential to any future coalition. The greatest increase in all turnout rates, for example, was that among unemployed people—nearly a 25 percent increase. This is particularly noteworthy because survey evidence has regularly shown that the unemployed were unlikely to vote. Blacks also voted in higher than normal proportions in 1982.

But the data that most analysts focused on in 1982 were the new "gender gap" and the even newer "marriage gap." These two newly visible factors are shown in table 12.1, with respect to voting in the 1982 congressional elections. Men and women differed enough for observers to start talking more seriously about a distinguishable "women's vote," which seemed to be revealed in several ways. Women consistently voted more Democratic than did men. They identified with the Democratic party by even larger ratios. Looking behind these data, most polls now show net differences in the attitudes of men and women of from 15 to 20 percentage points on such questions as which party is better able to keep us out of war or ensure economic recovery, or in evaluating Reagan's job performance.

TABLE 12.1

VOTING IN THE 1982 CONGRESSIONAL ELECTIONS

	Men		Women	
	Percent Democratic	Percent Republican	Percent Democratic	Percent Republican
Married	49	49	52	44
Single	59	37	63	34
TOTAL	53	44	57	40

SOURCE: *New York Times,* 6 January 1983, reporting data from the postelection analysis conducted by New York Times/CBS News poll.

Voting patterns of women are distinctive also in that they do not shift toward Republicans with age, as men do. Roughly similar party ratios exist at all age levels for women. This "gender gap" appeared clearly in the 1980 election, but seems to be widening in response to Reagan policies. The turnout rate of women is still slightly lower than that of men, and so the full potential effect of the gender gap combined with women's majority status in the population has yet to be brought to bear.

The "marriage gap" means that there is also a distinct difference between the voting patterns of single and married people. Table 12.1 shows that both single men and single women voted for Democrats in much larger proportions than did married men and women, with the ratio among women approaching 2 to 1. The contrast was constant and pronounced at all ages, income levels, and regions of the country. But the starkest contrasts occurred among younger and poorer voters, those most affected by the recession and the Reagan cutbacks. There has always been a thin difference between single and married voters in election data, but never anything like these margins or this focus among the economically vulnerable.

What seems to be happening is that a new set of positions is being taken by a large number of people in reaction to the cowboy capitalism of the Reagan administration. The trigger is clearly economic welfare issues and their effects on people. In a way, the terms "gender gap" and "marriage gap" are typically misleading media characterizations. These differences are not just "gaps" related to the fact of being a woman or single, but to the way that Reagan administration policies affect the vital economic livelihood of people like themselves. Such attitudes cannot be reversed by public declarations of respect for women or the appointment of a few more wealthy women to federal jobs. They can be addressed only by substantive changes in policy.

The only groups that show sharper anti-Republican voting are Hispanics and blacks, whose voting patterns undoubtedly have similar origins. These tentative interpretations find support in the escalating ratios by which people see the Reagan administration in class terms, as oriented toward the rich. Table 12.2 shows the trend in responses to the regularly asked question about which group Reagan "cares more about serving." Nobody was ever under the impression that Reagan cared most about the poor, but nearly two-thirds started with the assumption that as President he would work for all equally. That proportion dropped by half within two years, whereas the proportion who saw him as serving the rich increased by 150 percent.

TABLE 12.2

CLASS-RELATED IMAGES OF PRESIDENT REAGAN, 1981-83

(in percent)

Based on response to "Reagan cares more about serving . . . "

	February 1981	April 1981	November 1981	August 1982	June 1983
Low-income people	3	1	1	2	1
Middle-income people	6	6	7	8	7
Upper-income people	23	29	54	56	58
All people equally	64	58	35	29	32

SOURCE: *National Journal,* 2 July 1983, reporting ABC-*Washington Post* survey data, months indicated.

These new attitudes are being generated by economic conditions and what the Reagan administration has done. They are only reactions, so far, because there has been no visible alternative program to which voters could rally and which would provide an affirmative focus for developing new and deeper commitments to economic welfare goals. But some established attitudinal building blocks in the electorate show up repeatedly in various surveys. Presumably, these attitudes too are being sharpened by the recession and the Reagan policies. I have in mind the basic beliefs that Americans hold about the respective roles of business and government, rights to a job, and the rightful part to be played by working people.

Against a background of continuing support for the "free enterprise system," Americans generally endorse a major role for government in guiding that system and making sure that individual workers have jobs and income. In these respects, the general public holds attitudes in sharp contrast with the laissez-faire principles of business executives. Table 12.3 shows some of the most recent of these contrasts on selected issues of importance to this analysis. The proportions shown are those reflecting a relatively high degree of intensity of support, a "major contribution" to economic growth. The research was conducted just before Reagan took office, and it seems fair to guess that greater support for government action would be found under conditions of recession and unemployment.

These are data that by themselves equally show support for Yankee capitalist programs. But in the absence of public debate on any of these questions, what is most remarkable is that there apparently is a preexisting bias toward

TABLE 12.3

PUBLIC AND BUSINESS EXECUTIVE VIEWS ON ECONOMIC GROWTH, 1980-81

(in percent)

Based on proportions saying each step would be a "major contribution to economic growth."

	Public	Business Executives
Encourage greater cooperation among business, labor, government, and social-interest groups	59	51
Provide financial incentives to business for new equipment and facilities	52	86
Provide government funding to retrain and relocate workers in failing industries	49	14
Develop a national industrial plan in which the government would determine where and how our resources are used	40	3

SOURCE: Survey by Harris Associates cited in *The Confidence Gap* by Seymour Martin Lipset and William Schneider (New York: Free Press, 1983), 278-79.

some form of government responsibility even in a "free enterprise" society. Some of the same basic feeling is reflected in the regular majorities that support the idea that government has a responsibility to see that everybody who wants to work can get a job.

Even more important, particularly in view of the disfavor in which unions are held in the United States, are basic attitudes with respect to the proper role of working people. Americans may resent and reject unions, but at the same time they call for greater influence on the part of working people. Not only that, but there is a rising tide evident between 1972 and 1976—and likely to be rising still, perhaps even faster—in the proportions of Americans who say that working people have "too little influence" in American life and politics. Consider these contrasts:[8]

	1972		1976	
	Unions	Working People	Unions	Working People
Too much influence	56%	3%	64%	4%
Just about right influence	33	49	25	38
Too little influence	4	44	5	53

THE PROSPECTS OF COALITION

These sketchy findings do not demonstrate the formation of a new unifying consciousness among working Americans, nor should they be expected to. We do not know what form such an identity would take among Americans, but it is not likely to show up first in empirical data of this sort. A sense of shared risk and necessity is a qualitative change that takes time and practical experience to develop, and could escape pollsters' shallow inquiries in any event. What the data do show clearly is that something new is developing in the way of broad popular attitudes, that it focuses on economic well-being issues, and that it leads many people to see their side of those economic issues as opposed to what Reagan is doing. That is all anybody can ask at this point.

What are the prospects that these developing attitudes can help people cross the old barriers and fuse into an effective electoral coalition? The central focus of any such coalition would have to be economic welfare issues. Thus the early signs in the data are aimed at the right target. Many existing organizations and blocs of voters are well aware of the necessity and propriety of this focus as the basis for a coalition, and have started to try to build such a grouping. Leadership of a wide and participative sort needs to be developed around the specific cause of full employment and economic democracy.

The state and its proper functions should be one of the major issues raised, in order to keep economic entitlements united with the notion of political rights.

Who should be served by a democratic state in the 1980s? This is a focus in which public employee unions could play a constructive role, not as people whose interests are opposed to those of taxpayers in general but as people who have a conception of the good state and how it could do far more to serve the needs of the people if it were returned to their control. The notion of returning and taking back instead of "seizing power" is important also. It helps to emphasize the grounding of such a new movement in traditional American rights, reduces its apparent radicalism, and points to the unfairness of the Reagan redistribution from the poor to the rich.

Any new coalition of this sort must include minorities in a leading role. It must appeal strongly to women in a practical feminist manner, and to all those whose first concern is either reducing the prospect of war or enhancing the quality of the environment. Many of the latter are the same people, of course. But I am trying to stress a crucial unifying dimension: The notion of economic welfare must come to be seen as encompassing and being fundamental to the realization of the goals of minorities and women, *and* to the goals of the antiwar and environmental movements. Racial and sexual discrimination, and war and destruction of the environment, feed on the same values and assumptions that drive the capitalist economy. If these practices can ever be changed in the United States, it can only be together, never separately.

The Remaining Issues: Program and Organization

Insofar as it can be tested by the available evidence, the scenario sketched by Piven and Cloward seems to stand up. The Reagan policies are having the impact on people that they predicted, and a classlike reaction appears to be building. Many groups, representing a wide range of single-issue categories, have lined up in opposition to Reagan's policies. Their activities at the grass roots, and their occasional successes, have attracted national attention and even some comparisons with the rise of the New Right. But it is not yet clear what they are *for,* and it does not seem likely that they can sustain themselves for long on purely negative dimensions.

This is the point where the Piven and Cloward scenario leaves off. They seem to be content with the image of a protest movement combining many elements that mounts a massive voter-registration-and-turnout drive. This would of course be a major event in American politics, and they should not be expected to prepare a blueprint for every stage of the process of fundamental change in the United States. But the next steps do appear to be ones involving a *program,* and the question of what sort of *organization* is capable of carrying it out.

The question of what program could serve both to unite a viable popular movement and govern the country in a humane and democratic manner seems to me to have been answered in this book. Full employment-economic democracy in some combination is that program. Its specifics have been examined in great detail, along with all its problems in gaining acceptance by the necessary electoral coalition. This program, other evidence seems to say, must be at the focus of organizing efforts in order to mobilize nonvoters and regular voters. The classlike reactions to Reagan's policies will not get far unless they are focused in this fashion on an affirmative policy—an alternative that promises something different and attractive, with genuine importance to all potential members of the coalition.

Full employment and economic democracy can serve this unifying function precisely because they do not serve narrow material needs only. They mean an end to militarism; an opportunity to nurture children and the environment; full citizenship in which Martin Luther King's dream erases race, sex, and class lines; and a new vitality to people's lives built from economic and political challenge and experiment, participation, and achievement. And they must mean all these things at once and together. The task of leadership newly drawn from the ranks of these groups and movements is to articulate this combination so that the now-disparate elements can see their shared interests, and can feel them as including but being more compelling than their separate interests. Multiple self-interests will not suffice, even in the earliest stages, as the basis for a coalition. There must be something larger, grander, to restore what is missing in our public *and* private lives.

Acceptance of these programs as the focus of the new movement does not resolve the question whether a continuing organization is necessary to sustain the popular movement for the time that it takes to implement the far-reaching changes that are involved. Even if an organization is deemed necessary, there are still very serious questions about its appropriate form and practices. I do not see how any popular movement can be held together for any length of time without an organization of *some* kind, and the problem thus focuses on *what* kind.

This issue has bedevilled the American left for generations, and remains acute today. To enter the Democratic party is too often to submit to all the forces there—including Yankee capitalists—that resourcefully defend the status quo and assign first priority to the needs of the corporate-banking sector of the economy. But to try to gain recognition and support as a third party is very discouraging. One of the things that the American electoral system does best is to discriminate against third parties so harshly that they have little or no real chance of winning. And American voters are winner-oriented, so much so that a chance to defeat a disliked candidate by voting for the lesser evil almost always seems preferable to "throwing your vote away."

For the last two decades, a spirited debate has raged on the left between those who stood for "critical support" of the Democratic party and those who advocated an ideologically purer third-party approach to electoral politics. The former argued that labor and the minorities, essential to any democratic movement, were deeply invested in the Democratic party and could not be found elsewhere. Better to be in alliance with one's friends, even if it meant little in the way of policy achievements. The latter insisted that nothing of significance would ever be achieved within the Democratic party and that third parties, with all their problems, were the only conscientious and effective route.

This argument has apparently been won by those who want to remain a part of the Democratic party, with perhaps an important compromise. Piven and Cloward, for example, never give their Democratic party commitment a second thought as they design the campaign to bring the protest movement into its fold. Martin Carnoy and Derek Shearer, two of the leading thinkers of the economic democracy movement, first note that real reform has usually been achieved by extraparty movements and then declare that the only reasonable route is through the Democratic party.[9] Some major works in economic democracy never take up the subject, and some in each category clearly assume that the Democratic party is inevitably the focus for all political activity.

The compromise that seems to be developing is summed up by the term "party within a party" and has an equally long genealogy. Current advocates cite the many local groups, single issue and electoral, that have been the chief source of left successes in the last decade and urge a coalition of them within the Democratic party.[10] This coalition would have its own national network of communication and function both inside and outside the party, running its own candidates in primaries where appropriate but also supporting favored Democrats. In time, it might hope to encourage realignment toward a more homogeneous class-based party system, in which business would grudgingly leave the Democratic party to the newer elements. Many of these same thoughts were expressed by Michael Harrington as the way that democratic socialists could take advantage of the "invisible movement" for socialism that existed in the Democratic party. Others have also maintained that it was obligatory to work within the Democratic party until the moment was right to reveal true purposes and lead that party into the future.

In all this discussion of whether or not to enter or support the Democratic party, there is very little consideration of what a democratic political party would be like today. It does not seem that the typical hierarchical, money-manipulated, infrequently visible political party of our times is really a proper model for an emerging democratic movement. How a party-equivalent form of social organization might provide education, services, and social support on a full-time basis has never really been explored. Necessity may force such consideration soon, if the development of a class-based popular movement continues much longer.

Realignment and the Mondale-Ferraro Ticket

Very little has been written about the process of political realignment and the mobilization of broad new electoral coalitions, except after the fact and by means of great bodies of aggregate voting data. We do not know in any authoritative way what the most portentous realignment and mobilization would look like in its early stages. Thus left to our own devices, it seems to me that a plausible case can be made that the Democratic party nominating process in 1984 could be part of the realignment-mobilization of the constituency that I have argued in this chapter is essential. I refer less to the candidates, of course, than to the configuration of leaders, groups, and popular support in the process that led to their nomination.

I see this nomination process as a possible stage in eventual realignment-mobilization because it included several of the key groups that must fuse together, and because at least in major ways it has as its focus economic welfare issues. Blacks and other minorities have never had the representation and impact that they derived from the Jackson campaign, nor have they been so visible at a convention. Women certainly never wielded the power and influence stemming from a place on the ticket before, and the effects on women throughout the country could constitute a major turning point in the political emergence of a "women's vote." Disadvantaged people generally heard more rhetorical concern for their situation during the campaign and convention than has usually been the case.

Whether the potential for realignment-mobilization is ever realized is quite another story, and one that will not be known for several years. Blacks and other minorities will have to hold together, link closely with women and other elements in the coalition, and continue to expand their capacity to force party officials and officeholders to respond to their needs. Women will have to rally around a program that responds to the needs not only of women but of minorities and disadvantaged people, and that embraces full employment-economic democracy principles. They can be reabsorbed into the mainstream of American two-party politics very rapidly if they focus exclusively on gender and special interests rather than broader programs of social reconstruction. Much depends on the attraction that both candidates and programs have for the traditional nonvoters, whose increased turnout at elections is essential to the development of an effective new coalition.

There is no doubt that the Democratic party remained in the hands of the Yankees and their organized labor allies after the nomination of 1984, and every reason to believe that it would be distinguished by Yankee control to the extent that it was successful in the election. The "Yuppies" who rallied around Senator Gary Hart in the nominating campaign were at least temporarily repulsed by the alliance of regulars and the potential full-employment constituency. But they will be back in the future, perhaps next time in alliance with Yankees. One might argue that the most damaging possibility for the nascent full employment-economic democracy movement within the party would be for the Mondale-Ferraro ticket to win in 1984. Democratic party power in government at this early stage might mean the cooptation of many leaders, diffusion of loyalties, and the loss of organizing momentum toward nonvoters.

The strongest factor on the side of continued mobilization of a coalition of women, minorities, the disadvantaged, and nonvoters, on the other hand, is the continuing economic welfare emergency that nearly all such people face. The much celebrated economic "recovery" of 1983-84 is so sharply skewed toward the upper classes and professional-technical levels that it has only marginal impact on many millions of people lower down in the social pyramid. The transformation is steadily replacing relatively well paid blue-collar manufacturing jobs with much lower paid service jobs. The middle class is shrinking, with a few members rising into the higher-income levels but three times as many dropping into low-paid or even poverty ranks. The poverty population has been rising steadily since 1980, both in total numbers of people and as a proportion of the population. The "feminization of poverty" is now a standard of the American vocabulary.

Nor does the transformation show any signs of slacking off in its impact on people who might form part of the new constituency. Despite the recovery, and in part because of the continuing strength of the American dollar, imports are rising steadily and exports dropping in about the same ratio. The increased sales of imports mean fewer jobs for Americans, and the reduction of export sales has the same effect. Even more dangerous, the growing protectionism which American industries (and unions) have secured from the Reagan administration despite its free market protestations may lead to similar actions all around the world and eventually sharp reductions in international trade and employment levels generally.

The point here is not to welcome hardships imposed on working people, but to note that the "recovery" has not reached them in any broad way and the paramount issue for them remains economic welfare. The pressures on such people are therefore likely to translate into continued incentives to support new movements and programs for economic renewal.

What we seem to be arriving at is the realization that the unprecedented may be happening. In the 1980s, in the midst of another major political-economic transformation, we have the early signs and genuine possibility of something like a class-based political movement for a full version of democracy. Class-based movements are not unprecedented in the United States, but for the most part, they have been upper-class movements. The upper classes always seem to understand their interests and act accordingly long before anybody else has grasped the situation.

With so many encouraging signs, it is surely time to look about for danger. And there is no lack of potential and real threats to the coalescence of a democratic electoral coalition and popular movement I have been describing. The most obvious dangers come from diversionary national security events and appeals, and then from racial tensions. Faced with the possibility of a democratic electoral coalition forming around economic welfare goals, cowboy capitalists would undoubtedly find or make small wars, threaten nuclear war, and/or unleash sweeping internal security campaigns. Yankee capitalists' red-baiting might be subtler, and perhaps more effective. Any effort to build a coalition in the United States with minorities as full participants is bound to be difficult, and to offer a variety of vulnerable openings for opponents to seek to pry it apart.

These prospects should be assumed as part of the process of coalition building, and taken as natural obstacles to be overcome. If they are anticipated, they may be easier to deal with. They will provide an important test of developing leadership, and of the depth of the new class-equivalent attitudes among supporters generally. Most of all, they will challenge the breadth and subsuming nature of the definition of full employment-economic democracy I suggested earlier. If people do not see war and racial/sexual discrimination as flowing from the same values and dynamics that prevent them from reaching their economic welfare and democratic society goals, then the new coalition will disintegrate.

But if people *do* see their world together—if all the things that would divide and deflect and deny them their aspirations for economic well-being and a happy and democratic social life are understood to be part of one and the same system—then we cross a crucial threshold. We start to see democratic rights in a newly inclusive fashion, as including not only economic rights but also rights to a quality of life and human experience not before imagined. Decades of struggle in which the state has served as the arena have helped to pave the way for an understanding of politics in which economic, social, and political goals are once again integrated. Piven and Cloward have made this point well:

> Whatever the cooptive effects of particular social programs, . . . the welfare state nevertheless has had a transforming effect on popular understandings of what politics is about. It brought economic issues to the very center of democratic politics, and that is a development which is potentially activating and mobilizing. In this sense, the programs which promoted cooptation at one stage of American history have prepared people ideologically for political struggle at this stage.[11]

What is at stake here is nothing short of the reintegration of the notion of democracy—the final breaking of the walls of separation that have kept economics and politics apart and sustained the partial version of democracy that enabled capitalism to triumph over (full) democracy. I traced the historical rise of these walls and their service to capitalism in chapter 2. I suggested then that realization of full democracy in the tradition of the early democrats depended, first, on their elimination as conceptual barriers in American minds. This is precisely what is happening in the process of building the new democratic electoral coalition around economic welfare issues and goals. The dispossessed has returned, been recognized, and needs only a bit more help to reclaim the throne.

It should be clear by now that full employment and economic democracy must act together, complementing each other, to serve as the focus of a unified popular movement. Full-employment advocates have deep roots in party politics and political organizations, important legitimacy and experience, and only a modestly threatening program. Economic democracy embodies the full potential of the American democratic tradition, and has a grander vision of what is possible today and tomorrow as the social order is reconstructed. The two programs need each other in constructive tension to present American democrats with exciting new social purpose and possibility. It is not a matter of choice for them, but of necessity on the part of the people whom they serve.

The class-equivalent sense of shared risks and opportunities that is beginning to move Americans today is thus democracy itself, newly integrated into a full version unknown to more than a few since capitalism gained the upper hand. A full democratic vision, with human aspirations and moral claims new to modern American politics, is being explicitly asserted over the needs of capitalism in this popular surge. In the conflict that is underway in today's Great Transformation, democracy has found new champions. Whether it succeeds in the coming struggle, of course, depends on the unforseeable future. But much of that outcome is in our hands. Democracy is possible, in practical political and economic terms. Is it worth the trouble? Again, consider the alternatives.

Notes

CHAPTER 1. The Politics of Economic Renewal (pp. 1-17)

1. Charles L. Schultze, "Industrial Policy: A Solution in Search of a Problem," *California Management Review* 25, no. 4 (Summer 1983): 5-15.
2. George Gilder, *Wealth and Poverty* (New York: Basic Books, 1980).
3. Irving Kristol, *Two Cheers for Capitalism* (New York: Basic Books, 1978).
4. Bruce Bartlett, *Reaganomics: Supply-Side Economics in Action* (Westport, Conn.: Arlington House, 1981).
5. Milton Friedman, *Capitalism and Freedom* (Chicago: University of Chicago Press, 1962).
6. Lester Thurow, *The Zero-Sum Society* (New York: Basic Books, 1980).
7. Robert B. Reich, *The Next American Frontier* (New York: Times Books, 1983).
8. Martin Carnoy and Derek Shearer, *Economic Democracy: The Challenge of the 1980s* (White Plains, N.Y.: Sharpe, 1980).
9. Samuel Bowles, David M. Gordon, and Thomas E. Weisskopf, *Beyond the Waste Land: A Democratic Alternative to Economic Decline* (New York: Doubleday Anchor, 1983).
10. See Arthur T. Hadley, *The Empty Polling Booth* (Englewood Cliffs, N.J.: Prentice-Hall, 1978).
11. Ibid., 113.
12. Seymour Martin Lipset and William Schneider, *The Confidence Gap: Business, Labor, and the Government in the Public Mind* (New York: Free Press, 1983), 48-49.
13. Ibid., 411-12.
14. Everett Carll Ladd, Jr., with Charles D. Hadley, *Transformations of the American Party System* (New York: Norton, 1978).
15. For an excellent discussion of several aspects of that election, see Thomas Ferguson and Joel Rogers, eds., *The Hidden Election: Politics and Economics in the 1980 Presidential Campaign* (New York: Pantheon, 1981).
16. All data are drawn from *National Journal,* 23 October 1982, 1788-95.
17. Ibid.; see also table 5.3 for a detailed analysis.

18. See chapter 12, particularly tables 12.1 and 12.2.
19. See table 12.2.

CHAPTER 2. Democracy and Capitalism in American History (pp. 21-36)

1. Adam Smith, *The Wealth of Nations,* ed. R.H. Campbell and A.S. Skinner (London: Oxford University Press, 1976).
2. John K. Alexander, *Render Them Submissive: Responses to Poverty in Philadelphia, 1760-1800* (Amherst: University of Massachusetts Press, 1980), 31.

CHAPTER 3. The Stalemate in American Politics (pp. 37-56)

1. James MacGregor Burns, *The Deadlock of Democracy* (Englewood Cliffs, N.J.: Prentice-Hall, 1963).
2. Kevin Phillips, *The Emerging Republican Majority* (New York: Random House, 1968).
3. Kevin Phillips, *Post-Conservative America* (New York: Random House, 1982).
4. The phrase is that of Walter Dean Burnham, the most perceptive analyst of American elections and party politics. See his "American Politics in the 1970s: Beyond Party" in *The American Party Systems,* ed. William Nisbet Chambers and Walter Dean Burnham, 2d ed. (New York: Oxford University Press, 1975), 308-57.
5. John R. Petrocik, *Party Coalitions: Realignment and the Decline of the New Deal Party System* (Chicago: University of Chicago Press, 1981), 162.
6. Ibid., 162-63.
7. Phillips, *Post-Conservative America,* 49.
8. Committee on Political Parties, American Political Science Association, *Toward a More Responsible Two-Party System* (New York: Rhinehart, 1950).
9. Ibid., 26.
10. Bertram Gross, *Friendly Fascism: The New Face of Power in America* (New York: Evans, 1980; reissued in paper by South End Press, 1982).
11. Kevin Phillips, "Post-Conservative America," *New York Review of Books,* 13 May 1982.
12. Stephen Skowronek, *Building a New American State: The Expansion of National Administrative Capacities, 1877-1920* (New York: Cambridge University Press, 1982), 292.

Chapter 4. U.S. Decline and Transformation in the New World Economy (pp. 57-79)

1. Leonard Silk, "Capitalism and Crises," *New York Times*, 1 September 1982, 26.
2. Robert Reich, *The Next American Frontier* (New York: Times Books, 1982), 1.
3. James Cook, "The Molting of America," *Forbes*, 22 November 1982.
4. William J. Abernathy, Kim B. Clark, and Alan M. Kantrow, *Industrial Renaissance* (New York: Basic Books, 1982).
5. Barry Bluestone and Bennett Harrison, *The Deindustrialization of America* (New York: Basic Books, 1982), passim.
6. John Naisbitt, "The New Economic and Political Order of the 1980s" (speech delivered in Stockholm, Sweden, 20 September 1979).
7. For a full statement of this analysis, see Bluestone and Harison, *Deindustrialization of America*, chap. 2.
8. Sources for all comparative data in this chapter are the readily available *Economic Report of the President* (annual) and the *Statistical Abstract of the United States* (annual), both of which often employ data originally collected by the Organization for Economic Cooperation and Development and published in its monthly *Outlook*. Where other sources are employed, I so indicate. These comparisons, for example, are drawn from Ira C. Magaziner and Robert Reich, *Minding America's Business: The Decline and Rise of the American Economy* (New York: Harcourt Brace Jovanovich, 1982), 13.
9. Data in this paragraph are drawn from the *New York Times*, 14 November 1982, 14.
10. Magaziner and Reich, *Minding America's Business*, 16, portray these comparisons effectively. The basic data may be found in many sources.
11. A particularly effective tabular comparison may be found in Magaziner and Reich, *Minding America's Business*, 144.
12. Ibid., 23.
13. For these comparisons, the *Statistical Abstract of the United States* uses data from the World Health Organization.
14. For a full description, see the *New York Times*, 8 May 1983.
15. Wassily Leontief, quoted in the *New York Times*, 8 May 1983, 29.
16. James Cook, "The Molting of America," *Forbes*, 22 November 1982, 161.
17. Jonathan Alter, "Precarious Prosperity: The Siren Song of the Service Sector," *Washington Monthly*, December 1982, 7.
18. *The Economic Report of the President* contains quarterly as well as annual

inflation figures; quarterly data, as in this case, fluctuate more widely than the annual averages would indicate.

19. The gross totals of investment data are found in *The Economic Report of the President,* but more specific data on sources of revenue of U.S. corporations—particular the share derived abroad—are most readily provided by *Forbes* July issues. The data here are from the 4 July 1983 issue, 114ff.
20. *New York Times,* 10 July 1983, E2.
21. *Business Week,* 27 June 1983, 90.

Chapter 5. Cowboy Capitalism: A "Free Market" Solution? (pp. 83-102)

1. These estimates were orginally made by the Congressional Budget Office and are now widely used. Other data in this paragraph are drawn from *The Economic Report of the President.*
2. All budgetary data in this and the following paragraphs are drawn from the Office of Management and Budget, *The Budget in Brief,* 1984.
3. Estimates from the *National Journal,* 23 October 1982, 1791.
4. "A Bipartisan Appeal to Resolve the Budget Crisis," *New York Times,* 24 February 1983, 26.
5. Estimates vary, of course, depending on the assumptions made in reaching them. Representative Les Aspin (D-Wisc.), generally recognized as an expert in military affairs, estimates 48,000 jobs from $1 billion in military spending, and 100,000 from the same investment in education. The number of jobs created is not subject to proof, but the estimated ratios between military and (for example) education investments may be meaningful.
6. These proportions are much more reliable and may be found in the *Statistical Abstract of the United States.*

Chapter 6. Yankee Capitalism: Business-Government Partnership (pp. 103-20)

1. Ira C. Magaziner and Robert B. Reich, *Minding America's Buisness: The Decline and Rise of the American Economy* (New York: Harcourt Brace Jovanovich, 1982), 255.
2. Lester Thurow, *The Zero-Sum Society* (New York: Basic Books, 1980).
3. In addition to Magaziner and Reich, *Minding America's Business,* Reich is the author of many articles and a major book, *The Next American Frontier* (New York: Times Books, 1983).
4. Quoted in the *New York Times Magazine,* 28 August 1983, 63.

5. Rohatyn's ideas have been set forth in several articles in the *New York Review of Books* from 1981 to 1983. See the editions of 22 January 1981, 5 February 1981, 16 April 1981, 29 April 1982, 4 November 1982, and 18 August 1983.
6. Press release from the office of Representative Richard Ottinger, 24 May 1983. Mimeographed.
7. "America's Competitive Challenge: The Need for a National Response" (report to the President of the United States from the Business-Higher Education Forum, Washington, D.C., April 1983).
8. For example, see his response to Michael Harrington's "A Path for America" in *Dissent,* Winter 1983, 25-26.
9. Alexander Hamilton, *Report on Manufactures,* 1791.
10. Felix Rohatyn, "The Older America: Can It Survive?" *New York Review of Books,* 22 January 1981, 19.
11. Charles L. Schultze, "Industrial Policy: A Solution in Search of a Problem," *California Management Review,* Summer 1983, 5-15.

CHAPTER 7. Full Employment: Jobs Before Profits (pp. 121-37)

1. "An Economic Strategy for the 1980s" (report of the Full Employment Action Council and the National Policy Exchange, Washington, D.C., 1982), 6, 36.
2. Ibid.
3. Ibid., 51.
4. Robert Lekachman, "The Inevitability of Planning," *Dissent,* Spring 1978, 160.

CHAPTER 8. Economic Democracy: The Transition to Full Democracy? (pp. 138-54)

1. Martin Carnoy and Derek Shearer, *Economic Democracy: The Challenge of the 1980s* (White Plains, N.J.: Sharpe, 1980), 10.
2. Samuel Bowles, David M. Gordon, and Thomas E. Weisskopf, *Beyond the Waste Land: A Democratic Alternative to Economic Decline* (New York: Double Anchor, 1983).
3. Barry Bluestone and Bennett Harrison, *The Deindustrialization of America* (New York: Basic Books, 1982), 244-45.
4. Martin Carnoy and Derek Shearer, *A New Social Contract: The Economy and Government After Reagan* (New York: Harper & Row, 1983), 1-2.

5. Ibid., 23.
6. Bowles, Gordon, and Weisskopf, *Beyond the Waste Land,* 270.
7. Bluestone and Harrison, *Deindustrialization of America,* 232.

CHAPTER 9. Political Implications of Economic Renewal (pp. 157-71)

1. Herbert Croly, *The Promise of American Life* (New York: Macmillan, 1909).
2. Kevin Phillips, "Post-Conservative America," *New York Review of Books,* 13 May 1982.
3. Essential for understanding the Alliance, its lecturer system, and the Populist movement of the period is Lawrence Goodwyn, *The Populist Movement* (New York: Oxford University Press, 1977).

CHAPTER 10. The Politics of Institutional Reconstruction (pp. 172-88)

1. Stephen Skowronek, *Building a New American State: The Expansion of National Administrative Capacities, 1877-1920* (New York: Cambridge University Press, 1982).
2. Ibid., 285.
3. Ibid., 18.
4. Ibid., 289.
5. Ibid., 290.
6. Ibid., 291.
7. Bertram Gross and Kusum Singh, "Democratic Planning: The Bottom Sideways Approach," in *After Reagan: Visions for the 1980s,* ed. Alan Gartner, Colin Greer, and Frank Reissman (New York: Harper & Row, 1984).

CHAPTER 11. The Changing Shape of American Politics (pp. 189-208)

1. *Fortune,* 11 May 1983; *Forbes,* 22 November 1982.
2. Arthur T. Hadley, *The Empty Polling Booth* (Englewood Cliffs, N.J.: Prentice-Hall, 1978).
3. Ibid., 110.
4. Ibid., 115.

CHAPTER 12. Toward a Class-Based Realignment of American Politics? (pp. 209-25)

1. Frances Fox Piven and Richard A. Cloward, *Regulating the Poor* (New York: Pantheon, 1971).
2. Frances Fox Piven and Richard A. Cloward, *Poor People's Movements* (New York: Pantheon, 1977).
3. Frances Fox Piven and Richard A. Cloward, *The New Class War* (New York: Pantheon, 1982).
4. Ibid., 125.
5. Richard A. Cloward and Frances Fox Piven, "Toward a Class-Based Realignment of American Politics: A Movement Strategy," *Social Policy,* Winter 1983, 3-14.
6. Ibid., 14.
7. Data in this paragraph are drawn from *National Journal,* 3 September 1983, 1797.
8. Seymour Martin Lipset and William Schneider, *The Confidence Gap: Business, Labor, and Government in the Public Mind* (New York: Free Press, 1983), 210.
9. Martin Carnoy and Derek Shearer, *A New Social Contract: The Economy and Government After Reagan* (New York: Harper & Row, 1982), 227.
10. John Atlas, Peter Dreier, and John Stephens, "Progressive Politics in 1984," *Nation,* 23-30 July 1983, 1.
11. Francis Fox Piven and Richard A. Cloward, "The American Road to Democratic Socialism," *democracy,* Summer 1983, 65.

Index

About the Author

KENNETH M. DOLBEARE obtained his B.A. in English from Haverford College in 1951 and then served three years as a U.S. Navy officer. He worked for a major oil company while pursuing his L.L.B. at Brooklyn Law School and was admitted to the New York Bar in 1959. He began teaching political science at Hofstra University in 1960 and remained there until 1965, when he received his Ph.D. from Columbia University. Moving to the University of Wisconsin at Madison, he served as assistant and associate professor, publishing three research monographs in law and public policy, and was awarded a Guggenheim Fellowship in 1969.

In 1970 he was appointed professor and chair of the Department of Political Science at the University of Washington, where he served until 1974. From 1974 through 1981 he taught American public policy, political economy, and political thought at the University of Massachusetts at Amherst, serving also as president of the Policy Studies Association in 1979-80.

Since 1981, he has taught political economy and public policy at The Evergreen State College in Olympia, Washington, a relatively new (1971) and innovative liberal arts college with a growing national reputation for team-taught interdisciplinary studies. Professor Dolbeare currently serves as director of the Graduate Program in Public Administraiton. His most recent books are *Neopolitics: American Political Beliefs in the 1980s* and a historical anthology entitled *American Political Thought.*